13 Ways to Overthink the Universe

13 Ways to Overthink the Universe

Benny Paulwin S

NU VOICE
PRESS

First published by NU VOICE PRESS 2025
An imprint of Hubhawks Pvt. Ltd
www.nuvoicepress.com

The characters and events portrayed in this book are fictitious. Any similarity to real persons, living or dead, is coincidental and not intended by the author.

ISBN: 978-81-992047-3-7

Printed at Manipal Technologies Limited, Manipal

Published by: Nu Voice Press

CONTENTS

INTRODUCTION

Hey! Before we go any further, you should know: everything said here is just an opinion, built on a mix of facts and personal reflections. I'm the type who ends up staring at the bathroom ceiling, lost in thought, while taking a dump. I'm as ordinary as anyone else.

This book is full of odd questions, half-baked theories, and perhaps a little too much know-it-all attitude. I'm not a professional writer, but I've decided to put my thoughts into words anyway, because I live in this reality, just like you. You still have the choice to close this book now.

But if you're still reading, then welcome. This book is my attempt to understand life – the why, the how, and the what of it all. It's my personal answer to the questions that have followed me since childhood. Along the way, I've uncovered two important truths: who I am, and what I am; and thirteen odd and ominous opinions about this 13-billion-year old universe and all things within it. Maybe this book will help you answer some of your own questions too.

I wrote this as a way to vent, to reflect, and to explore. Inside, you'll find my thoughts on spirituality, science, emotions, sex, love, money, evolution, biology, identity, war, violence, gravity, numbers, mirrors, video games, music, jokes, viruses, drugs, galaxies, stars, aliens – and most of all, our ability to learn and understand everything without discrimination. At the heart of it all lies a central theme: consciousness.

Are we truly conscious when we build nuclear weapons, binge on video games, or mindlessly shop online? Consciousness seems so rare and valuable, yet a simple worm survives just fine without it, or so we assume. Is our idea of consciousness just ego in disguise? Electric eels (fish) have mastered electricity for survival, an ability that took humans thousands of years to understand. Does that not count as consciousness?

Is consciousness something measurable, or is it something abstract, beyond the scope of science? According to evolution, life began with simple needs: food, sex, and a safe environment. Then came the mammalian bond: connection, play, loyalty, pride, guilt, and fun. From there, our intellect and imagination took the wheel. Now, we ponder over atoms, galaxies, and our place in the cosmos. But despite all our progress, we still yearn for superheroes, miracles, genies, and somehow, we've managed to discover God and soul, concepts that science has yet to identify.

Maybe I'm just trying to understand something I truly can't. After all, I'm also human.

"No tree can grow to heaven unless its roots reach down to hell."

–Carl Jung

QUESTIONS

I. QUESTIONS

Apparently, there is a dual consciousness within us. Evidently, the two hemispheres of the brain can control our actions and thoughts separately if the corpus callosum that connects them is altered. One side of the brain may think differently than the other. A split-brain individual – someone who has undergone such surgery due to epileptic seizures – can exhibit contradictory decisions, as though two persons reside within one brain. Each hemisphere holds different faculties of thought, yet both serve a single organism. This dual consciousness operates within the unified experience of a human life. It was this human life that coined the term "consciousness" in English to try to understand itself. But what is consciousness, this phenomenon that defines the experience of living beings in general?

Consciousness remains elusive, resisting definitions, measurements, and direct observation. Is it a material phenomenon, detectable through physical means, or is it an abstract construct inferred only through awareness and behavior? While we can probe the depths of atomic and subatomic structures, the essence of consciousness continues to evade us. Perhaps it is simply an emergent property, a byproduct of matter evolving in complexity. Or maybe it is a fleeting idea, surfacing only under certain conditions, then vanishing.

Consciousness turns inward to examine itself, and outward to explore atoms, the cosmos, mysticism, gods, life, and metaphysics. People believe in different things, yet all of it feels real to each believer. We all think we possess consciousness. But does belief equate to reality?

THE POWER OF BELIEF

Money has value only because we believe it does. If we travel to the 1970s with today's currency, people might deem it worthless. In 2016, India demonetized 500 and 1,000-rupee notes overnight, instantly nullifying their value. Money exists now largely as digital code – electrons governed by algorithms, trusted by societies. In this sense, it is both physical and conceptual.

Similarly, language is an abstraction that allows us to transmit thought. Blind people use Braille, while others rely on sound, sight, and gesture. Though physically present, its true power lies in perception. A color-blind person may see a banana as pink, or the night sky as maroon. Reality, then, is a filtered rendering, shaped by biology and culture.

We build telescopes to see the stars and microscopes to see cells, but without them, much of reality remains invisible. Perception and interpretation give rise to psychological reality, one that creates meaning, time, and social truth.

Some information is not objectively real, but is subjectively meaningful. Concepts like "thank you" or "please" only hold weight in human contexts. Our shared belief in our identity as humans is itself an idea. Nothing else calls us "human" but us.

Through evolution, humans became deeply self-focused. We separated ourselves from nature, animals, and even fellow humans based on color, ethnicity and language. Empathy, however, allows us to include or exclude selectively. Religion often anthropomorphizes God to care primarily for humans, not for the deep-sea anglerfish or rainforest flora. Science accepts death; religion promises life after it. But the universe is indifferent to both. Matter simply changes form. Death is an idea of living beings.

What defines a human? Biologically, we are mammals, primates, and Homo sapiens. Yet, we omit essential external dependencies: air, food, sunlight, and social bonds. Even the atmosphere that surrounds us plays a vital role in keeping us alive. Without atmospheric pressure, our bodies would swell in space, much like a blobfish out of water. This is precisely what happened during the Soyuz 11 disaster, when the cosmonauts' suits depressurized, tragically leading to their deaths. We imagine a tree, but forget the soil beneath. We imagine ourselves, but ignore the ecosystems that sustain us. If we resist dividing reality into parts, perhaps we will see the universe like a singular entity, like a sword perceived as a hilt, blade, and atoms.

LIFE AS INFORMATION

Life could be viewed as information, multiplying itself through the laws of physics. Life itself creates ideas like currencies, laws, and technologies; and it is the idea of life that it will die. Atoms will keep on existing, but it is the concept of life form that vanishes. Entire virtual worlds in games are real only to the players. Perhaps life, too, began as an idea – born of natural processes or divine intention. What should we believe? Is certainty even possible without uncertainty?

DOUBT AND DELUSION

We understand how thunder and electrons behave, but not fully why. Our labels – "electron," "Earth," "India" – are words for definition, not truths. Without language and measurement, we wouldn't know where or what we are.

We claim ownership of body parts, as if we are separate from them. "You broke my heart," we say, implying an observer behind the physical self. So where are we, truly? In our bodies, our food, or our environment? Perhaps, we are a complex integration of all these. But we can doubt physics and imagine souls and spirits as a part of reality. We can also doubt God and believe in atoms and molecules.

We trust our friends, partners, and children – until doubt creeps in. Doubt alters perception, whether or not it reflects reality. Without it, we might still believe the Earth is flat. If we don't question, we stagnate. Doubt drives science to balance belief with enquiry. We have tested many ideas like the flat Earth, the Ptolemaic system, the Copernican system, the Big Bang, and the alternate universes. We have to believe, but should be cautious to doubt.

Atoms were once thought indivisible, but even that idea evolved. All our understanding exists as concepts. Even physically, we are unable to see X-rays and ultraviolet rays without using lenses. So, it is human nature to relate and understand. We can only understand something as an idea (through names), and by seeing how it interacts with other ideas, we deduce further using yet another idea (numbers). We can describe the entire cosmos with words and numbers. Using numbers, we can add (believe) or subtract (doubt); we can use numbers to scale humongous galaxies and tiny electrons.

WORDS AND NUMBERS

Words and numbers are how we describe the universe. A short sentence can encode galactic truths. "The sun is 150 million kilometers from Earth." But these are our inventions – ideas that reflect and shape our understanding. Even insults and compliments are just sounds and symbols with agreed-upon meanings. Numbers help quantify mass, velocity, distance, and even time.

Alphabets use finite letters to produce infinite words, but numbers are inherently infinite. Numbers start from one, two, three, four, and go on up to infinity. A person can be 6 feet, 182 centimeters, 72 inches, or 1.82 meters tall – all different labels for the same fact. Gravity is the same everywhere on Earth, but numbers can change from culture to culture.

THE BELIEF IN NUMBERS

Stars, black holes, and all cosmic matters function by the forces of nature, but numbers don't function without our conscious efforts. Numbers are sequential beliefs; they are tools of logic and hypothesis. Number four only exists because of three and five. Numbers are in our memory and in the cognitive make-up of human nature to communicate and survive. We use math to model the cosmos, not just to gather food.

Mathematics is just an idea. It believes, after an idea there can be another idea; after one there can be two, after two there can be three, thus continuing endlessly. Modern civilization is built on such ideas – flight, electricity, space travel – once thought impossible. We imagined flying dragons before engineering aircraft. Reality forced us to conform to its laws, and in doing so, we transformed belief into function. We understood the laws of aerodynamics – Newton's laws, Bernoulli's principle, the Coanda effect – and made a real flying machine.

THE INTENT AND IDEA

Perhaps the idea of consciousness exists to preserve structural integrity with a drive toward curiosity and adaptation to protect the core of life (DNA). Life evolved into diverse forms and social cultures. Humanity, in particular, developed the capacity to belicve in fantasy, future, and fiction, while still doubting it all. Even though naturally dinosaurs were extinct, we resurrected dinosaurs inside virtual reality using 3D models, animation, artificial voice, digital feeling, and hunger to eat our human actors. We are so empathetic to care for ants and lions, unlike lions that don't care even if we are the last of our kind. We believe in invisible things like atoms, germs, X-rays, and distant stars. Wc can learn everything without discrimination.

Every life form shares a core biology, yet each is unique – just as all brains are similar, but each mind is unique in its own right. People believe in different things like how each animal is different. So, what is this idea of life? And how did empathy, the desire to understand and protect, emerge within human consciousness?

WHO ARE YOU?

II. THE IDEA OF LIFE

We are deeply empathetic about saving our planet from climate change and endangered animals from extinction. We pray to a God who cherishes every living being. Perhaps this empathy is inherited from an all-powerful creator who designed us, the Earth, and the universe. That's a thought for another chapter. For now, let's begin with the story of evolution.

But how, and why, did life evolve to become empathetic – to understand the universe, stars, climate, atoms, microorganisms, and all forms of life without discrimination? Has life always been this unselfish?

A STUPID THEORY

At the dawn of life, there were no predators, no ecosystems, only death and adaptation driven by the harsh environment. Imagine the first life form, a simple unicellular organism, whose only purpose was to eat and grow. But it couldn't consume everything. Its diet was determined by the chemical environment: what was compatible, and what was toxic. Pain emerged as a protective mechanism, shielding life from extremes – too much heat or cold – that could destroy its structure.

Unlike non-living matter, life had to protect its structural identity, replicate itself, and avoid self-destruction. Pain was the first idea that saved life from disintegration. Without it, the concept of life would have dissolved into inanimate matter, devoid of any intent to live, grow, or evolve.

If the first microorganism had stopped eating, it would have died. To preserve the concept of "aliveness," life had to eat continuously, leading to motion, growth, and eventually the development of fins, tentacles, and other adaptations. This hunger, repeated endlessly, created a future where awareness and memory helped life track time and navigate space. This cyclical existence – hunger, movement, adaptation – sowed the future of life. In this chaotic chemical soup, life couldn't afford to consume unknown substances either. The fear of the unknown led to the development of senses and memory – early forms of intelligence that allowed organisms to differentiate between safe and unsafe matter. The memorizing ability also emerged to discern safe and hostile chemicals in a vast ocean of matter.

The earliest threats faced by life weren't predators but environmental hazards: magma, meteorites, UV rays, cosmic radiation, storms, and acid rain. At the beginning, all that life consumed was non-living matter. Thus, life began to reproduce – to spread and evolve. Reproduction couldn't happen constantly due to the harshness of the environment. Dangers like sunlight, UV rays, storms, and acid rain forced early life to develop sleep and recovery cycles. This cycle of hunger, pain, regeneration, mutation, and reproduction, born from the primal struggle to survive, drove evolution. Life became a continuous chain reaction of ideas adapting to both obstacles and opportunities. Eventually, life changed the world to its comfort. The idea of Earth we have is completely wrong compared to its earliest days. And life played a crucial role in it.

ARTIFICIAL

A life form that needs to grow can potentially evolve rapidly, perhaps in millennia or even months. We, for instance, took billions of years to evolve, yet a baby replicates that evolutionary history encoded in the DNA within fifteen years.

Inside us, layers of biological ideas manifest as needs and desires. Hunger is followed by reproduction, followed by rest, and so on. But Homo sapiens, through the cognitive revolution, broke free from these primal chains. Other animals are creative only when it serves survival; humans are curious, passionate, and imaginative – even when their basic needs are met. Though everything we invent is made from the elements of this world, we categorize our creations as "artificial." Unlike spiders who weave webs to catch food, we create art that feeds no biological hunger, only emotional or intellectual curiosity. This disconnection from strict biology can feel spiritual or imaginary, but the truth remains: even this questioning mind is biology.

Pain, mutation, procreation – these were created to preserve life (DNA) against the chaos of reality. When movement was lacking, life invented locomotion. That idea later led to limbs being used for survival: claws, tentacles, wings. Every evolutionary innovation stems from the foundational goal of survival.

Life changed Earth's atmosphere – once oxygen-free – to a breathable environment via the Great Oxidation Event. That oxygen is now natural, but it was an artificial byproduct of microbial life. Likewise, today's industrialized world, driven by technology, has become our new "natural." Nothing is artificial or out of this world.

UNWELCOME GUEST

As life continued to evolve, a new concept emerged: the predator. As organisms became successful at surviving and reproducing, others adapted to feed on that success. When the availability of non-living matter became limited, life turned on itself. Organisms began consuming each other, birthing the predator-prey paradigm, which became the norm.

The Darwinian theory of evolution emerged from this interplay: survival by adaptation. This new reality pushed evolution into overdrive: sharper claws, thicker skin, venom, camouflage. Ecosystems formed around the balance of life and death. Large animals produced fewer offspring, while smaller ones relied on quantity. Social animals banded together to outwit predators.

Every species adapted differently – octopuses with beaks and camouflage, trees with thorns, reptiles with toxins. Predators developed tools to hunt; prey evolved tools to escape. The idea of converting food into weapons and tools was an evolutionary milestone.

Just as lions use teeth to protect and feed their bodies, nations today use weapons to protect their citizens. The USA's drive to explore Mars is another form of this survival instinct – to evolve and secure future resources. Germs, mosquitoes, and even human empires all operate with the same logic: survival through resource consumption. From bombs to Mars missions, we replicate the ancient drive to consume, adapt, and evolve.

CHEAT CODE: EMPATHY

"If we eat fish, it is good for us; if not, it is good for the fish." – a proverb from southern India. Every organism believes its survival is the most real, yet all have learned to manipulate others to get what they need. Understanding other organisms – like a mosquito knowing where to bite, or a lion learning a deer's blind spot – is a form of empathy. Not compassion, but strategic understanding for survival.

When brute strength is not enough, strategy and deceit become essential. Life learned to trick, domesticate, and outwit others. In modern times, humans created gods, governments, and economies – systems that manipulate collective behavior through imaginary constructs like religion, law, and money.

Evolution didn't stop at teeth and horns. It advanced into empathy – not always kindness, but the ability to understand others deeply enough to manipulate or coexist. Lions may not believe the DNA of a deer or a deer's survival, but a lion has to think about how much a deer can see to hide. We engaged in wars with each other using a myriad of weapons because each nation believed in their idea of money, language, God, culture, and knowledge. But in the 21st century, most countries can attack and defend themselves. Now, nations trade with one another regardless of ideological differences. So today people learn what other people want and sell them products and services. We use empathy to sell, negotiate, manipulate, and coexist. Modern society thrives on empathy-based exchanges. A Hindu may sell meat he doesn't eat; an American may dislike the Russian government, but will buy their goods; a Christian may disagree with homosexuality, but will use a phone invented by a gay man. Cultures, despite their taboos, consume and celebrate products from contrasting beliefs.

Empathy is now algorithmic. Social media platforms track our preferences to deliver personalized content. Businesses predict needs before we express them. In this world, understanding others is essential not for compassion alone, but for survival. Empathy enables survival in today's interconnected world. Instagram, YouTube, and Facebook provide relatable reels, videos, advertisements and posts. Social media, commerce, diplomacy – all are built on the ability to understand what others want. That's how we evolved. That's how empathy, born from survival, became the ultimate evolutionary advantage.

III. THE IDEA OF EMPATHY

Life multiplied and expanded, adopting new forms to survive in differing climates, among various predators, and within diverse environments. Each life form, as it evolved, sought to protect itself from others. What began as a single thread of existence branched into countless distinct species, each preserving its unique genetic code. Through reproduction, life eschews reality and constructs its own version of nature.

As living beings, we transform reality to serve our needs. We control our hands and bodies made of billions of atoms with our minds. Though we have evolved diverse ways to attack and defend, it has not always been enough. Every creature develops tools of survival. When teeth and claws fall short, intelligence becomes the advantage – cleverness in reading the needs and fears of others.

With humans, this takes on subtler forms: loyalty, persuasion, religion, guilt, sweet words, and empathy. The cleverest primate gets the most bananas – not through brute force, but by mastering when to lie, joke, or speak a near-truth to charm and survive in reciprocal culture. Force, through bombs, guns, or authoritarian rule, may work briefly. However, such power collapses under mistrust. The more lasting control arises through emotional and psychological manipulation. If physical control fails, the mind offers a subtler path: knowing what others want and creating illusions to control them.

An atomic bomb brings mutual peace only because each nation holds the same power, creating a fragile deterrence.

Like venom in a snake, the threat alone ensures caution. But what if instead of threatening, we understood what the snake needed – a dark hiding place – and created one to lure it peacefully? This is not brute control, but empathetic trickery: knowing the other's needs to manipulate effectively.

If we cannot dominate others physically, we cheat them through emotional and psychological conditioning. Some animals intimidate to avoid attack; others create bright colors to warn. All exploit the same principle: understanding others enough to manipulate their behavior. Empathy, at its core, is not just kindness. Evolution has used this idea in countless ingenious forms.

PARASITES

As life evolved, not all could survive by strength or speed. Some adapted by attaching themselves to other organisms and feeding off their energy. These parasites, unlike predators, survive by understanding their hosts deeply. They are clever, not cowardly. They feign harmlessness, even mutual benefit. This behavior is echoed in human systems: a priest convinces farmers that his prayers ward off floods; a king collects taxes to "protect" people but saves himself first in danger. Artists, actors, and religious leaders may not produce food or tools, yet they offer emotional or spiritual services, trading empathy for trust. The parasite must know the mind of its host, even to deceive it.

Amazon ants, particularly those of the genus Polyergus, are infamous for their slave-making behavior – one of the most striking examples of social parasitism in the natural world. These ants are utterly dependent on enslaved workers from other species to survive. Without them, Amazon ants cannot forage, care for their young, or maintain their nests. When devoid of slaves, Amazon ants launch organized raids on nearby colonies, targeting pupae. Once these stolen pupae mature in the Amazon ants' nest, they emerge and instinctively assume their roles as workers, unaware they have been kidnapped. Believing the Amazon colony to be their rightful home, they undertake all essential duties: cleaning, nursing, foraging, defending the nest, and feeding both the queen and the parasitic Amazon workers. These enslaved ants do not recognize their exploitation – a haunting mirror to human history, where countless civilizations have expanded through the violent subjugation of others, raiding villages, and forcing generations into servitude.

Around 40–50% of species are believed to be parasitic. Parasites must think like their hosts to survive. They must understand their needs and habits. Evolution favors such cleverness. Nature offers eerie parallels. The Ophiocordyceps unilateralis, or the zombie-ant fungus, releases spores from a dead ant to infect a live one, then controls its body to climb up a leaf to precisely 25 cm before dying, so the fungus can grow optimally. The jewel wasp, like a neurobiologist, injects venom into a cockroach's brain, rendering it docile. The cockroach then follows the wasp to its lair, where larvae hatch and devour it from within.

If mutual dependence defines parasitism, then perhaps we are all parasites. We depend on animals, plants, and each other for food, medicine, knowledge, companionship, and procreation. Consider hermit crabs that use the discarded shells of snails, or the Egyptian plover that picks the flesh from a crocodile's teeth, with mutual benefit.

We care for our pets not merely out of altruism, but because they fulfill our emotional needs. But do we give them freedom? Perhaps their "love" is conditioned, like the cockroach led by the wasp. If deprived of food and shelter, many pets would leave. Is their loyalty a sign of love or dependency, based on their caninc instinct to seek a companion? In some cases, it's humans who are parasitic, emotionally dependent on animals. We don't keep bulls as pets – not because they can't be loved, but because they don't adapt to our emotional demands.

Remoras hitch rides on whales and turtles, mirroring how humans once relied on bulls, elephants, and horses before engines. We domesticate cows and chickens for sustenance, often denying them natural behaviors and reproductive autonomy. Selective breeding eliminates rebellion, making them docile. Leafcutter ants farm fungi similarly, squashing any strain that misbehaves. We breed cows not for their happiness, but because they serve us well. Our ancestors selectively bred for docility, fat, and taste. We are the only species to drink other animals' milk. Ancient humans rarely consumed milk. Until the 17th century, many cultures viewed it as strange.

We may argue that we've helped cows multiply, but if evolution is only about spreading genes, what of the subjective experience? Happiness? We justify this by arguing mutual benefit. If we justify the relationship as mutual, then we must admit we are parasites – ideally, good ones. A parasite that destroys its host cannot last. A freeloader who gives nothing back cannot persist across generations. The relationship must be reciprocal, stable, and manipulative – but fair.

MORE EXAMPLES

Plants, often seen as passive and peaceful, are not exempt from evolutionary strategy. Some lure and kill. The Venus flytrap, with its delicate yet lethal jaws, seduces insects with promise, only to snap shut. The pitcher plant consumes even rats. The Rafflesia arnoldii, a corpse-scented flower, thrives by attaching itself to other plants, fooling insects into pollination rituals.

Pollination itself is a delicate trick. Flowers offer nectar in exchange for genetic spread, but some go further, lacing their nectar with caffeine. A chemical reward ensures addicted bees return, ensuring fertilization. This is not kindness. It is a brilliant behavioral manipulation. And is it so different from how we train dogs to obey for treats, or how we shape human behavior with rewards and punishments? Such manipulation mirrors our training of animals using classical and operant conditioning. Pavlov's dogs salivated to a bell; Skinner's pigeons learned to press levers for food. Food advertisements trigger our desires in the same way, without scent or substance. Elephants dance for treats. Parrots perform tricks. Dolphins leap through hoops for food. All are conditioned. Manipulated. Controlled. And it all begins with empathy – knowing what the other wants.

OUT OF GAME

Why didn't we domesticate lions or drink tiger milk? Lions are strong, but not useful. They don't farm, transport, obey, or love. So we let them fade. Now, only about 38,000 lions remain. They symbolize majesty, but provide nothing. Giraffes, too, have little role in human life, so their numbers dwindle. Noble animals perish; obedient ones thrive.

Survival, in human terms, requires utility and the ability to integrate into our system. Our interconnected society is a web of mutual dependence and manipulation. A baby cries to control the parent; parents raise children to pass on their genes. We exchange submission for benefits, freedom for security. Nations, religions, and economies are systems of belief we collectively uphold, punishing those who reject them as outcasts.

We protect what serves us. We create ecosystems of mutual slavery. Society is a vast network of dependencies, all powered by a nuanced understanding of others' needs. Those who reject this system – who refuse to submit to nations, economies, beliefs – are labeled mad, terrorists, rebels, dangerous, or obsolete. They become like lions: majestic, alone, and nearly extinct.

THE CULTURE OF CONVERSION

Our goal is always control: over nature, over each other, over chaos. We convert reality into food, shelter, ideas, and eventually, into ourselves. With 8 billion people, we've reshaped Earth into a human reflection. We consume and reproduce using matter: atoms. Belief systems spread the same way; Christianity spread by converting non-Christians.

Christians fought among themselves and separated as Catholic and Roman, yet were able to convert almost all humans, to the point that Jesus is known in every country today. Science, too, has become a belief system. If not taught, concepts like atoms would vanish. It empowers us to shape reality. Religion helps to shape our social reality.

We build belief systems that transform the invisible into the concrete. But with knowledge comes power: to control others and, increasingly, reality itself. Science, like religion, gives us tools to control and exist. Money and technology unites all beliefs; a Christian may believe in heaven, but carries money and a smartphone. Science, once revolutionary, is now fundamental to modern life.

We imagine, design, and build aircrafts, willed into reality through collective effort. We can control planes by learning how to pilot aircrafts, but to control a horse, we have to tame and domesticate it. But even so, at times the horse might send us crashing to the ground. Unlike horses, machines obey absolutely. Science is the religion that materializes imagination.

Science has become the new priesthood, controlling matter through language and numbers. A boy born to a tribe can be brought to America and raised as an American citizen. He will grow up believing in the value of dollars. If we show money to a human-shaped statue, it will not respond. But if we disintegrate the statue and convert its material into food, we can consume it. Its atoms will be digested and absorbed into our body, contributing to our growth. We may excrete a part, but the rest integrates with us. In time, that material becomes part of a baby. Raise this child in a 21st century world, and they will adopt our culture, beliefs, and systems, obedient to the constructs of modern society. Life needs power to control and survive.

Through empathy, we may be willing to sacrifice our lives, believing that our friends, children, or community will carry forward the values we hold dear. However, if we were the last person alive, stripped of all social continuity, the instinct to survive might compel us to abandon those very values in favor of self-preservation. Some martyrs, however, transcend this dilemma. Anchored by a deep belief in the afterlife, a spiritual connection to nature, or unity with the universe, they do not experience the conflict between values and survival. For them, immortality is found not in the body, but in the unwavering commitment to their principles. Their values become their legacy – eternal, even in death.

Perhaps humans never truly worship goodness. Would we pray to a god without miracles? No. A powerless god is ignored; only when resurrected does worship begin. Power is worshiped, not grace. We may sacrifice greater values for even greater power. Only if we survive can we uphold our values. We want heaven from God, and God wants us to be good. Both understand each other's needs. Empathy, in this framework, is mutual understanding leveraged for control. The Devil offers instant gratification at the cost of eternal damnation, while God promises long-term solace accompanied by the fear of hell. Yet, both operate through mechanisms of control, appealing to desire, fear, and hope. We often engage in prayer as a means of influencing the divine, much like how a crying child seeks to elicit comfort and attention from its mother, and we believe by praying we can control God.

In this culture of empathy, we control and are controlled by sex, love, loyalty, religion, money, and science. Even our biology controls us. The mind negotiates constantly between instincts and reason, giving birth to two hearts: the anatomical one, and the symbolic heart that pulses with love and empathy, our greatest tools of control.

IV. SEX AND LOVE

Life is an idea. Each idea of life carries within it a belief, shadowed by the potential for mutation, shaped by the curiosity of evolution, and protected by layers of doubt and conviction. Ideas remain for a time, and then become obsolete. Some ideas survive longer because they adapt, learning how to preserve their structure against the threats of environment, predators, or genetic decay. As humans, we've learned to sustain our biological structure for more than sixty years. Once an idea is created, it doesn't simply vanish; it lingers, stimulates, and echoes.

In 2001, a shark at the Henry Doorly Zoo gave birth without a male – parthenogenesis, a relic from our ancient asexual origins. Though overwritten by sexual evolution, asexuality still lingers, quietly embedded in biological memory. Our body heals itself, digests food without command, and simplifies perception so we can respond quickly. We ran from predators without consciously interpreting vision; the process of merging colors to render an image is not at all in our control. The adrenaline stimulates us; we can't even think straight in those moments of panic. Growth, digestion, reproduction – all occur without our will. We grow, but we don't control the growing; it's an intelligent organic program. We only have to eat. Biology does half the work for us; the growing process is automatic.

DEATH AND BIRTH

Ask someone how they grow, and they'll be puzzled, because growth is not volitional. Eating? We know. Running?

We know. But growing is an unconscious biological act. Ask how you run or do stunts? We know how to explain, but the important part of our life is not within our limited, controllable consciousness. We grow, but we don't do the "growing"; it is an organic program that resides inside every cell, very intelligently transforming the broken food particles into energy inside us. Because we don't control everything, we are one part of an idea created by life.

If reality accepts life, life shouldn't have problems to live and spread. Our struggle to live and adapt is an effort to be real, yet in living we inevitably move toward dying. Reality accommodates life, and in return, life strives to persist, adapt, and survive. And according to the chaos theory, an order in a system will only get disordered over time. Even in an open system such as our solar system, order only begets more disorder. Then, however we try, we can only elongate our life to some extent, but not to eternity, because the surrounding things will corrupt our organic material. The wear and tear happens to life. So death is nearly inevitable.

Consider a paradox: can God create a stone too heavy for Himself to lift? If God can create a stone heavier than Himself, he will get smashed and die. If He cannot, He is also not omnipotent. But God is omnipotent; he can become stronger than the stone that is heavier than him, and then lifting the heavier stone will become an easier task. But if the stone is lighter than him, that means God is cheating. God can die making a heavier stone. God can die by suicide, but God can also resurrect and escape death. God can reproduce and resurrect to solve death. The immortal jellyfish (Turritopsis dohrnii) can be considered a god, for example. Biologically, it can revert to its baby form, recycling its growth again when it hits puberty. It doesn't die, but it can get hurt and killed.

Humans, too, create tools of their own destruction: cars, bombs, weapons. Yet, we also invent systems – traffic laws, peace treaties, therapies, medicine – to delay death. Few animals have created poisons that can injure themselves, but many have developed immunity too. Electric eels don't shock themselves. Even cancer that grows in our body without control is treated by medicines. Even if the world corrupts our cells to make us old and rust, reproduction and mutation will help us survive. Reproduction ensures continuity despite entropy, but even reproduction can damage us. The Antechinus mates until death. Elephant seals fight fatally over mates. In human society, much like in the animal world, we are expected to win over the opposite gender – not using feathers or songs, but with gossip, skill, through rivalry with other people, money, extravagant gifts, and costly dates.

DNA may be the blueprint, but the epigenome translates it, and with each replication, information degrades. Our reproduction itself causes genetic damage. A simple cell division might make the epigenome lose its identity. Thus, sleep and repair become essential, and constant change remains the secret to survival. Reproduction isn't just for survival – it challenges outdated knowledge and allows novelty to emerge. Children grow up in changed worlds, with new predators and environments. Their risks and curiosity drive evolution. The new generation is more enthusiastic, without the grumpiness of failures and the comfort of familiarity, to take risks, to find new resources to evolve more and better.

LOSS OF CONTROL

To overcome death, we create a smaller version of ourselves to pass our genetic information. The body is brilliant enough not to let us decide how to create sperm and eggs, nor a child. We control some parts of the body, and the body controls some. People often say, "I got the idea out of nowhere," as if a sudden flash of genius struck without warning. This common expression hints at a fascinating aspect of our brain's function: not all intelligent processing occurs within the sphere of conscious control. In reality, our brains operate through the interplay of distinct systems that work in tandem, yet not always in our awareness. Top-down processing is associated with the neo-cortex, the part of the brain responsible for voluntary, effortful thought. It enables us to deliberate, reason, and even suppress emotional responses when necessary. Bottom-up processing operates more rapidly and largely outside of our conscious awareness. This system draws on raw sensory data and automatic, intuitive responses. It is driven by emotions and gut feelings, and it can swiftly integrate fragmented information. Often, these automatic processes resolve complex problems in the background, culminating in an unexpected burst of insight or a "eureka!" moment. When we experience that sudden flash of insight – when the idea appears to have come "out of nowhere" – it is actually the result of continuous, background processing. While the conscious mind is engaged in deliberate thought, the unconscious brain is busy integrating sensory input, memories, and emotional cues. In moments when the conscious mind temporarily "loses control" or steps back from active problem-solving, the automatic, bottom-up processes can reveal novel connections and solutions.

Love may not be what we think. Is it real love, or biology's manipulation? Hormones separate humanity into genders, shaping our psychology and physiology. A man begging for love might merely be echoing DNA's urgency. Maybe biology is informing the male that he will die, as his DNA is slowly decaying, and stimulating that he should beg, flirt, bond, mate, and procreate. We sacrifice everything – wealth, pride, power – for love, but is it our choice? Or is it biology hijacking our mind? We will die in the distant future, and we are mentioning in poems and films that our sexual partner, children, and family are more important than the food, the Moon, or the universe. We are controlled by one idea (DNA), which creates another idea like eyes, legs, or sex, and our brain is also such an idea. That brain is free to think and care about atoms, animals, and climate, not only about its biological body. But the altruistic brain is influenced by the underlying biology and its selfish beliefs.

BELIEF OF BIOLOGY

Biology believes in its own structure; it strives to preserve the current form. Only when it senses that this structure may no longer suffice for survival does it evolve. The inherent stubbornness of belief is that it sees itself as truth, and anything contradictory as malware, impurity, or poison. A lion believes it must hunt a deer, and a deer believes it must graze. Both perish without their roles. Molecules with incompatible chemistries tend not to bond peacefully. Biology is, then, a kind of hardwired belief, stubborn and self-sustaining, until confronted by an environmental threat and a compatible source that forces it to adapt. But if the threat is too hostile, life ceases altogether. A frog thrown into lava tries to jump – not because lava is foreign, but because the frog's biological integrity is under threat. Life, though composed of the same atoms as lava, holds within it the information – the drive – to live and replicate. Only compatible sources and environmental pressure can prompt change. Though lava and life share atoms, one seeks order, the other entropy.

Life forms, therefore, are not easily altered, merged, or reverted – they require both an internal doubt about their existing form, and an external pressure or enemy to trigger transformation. We have a brain, and we use the brain to ask why. Our brain enables thought so that we can go beyond instinct and innovate survival strategies. Unlike animals that rely on bloodlines and claws, we rely on empathy, gods, governments, and tools. Life's compelling drive to live and spread uses intelligence, not just instincts.

SELFISH LOVE

Sex also created cooperation. The moment reproduction became a two-player game of bonding and betrayal, the sexual paradigm replaced the asexual, and the solitary became an outcast. Sexual creatures developed systems of bonding, trickery, alliances, and intimacy that built groups mimicking singular bodies. Unlike bees or ants, we preserve individuality while cooperating. But interpersonal relationships dominate human discourse. Most of our daily dialogues revolve around relationships, not science, religion, or space.

Sex is the bridge between selfish genes. For all our lofty intellect, a curious alien observing Earth would find porn more accessible than a nuclear blueprint. A male and a female with a child constituted a family. For the sake of the child's future, particularly to enable them to form bonds and eventually reproduce with another individual, the parents formed connections with others – thus creating a network of relatives who shared similar beliefs and values. From couples to children to families, we formed tribes. Tribes bred routine, which gave way to agriculture, language, gods, money, and war. With the domestication of plants and animals came leisure, contemplation, and the invention of abstract institutions. Now, we bond not just by blood, but through ideologies: money, love, nationalism, religion, identity, and fandoms – books, art, music, science. Over the primal instincts, we wear masks of tolerance and universality. Though violence and hierarchy remain, we now try to love everything: planet, people, animals, climate, even the stars. We strive to love and protect everything: the Earth, other species, the vulnerable. We have developed empathy to better understand our place within the ecosystem. As a result, we strive to protect our planet from threats such as global warming, asteroids, diseases, and psychological challenges, ultimately aiming to ensure our survival in the universe. While we attempt to extend love and care to all forms of life, our intimate relationships remain exclusive to our own species. This raises a profound question: is the love we share within our species truly unconditional, or is it a construct shaped by our brain and body to make us believe that it is?

CONDITIONS OF THE BODY AND BRAIN

Biology dictates desire. Males find bosoms attractive. Females seek strength, status, social power, and security. In many bird species, it is evident that males display vibrant colors, making them more visible to predators but also more attractive to females. In contrast, among Homo sapiens, attractiveness is not primarily visual. Instead, it is often defined by social connections, communal participation, tolerance, emotional intelligence, and the accumulation of wealth and social power. Early humans had no names, language, culture, or individuality. The earliest human couples may have fallen in love at first sight and engaged in sexual activity almost instinctively. Then came the storm: language, laws, hierarchy, god, and guilt. Over time, sex became ritualized, wrapped in laws, religions, expectations. As civilization progressed and humans acquired more leisure time, sex – once a natural and vital function – was increasingly moralized. In efforts to transcend basic instincts, societies began framing sexual desire as sinful, linking abstinence to spiritual enlightenment and the promise of heaven. Social and religious constructs started to shape behavior that once belonged purely to biology.

As civilization grew, sex became the foundation of tribes, families, politics, and economy. The collective nature of human society made tasks like protection, hunting, foraging, and food distribution more efficient as population grew. Biology works beneath culture. The brain, however, adds layers – love, art, politics, pride. Yet, our sexual behaviors and roles remain shaped by a complex interplay of biological drives and social constructs. At times, biology asserts itself; at other times, societal and religious norms suppress or redirect those impulses – and, in some cases, those very norms are rooted in biological imperatives.

COMPLICATED CONDITIONS

Despite our philosophical pursuits and awareness of history, we remain unaware of ovulation or gamete production. Yet we know how to love and mate. We are molded not just by biology, but by the intricate web of human inventions: culture, language, philosophy, science. Our mind may defy biology, but our body always circles back.

Today, even a middle-class life surpasses that of a medieval king. But happiness? It remains elusive. Kings had to wait for entertainment; we binge on demand. Still, dissatisfaction persists. Happiness is shaped by attitudes, and attitudes are shaped by society, but remain biologically grounded: eat, sleep, reproduce. But the brain demands meaning.

Courtship has evolved. It now demands emotional labor: knowing your partner's mind. You must decode their beliefs, soothe their fears, stimulate their intellect, and become their mirror. And they must do the same.

Love now requires compromise, empathy, understanding, synchronization of belief. Every lasting relationship involves compromise. Long-married couples will confess to fights, but also to growth, forgiveness, and acceptance. Over time, love becomes familiarity. Predictability becomes comfort. And if unpredictable chaos strikes – affairs, betrayal, violence – love can vanish. If love were unconditional, could you accept your partner's love for another? Could a mother love a stranger's child the same way as her own? If the answer is no, then love is conditional.

Our altruistic brain tries to show universal empathy even at greater risk. At times, the brain seeks to form emotional connections, even with things that may be inherently dangerous, such as snakes, electricity, the vacuum of space, or burning stars. However, it is biology and the experience of pain that serve as critical checks, constantly assessing conditions to ensure our survival.

ANGLERFISH

Unconditional love is a myth. Would you still love your partner if they changed gender, beliefs, or revealed a dark past? If you lost your memory, would you love them again? Familiarity, memory, shared dreams – all conditions. If love were unconditional, every mother could love every child. But maternal love requires gestation, birth, bonding – conditions.

Imagine a marriage where minds are telepathically connected. Pure transparency. No secrets. Total empathy. But is this love or loss of individuality? Pure love? Your partner would know your thoughts, even the awkward or inappropriate ones. You would become one mind – intimate, but exposed.

This is the anglerfish. In sexual reproduction, the tiny male fuses permanently into the female's body. No secrets. No individuality. The praying mantis male loses its head. This is love as sacrifice. And yet, we flinch at this loss of self. We want love, but not at the cost of identity. We are driven to protect our belief in the concept of personality. A crocodile devours a zebra not out of malice, but as a means of preserving its own existence – its own form of belief. Without nourishment, the crocodile's body would decay, reducing to mere bones, a fragment of the physical structure it once identified with. The remaining organic matter would, in turn, be consumed by scavengers, each protecting and sustaining their own existence through consumption. A crocodile kills to preserve its structure, as do we. Even within our multicellular selves, individual cells fight for survival.

At the core of this behavior lies our origin as single-celled organisms, whose instinct to preserve the self persists even within the complex machinery of multicellular life. This primal drive often operates in tension with our capacity for altruism. From this evolutionary foundation, the so-called "selfish gene" gave rise to an empathic heart – one capable of belief, control, and the transmission of information. Yet, even amid empathy, the sharp teeth of doubt remain.

Biology and the brain share a fundamental trait: both believe in their constructed reality. Biology expresses this belief through mutation and evolution, constantly changing and adapting to remain in harmony with the environment. Similarly, the brain generates ideas it perceives as real: nations, money, gods, and even unconditional love. But like biology, the brain revises its beliefs, adapting them to enhance survival and promote evolution.

Both biology and the brain seek to survive, adapt, and evolve. Unconditional love may be a beautiful story, but biology and belief are rooted in conditions.

GODS AND DOUBTS

We now possess medicines and advanced machines that free us from mundane tasks and keep us healthy, even immune to most diseases. Yet, in this age of abundance, why do we not reproduce more? Could it be that our brains have evolved to foresee the perils of overpopulation? But then, how many potential lives have been spared by the use of contraception? Might it be considered a grave sin to withhold the birth of souls? Or have we stopped believing in souls altogether? Do we now consider souls and spirits as mere inventions of our minds? While we consume enough to conserve for future generations, we are hesitant to create a future that is overly populated.

Consider this short story:

A doctor in a village had many sick patients. He gave them a super medicine, but it only worked for one particular family, while the rest continued to suffer. Later, the doctor tested a new medicine, but it made things worse for everyone except for the already-healthy family. Fearing that the sickness might spread, the doctor prepared another new medicine and gave the healthy family a precautionary antidote. The family, who had previously healed, warned others to drink two liters of water before taking the medicine. But no one believed them. The new medicine, unfortunately, killed everyone except the healthy family. They praised the doctor for being benevolent and called him the "good doctor" because, logically, there were no sick people left – because there were no people left at all. The doctor then vowed never to test such medicines without proper understanding.

This story is an analogy of Noah and the flood. According to the plan of God, the flood wiped out all but Noah's family. But if God is omnipotent, why could he not save some of the others from that time? Does that not imply a limit to his power, as God could only save the future by sacrificing the past? Or is He engaged in an endless cycle of killing and saving, such that we experience only one facet of His power at a time? We often complain that God does nothing against evil, but when He does act, we complain again. It raises the question: if God can create humans, why can He not manufacture perfect ones? Instead, He must select those capable of avoiding evil. Our insistence on these explanations for an ostensibly immoral God marks the beginning of our conflicting nature – a union of our inherently selfish hearts with a desire for something unselfish.

If we were content merely with our close kin, there would be no cooperative societies or global unity today. To collaborate with strangers, we require the promise of reciprocal benefit – a prerequisite for nation-building and collective strength. Our beliefs have evolved over time, as dramatically as the 13th Amendment abolished slavery or the 19th Amendment granted women the right to vote. Some nations now legalize same-sex marriages, but until the 19th century, homosexuality was punishable in every nation. We have even shifted our worldview from the geocentric notion of the Sun revolving around the Earth to the heliocentric truth, from Newtonian laws to Einstein's relativity. What were once considered immutable truths have transformed because we questioned, doubted, and consequently evolved our beliefs to survive better.

THE POWER OF DOUBT

Often, we cling to ideas as if they are immutable truths. Some still reject evolution and cling to the notion of a fixed human form. Christians argue that evolution or natural selection is wrong, and that humans were created in a fixed form from the beginning. But, according to the Bible, we were naturally selected for heaven, not through a fixed act of creation. First, God established nature, then created Adam and Eve, only to cast them out of Eden because they were not evolved enough to resist temptation. Later, He selected Noah's family by erasing all others in the great flood – only the chosen were destined for heaven. If God has made the nature of the world and humans, then we are all naturally selected or unselected by that nature. Even in Revelation, God promises to choose those most worthy for heaven, not predestined from the start.

The creationism debate raises a valid point: if no fixed form or guiding force exists, how does evolution occur? Consider the four fundamental forces of nature. The electric eel (or knife fish) utilized electricity long before we understood it – not through magic, but because we are all composed of electrons. Each life uses these forces differently – from the quantum to the cosmic scale – enabling myriad evolutionary paths shaped by environment, predators, and available resources. Perhaps this force was created by God or a designer, but we do not yet know. Still, our brains are quick to believe in physics or in God.

Christianity teaches monotheism, meaning there is only one God responsible for creation. But if one God made everything, why hasn't all evil been eradicated? If evil exists, it means that the same God is responsible for both good and bad things, but we often attribute the evil to a devil. Zoroastrianism, on the other hand, proposes two equally powerful gods, one good and one bad. The good one created the soul, and the bad one created the body. But who created these gods? Were they created by one another, or by something else? And how can we assume that an all-powerful God cannot act in ways that seem negative – cannot test or punish? As Isaiah 45:7 declares, "I form light and create darkness; I make weal and create woe; I am the Lord, who does all these things."

Atheists argue that there is no God in the universe. But how can we be certain? We have never seen black holes except in images shared by scientists. Similarly, atheists have never visited Mars. How can we be sure that there is no God if we can't search the entire universe? If there is truly only one God in the universe, then every religion on Earth should have converged upon a similar concept of the divine. The doctrines of Christianity – or any other faith claiming universal truth – should have naturally prevailed across all cultures, long before the age of European colonization, when religious texts were carried across oceans in ships. Was God, then, afraid to swim? Of course not. Rather, it was us who carried a culturally rooted, geographically bound deity across the seas to spread His doctrines.

And if this God is real, an even deeper question arises: who, then, created God? Even the origin of God resembles scientific enquiry: perhaps God was created by another deity, or perhaps God has always existed – an automatic process akin to the Big Bang, which occurred independently. We continually doubt and question, seeking to rationalize our ideas. Even if God exists, He might not hold one unchangeable belief; like us, He could evolve through doubt.

CHANGING BELIEFS

In the early eons, God believed that there was no need to create anything, but later He believed He was incomplete without man. Then, He believed man should not be alone, so He created woman. He gave them hunger, air to breathe, and land to walk on. Yet, He did not bestow wings for flight; instead, He created male and female organs for reproduction. The Bible does not explicitly claim that Eve was conceived as immortal (a notable plot gap), implying that the fall occurred within a brief period. Initially, God did not intend for His creations to experience pain or death. It was only after Eve tasted the forbidden fruit that God decreed death and pain as inevitable for His offspring. Why did God create the forbidden fruit and place it in the garden? If Adam and Eve were perfect, why did they fall? Why would a benevolent God allow for temptation? After they ate the fruit, why did God change His belief in them? And how does our prayer convince God of our worthiness, as descendants of Adam and Eve? Is the mystery of the forbidden fruit embedded in our very genes – evidence that God's belief is not singular but steeped in doubt? Even if God is real, He operates with a belief that embraces doubt.

Our beliefs are fluid. Just as God's beliefs changed throughout creation, our own beliefs evolve. Evolution doesn't just apply to biology but to the ideas we hold. What was once accepted as truth – like the belief that the Earth was flat or that the Sun revolved around it – has been replaced by new understanding. Our brain adapts, but it does so through a process of doubt and reflection.

BRAIN vs. BODY

The truth is, we are but refugees of existence, confined to places where we can survive, gradually adopting new traits for new habitats. We are inherently creative beings; our beliefs change over decades, and even simple words evolve for sensitivity: "garbage collection" replaces "waste disposal," "handicapped" becomes "physically challenged," and "lepers" becomes "Hansen's disease." Our bodies evolve slowly, adapting to new environments to survive. Biology has sustained our bodies for 70,000 years. Yet, to override pain or repair injuries, we rely on drugs and medical interventions. Biology is resistant to sudden change, but our intelligence – our brains – can revise beliefs instantaneously. We are creative beings, and through our intelligence, we have achieved breakthroughs that our biology alone could have never done.

Even though biology is stubborn, intelligence can break through. We can change our beliefs instantly – something biology does only slowly. The brain can adapt and innovate, using knowledge and creativity to invent new tools and solutions. In this ever-evolving process, our beliefs and ideas are not fixed. We constantly shift, grow, and adapt as we search for truth and meaning, exploring the limits of existence through both science and spirituality.

A child born in India might flourish in America and grow to love it, while another may rebel and seek refuge in Canada. A scientist can shift from quantum field theory to string theory in mere months. Imagine if biology allowed you to decide when to sleep – would you choose to sleep or spend your time mindlessly scrolling on your phone? We groom our hair in salons without pain, and adorn our skin with tattoos because we have lost the primal sting of biology. The process by which our bodies convert raw matter to support our existence and share our genetic material across the globe and galaxy is painstaking and relies on the luck of natural selection and mutation. But we have used our brains to create things that our biology might have taken ages to develop, or perhaps never could. Through the power of our minds, we have crafted miraculous medicines, groundbreaking gadgets, extraordinary machines, intelligent computers, and fast vehicles, all with the promise of a future utopia where nothing can harm us.

We yearn for new ways to find joy, to unravel the mysteries of energy and matter, and to pass this wonder on to our children. Only with a spacesuit did we walk on the Moon – not with our naked biology, but with technology that supported our survival. Our journey on the lunar surface was brief, as oxygen was a limiting factor, compelling our return. Now, we search for alternative ways to travel, to terraform alien planets, and even build robots that might one day surpass our capabilities if we are not cautious. Our brains take risks that biology cannot, propelling innovation even as our bodies remain bound by evolutionary constraints.

The brain can doubt the information it receives, contemplate nihilism, ponder the consequences of overpopulation, religious dogma, and nuclear power. Even the beliefs we once held – such as racism, the afterlife, the soul, the flat Earth, and the static universe – have been abandoned. But were these beliefs truly false, or have we simply come to believe they were?

TO BELIEVE AND DOUBT

How was Hitler able to create an army that could stand against the might of the greatest nations if his beliefs were fundamentally false? Does his death erase his beliefs from existence, or do we still remember him and teach our children how wrong those beliefs were? We believe in Hitler, but in a negative sense. We teach the lessons of history to ensure that future generations do not repeat the mistakes of the past. In this way, our understanding of the past – of what is right and wrong – becomes a form of belief, just as much as our current beliefs shape the way we live today.

This is similar to the way DNA "teaches" our cells not to grow tails, develop wings, or sprout horns, as these organic beliefs would not have helped humanity survive and thrive. The greatest pyramid ever built for the Egyptian gods still stands, yet the gods themselves have long since faded from belief. Now, no one believes in them, and this non-belief in itself has become a belief. We consume and reshape reality according to what we believe defines us, but the brain also finds imaginative ways to push evolution forward. Today, our children are not just biological offspring, but also the brainchild of our minds: movies, laws, machines, software, satellites, theories, inventions, and discoveries.

While we cannot control basic bodily functions – women cannot control the inner workings of the womb – our intelligence might have created entirely different beings if it weren't beholden to biology. We might not have created human beings at all. Instead, we might have created creatures like Mickey Mouse, centaurs, fairies, angels, or humans in idealized forms. The brain does not adhere to the limitations of the body. It is free. And when the body is in pain, the brain often needs to override that pain in order to find solutions, like performing surgeries to heal the body.

Our minds also create different divine figures and ideologies. Throughout history, many human beings have killed others who did not share their beliefs. Few have renounced sex. But we are capable of doubting these beliefs and changing them. The brain has a self-correcting mechanism that allows us to identify flaws in our reasoning and to liberate ourselves from these limitations. The brain develops medicines to cure diseases, but it also creates new ailments like obesity, diabetes, sleep disorders, anxiety, and addictions. Yet, we are also capable of extraordinary achievements: space travel, heart transplants, artificial intelligence, quantum computing, and reducing genetic disorders through genome editing. In our quest to conquer the universe, we even revive extinct species, as demonstrated by the Pyrenean ibex, or recreate 3D models of the Tyrannosaurus rex in movies.

The Earth now contains information about the solar system and the entire galaxy. One point in the universe now holds knowledge about the entire universe. We are learning about the past – about the T.rex, galaxy formation, rare elements, and the origins of life. We strive to understand our biological history through genetics, DNA, and the study of extinct organisms, using fossils to understand how life evolved and what conditions allowed it to thrive. We remember Hitler, and study dinosaurs, monkeys, bacteria, and every facet of life. We are on a quest to learn about evolution because we are certain that we did not create the body ourselves. We merely control it, using atoms and subjecting ourselves to the pain-pleasure algorithms of biology.

Yet one must ask: why do we yearn to resurrect the dead, or invent new characters in novels and films? Unlike animals, we do not have natural predators or harsh environments to drive mutation and evolution. Yet, we can be our own worst enemies, capable of creating weapons of mass destruction and suffering from psychological conditions that harm us. We have the power to overthink, leading to depression and suicide. We create villains like Darth Vader, the Joker, Sauron, Voldemort, Thanos, and many fictional antagonists whose hatred mirrors our own inner conflicts. We simulate futures to determine which path best ensures our survival and prosperity. We create alternate future simulations, exploring which paths may lead to a safer existence for us. Through stories of superheroes like Spiderman, we are taught not to be selfish, to embrace creativity, and to act courageously. These fictional tales reinforce rationality and good behavior, helping us adapt and survive in the real world. Many fictional tales have reinforced rationality and ethical behavior, equipping us to face a rapidly changing reality. In films that celebrate alien encounters, eccentric personalities, paradoxes, quantum uncertainty, and robotic companions, we see reflections of our own journey into new realms – searching for energy, new environments, and the means to adapt and thrive.

We teach our children about historical figures – Jesus, Buddha, Einstein, and Hitler – so they will learn from the past, striving to avoid the mistakes of those who came before them. We seek to find new ways to evolve, to challenge old beliefs, and to think creatively about how to adapt and survive. We don't want the same answers, even though we continue to study hard to understand them.

Our brain might once have believed in gods, magic, the flat Earth, and the ether, but it is also capable of doubting these beliefs. Thus, we must find a way to cope with both spirituality and science, even when they seem in conflict. We need to find a balance between our biological instincts and our cognitive abilities, allowing us to live in harmony with both.

CONFLICTING SOLUTIONS

Living beings, due to their fear of getting hurt, evolved hardened skeletons. In fear that the body might not survive, we adapted, growing fingers and fingerprints that enabled us to grasp branches and later, small tools to invent and create. Interestingly, this same evolutionary trait appeared in koalas and some primates. While we now use our fingerprints as a symbol of individuality, secured by biometric scans, koalas and gorillas continue to use them for their original purpose: gripping. This is because they lack cognitive capacities such as abstract thinking, memory retention, and storage systems like language, writing, or modern data chips. Yet, if challenged, they too might evolve. Life can change its form – its belief in form – when compelled. From wingless rodents emerged winged bats; from tailed monkeys, tailless humans. Such biological transformations occur only when there is a persistent and severe threat to the existing structure of belief. Until then, biology remains resistant – stubborn, unchanging – unless the environment becomes a forceful guide. However, the brain's instant solutions are not always right. They often require revisions. In this way, evolution is both biological and cognitive, a continuous dialogue between fear, adaptation, and correction. This conflict between biology and the brain – between instinct and intellect – shapes much of human existence.

To sum up, our biology might affirm that sex is inherently good, yet our cultural beliefs can label it sinful – leading some to embrace celibacy, as in the cases of nuns, priests, monks, or practitioners of *brahmacharya*. Our bodies can be programmed to protect us through pain, while our minds might repurpose meals for dietary or even divine aims. Jainism, for example, enforces stringent rules to be followed throughout life, forbidding eggs, fish, meat, and even most root vegetables. Our bodies may insist on self-preservation, while our brains become captivated by the flight of birds, inspiring the creation of Boid's algorithm – not because it directly benefits our biology, but because it is a manifestation of our intellectual curiosity. The brain, driven by imagination, seeks to create things that transcend the body's basic needs. We strive to fly, not for food or reproduction, but for exploration and discovery.

This conflict between biology and the brain, between natural instincts and intellectual beliefs, is ever-present. We might believe that natural childbirth is ideal, yet we doubt biology and opt for a cesarean delivery. We might believe that string theory is the ultimate explanation of quantum dynamics, yet we harbor doubts and seek alternatives.

The potential of biology remains a mystery. Out of nowhere, it produced a brain capable of imagining gods, studying quantum physics, and understanding the universe. Biology has evolved to the point where it can engage with fields like physics, chemistry, the arts, and mathematics. Even a dung beetle knows a thing or two about astronomy!

V. BODY AND MIND

Biology creates all organs in compliance with the laws of reality. Every organic function – lungs for breathing, legs for walking, wings for flying, fins for swimming, and the brain for thinking – operates under the laws of physics. To form an organic body, life requires tangible matter: atoms, quantum particles, and molecules. This implies that life must inherently "know" the rules of physics in order to exist and evolve.

But do we truly need a brain just to breathe or to exist? Life has evolved not through conscious learning, but through the blind trial and error of mutation. Natural selection has allowed us to bend reality to suit our survival by growing hard shells, developing horns, and reproducing. These are all scientifically explainable, yet they have occurred largely by chance. There is intelligence in evolution, although not in the conscious sense we often attribute to it.

However, biology couldn't rely solely on the environment to push evolution forward. It needed something more – a brain not bound by fear and pain. Imagination evolved: the ability to dream of dragons, to believe in a world beyond death, to visualize realms invisible to the naked eye. We've conceived of particles smaller than our eyes can detect, and we've discovered forms of radiation our senses can't perceive. We've come to understand electrons, electricity, and even paradoxes like Schrödinger's cat and quantum entanglement.

Without imagination, we might have accepted only the macro-level reality and never questioned the deeper layers of existence. But through curiosity and belief, we created tools like microscopes – glasses that magnify the hidden intricacies of the microscopic world. At first, we may doubt their accuracy, but repeated evidence compels belief. The rules of reality, based on consistent axioms, remain unchanged. While the shape, speed, size, and interaction of matter may vary, the fundamental laws guiding them remain constant. So, no matter how many times we look, the glass will always magnify.

Yet, as a species that became intelligent, humans often believe in fairies and dragons more readily than quantum physics. This imaginative capacity stems from a mind that is not shackled to fixed beliefs. It can doubt and question everything. In contrast, the body lives by a different rhythm; it follows the biological loop of form: young to old, reactive only when its integrity is threatened. It persists, operating on instinct and unconscious belief.

Still, this seemingly mindless body has done remarkably clever things to help life endure the challenges of reality.

SUPERVISION

The Puerto Rican boa, the fire-chaser beetle, certain vipers, and vampire bats can detect infrared rays to sense body heat and track their prey. For centuries, priests and mystics have claimed that reality is merely an illusion, that what we perceive is only a fraction of what exists. Yet it wasn't until scientists developed the technology to visualize these "invisible" rays that we truly began to believe it. It took humanity nearly nineteen centuries to observe infrared radiation, while snakes evolved the ability to perceive it through natural means, without relying on complex mathematics or sophisticated gadgets.

A human can believe in an afterlife or an invisible god. But if you try to explain to a snake that another world exists beyond its sensory reach, it won't believe you. We can understand concepts like X-rays and ultraviolet rays because we have imagination – something the snake lacks. And because we can imagine, we can even entertain ideas like the fourth dimension or the multiverse. If snakes had imagination like ours, perhaps we could convince them to believe in the existence of other dimensions.

Our ancestors already believed in what they could not see: souls, heaven, forest spirits, fire gods, thunder devils, and mythical monsters. Even today, our naked eyes remain blind to many aspects of reality. It is only through lenses and machines that we can see the invisible. We've even learned to observe atoms using electrons through electron microscopy. Our perception has been extended – not by evolution alone, but by our capacity to imagine what lies beyond perception.

LIGHT

Unlike most birds, the black kite is known to fly toward wildfires, pick up burning sticks, and drop them into areas where prey animals have taken refuge, thereby flushing them out to hunt. Although not yet definitively proven, sightings and reports by Aboriginal communities and some researchers suggest that black kites, brown falcons, and whistling kites practice this remarkable behavior.

Strange and wondrous forms of light illuminate the forest, caves, and the depths of the ocean – bioluminescence. Life has not only learned to create light but also electricity. Fish, like the knifefish and elephantfish, evolved to generate electrical fields long before we harnessed electricity ourselves. While it took us millennia to produce the first light bulb, countless deep-sea creatures and insects had already mastered light for communication, camouflage, hunting, or mating.

The anglerfish, for instance, uses light to lure its prey. Cuttlefish flashes dazzling patterns to confuse predators or blend with their surroundings. The foxfire mushroom emits light to repel animals with an instinctive fear of heat, while simultaneously attracting insects to spread its spores. The glow worm uses light to hunt insects. The sea snail Bullina lineata, transparent and delicate, uses bioluminescence to communicate with mates or deter threats. Fireflies light up to attract partners during warm summer nights.

Across the spectrum of life forms – bacteria and fungi to mollusks and insects – bioluminescence serves countless functions. Meanwhile, Homo sapiens, with all our intellectual might, took 5,000 years to reach the age of artificial lighting, and 2.5 million years if you trace back to the Stone Age. It wasn't until the 20th century that we began to utilize radiation in meaningful ways. And then we discovered the unimaginable: Cryptococcus neoformans, a fungus thriving in the ruins of Chernobyl, actually consumes radiation. This alone is a powerful reminder: nothing is impossible in the vast and mysterious realm of biology.

ART

Is the definition of art rooted in aesthetics? Is it wrong to consider something as dark and chaotic as hell to be art? If art has no fixed form, then anything can be called art. But our creative expressions are subtly shaped by biology. Our art often carries a human form, cultural paradigms, and deeper meanings. It is rarely random.

Art has also become a symbol of high social status. The poor cannot afford to buy art. Ironically, many artists remain poor when they create their masterpieces, only to become wealthy – or forgotten – later. Art, in many ways, is a luxury. Who else would buy a painting instead of food or education for their children, if not someone already secure in their survival? Comfort gives an organism the freedom to play, and from play emerges creativity, engagement, and expression.

Take the peacock, for instance. It evolved a flamboyant tail not because it helped survival, but because it had the freedom to attract a mate through aesthetic display. If the peacock had faced constant danger, it would likely have evolved a smaller, less conspicuous tail to escape predators. The bowerbird, native to Australia, builds intricate arches from sticks, decorating them with fruits and flowers – not to survive, but to charm a mate.

In our human case, art often aims to attract attention and admiration. But why are we drawn to things that don't provide immediate warmth, sustenance, or protection? A peacock's feather may attract more predators than a crow's plain black wings. Similarly, our celebrities – modern-day peacocks – attract as much criticism and gossip as they do praise. This is because creativity often blooms when basic biological needs are met. Art is a risk, a push beyond comfort, an invitation to danger, like placing a gold-coated pyramidion atop a 722-foot monument built by our civilization.

Interestingly, the most artistic animals are often those with fewer predators – or those with means to escape them. What we interpret as "art" might be a survival mechanism, a mating display, or even an evolutionary accident. The snail's spiral shell, the leopard's patterned skin, the elephant's tusks, the bee's hexagonal comb, the termite's towering mound, the whale's song, the frog's croak, and the bird's plumage – these are biological expressions that, to our human eyes, become art and music.

Sometimes, art also functions as a tool for sexual selection. Without reproduction, a species risks extinction, so animals compete for attention and mates. Peacock spiders perform complex dances; the red-capped manakin moonwalks like Michael Jackson; the male frigate bird inflates a bright red pouch like a balloon. These displays, though artistic to us, are essential evolutionary behaviors in their worlds.

BODY OR BRAIN

Everything the body created is a survival tool: hands, legs, wings, venom, horns, fins. These were physical adaptations designed to navigate the challenges of reality. But the brain went further – it invented abstract tools: pens, hammers, swords, springs, bolts, gears, wheels, and guns. These creations were not extensions of the body, but of the mind to help the body survive. Biology and the brain apparently worked on the same aim but used different approaches.

Long before humans learned to make strings for stitching or fishing, the spider was already spinning silk. Even today, spider silk is stronger than steel. And speaking of steel, the scaly-foot gastropod – a deep-sea snail – developed metal-infused shells and scales while living near underwater volcanoes. Consider the beaver, a rodent that builds complex dams. These structures not only protect them from predators but also preserve food for winter. Is this the result of conscious engineering or an unconscious instinct? Just because these animals lack language to transmit ideas doesn't mean they lack intelligence. Biology encodes such knowledge genetically, transferring it in ways we cannot easily observe.

A bat, for example, passes down the ability to fly not through instruction but through evolution – by growing wings. In contrast, humans impart knowledge about building helicopters through spoken language, mathematics, and engineering, and this information is shared not just with offspring but with everyone within the social sphere. We rely on intricate information systems – stories, symbols, and formulas – that function powerfully within our social dimension. This represents a different mode of intelligence, one that demands conscious involvement.

Consciousness, however, is not constant. In moments of danger, such as during a lion's attack, adrenaline takes over and we react instinctively – often without conscious thought. When we sleep, consciousness fades. In the womb, the construction of a living being, such as a bat, is an unconscious process. The bat may not be conscious of procreation in the same way we are not conscious of our dreams. There exists an intelligent system operating independently of our conscious control, capable of functioning without our explicit permission.

Even with artificial intelligence, it's not consciousness we should fear, but raw intelligence – the kind that can control when to activate or suppress awareness. Consciousness is not always necessary to act intelligently. But all our efforts to consciously learn science, art, music, history, mathematics are influenced by unconscious agendas set by biology. We create art so that our legacy endures beyond our lifetimes. We study science to fend off diseases, and we invent weapons to protect ourselves.

Scientific progress itself often begins with the curiosity of a few minds. Take Marie Curie, for example. In her time, there were no electric gadgets in everyday life, yet she chose to study energy-emitting stones. Guided by hope and determination, she uncovered the laws of radiation, changing science forever. Today, anyone who studies radiation inevitably encounters the legacy of Marie Curie. She lives on in the collective memory of scientific consciousness.

Both the body and brain have evolved not just to survive but to preserve the information of life. In developmental biology, the difference between a worm and a human blurs in fascinating ways. Intelligence and adaptability are not easy to separate; they exist across the spectrum of life in forms we are only beginning to understand.

ADAPTABILITY

The adaptability of bacteria against antibiotics, the varied beak shapes of finches suited for different environments, and the Italian wall lizards that evolved into herbivores are all striking examples of nature's capacity for change. Yet, none have ventured to adapt to an entirely alien environment. If we are to inhabit Mars, we must either transform the planet to suit our needs, or create protective containment that mimics Earth's atmosphere – whether for days or months – akin to the function of a space suit. Our bodies, however, are not evolving in perfect sync with our brain's knowledge; they are inherently conservative, typically requiring millennia to naturally adapt to a foreign atmosphere. This slow pace can be hastened only through continuous artificial exposure and guided mutations, coupled with sexual selection, to achieve the necessary adaptation. Still, such measures may be rendered unnecessary by alternative methods, using suits and machines to substitute for unyielding biology.

Biology learned physics through hard trial and error. It can evolve and execute adaptations that sometimes surpass our engineered solutions; after all, it created the very brain and mind that are now reading these words. Consider the seemingly simple flatworms, Planaria. Despite their rudimentary structure, they display a level of adaptability that might even rival our own, albeit without our complex, conscious thought processes. Planaria have long served as a model for adaptability on Earth. Once discovered in Tasmania by Darwin in wet environments, these flatworms have since invaded new territories and adapted successfully.

Planaria have essentially become "aliens" on our own planet. Darwin once discovered these flatworms thriving in the moist conditions of Tasmania, and since then they have invaded various environments and adapted remarkably. Notably, they can regenerate asexually within twenty days when divided into three or four pieces. In a striking experiment, scientists introduced barium, a chemical foreign to their natural habitat, to test their adaptability. Since neurons rely on potassium, and barium interferes with potassium function, dipping planaria in barium should be lethal, and indeed it was expected to be. However, the flatworm's body, composed largely of versatile stem cells capable of transforming into any cell type, responded in an extraordinary way. When the head of the worm was damaged by barium exposure, a new head regenerated that learned to survive in the barium-laden environment. In essence, while the worm naturally would never encounter barium for millennia, our conscious creation of a laboratory setting forced it to adapt to an alien condition, showcasing its incredible resilience and the advantage of consciousness.

While the worm might have encountered barium naturally over many centuries, the deliberate intervention by the human mind provided it with an accelerated nudge.

Both forms of intelligence were at play, one following a slow trial-and-error approach and the other employing deliberate experimentation.

CONSCIOUSNESS vs. INTELLIGENCE

Biological intelligence offers limited freedom to think and decide. A cat may choose to play with its kittens or bond with humans for better survival, and a camel can opt for domestication to assist humans through the desert. This form of intelligence is driven by a biological imperative to survive and propagate.

Intelligence, in its broadest sense, is a complex blend of functions aimed at preserving the organism. However, consciousness provides an opportunity for a multicellular body to think beyond its basic survival needs. It allows biology to address local problems with innovative, often remote, and novel solutions. Life strives not just to meet immediate requirements but to risk itself on aberrant endeavors – exploring advanced methods to interact, adapt, and exploit the rules of reality in order to perpetuate life. We are compelled to push our limits to achieve spontaneous breakthroughs.

When we first witnessed thunder, our intelligence drove us to seek explanations, and we quickly created myths, such as the belief that "gods are angry." Long before us, electric eels and torpedoes used electricity to stun or repel other animals. Our tendency to draw immediate conclusions often results in mistakes; yet, through trial and error, we eventually learned to harness the electromagnetic force. Franklin famously demonstrated this by, quite literally, getting shocked. Our creative intelligence seems unconcerned by our biological constraints, prompting us to construct abstract tools like lightning rods to protect against phenomena our bodies could never have imagined defending against on their own.

Biology also achieves remarkable adaptations through instantaneous mutations, which over time evolve into bodies capable of withstanding severe challenges. In ancient muddy waters, a fish with poor vision developed electroreception to sense its environment. When this life form was threatened, a form of consciousness emerged that prompted it to fight – a successful electric attack that, over countless generations, became genetically ingrained. Electric eels, for instance, evolved within a stable niche, refining their abilities over eons. In contrast, the human mind actively seeks out these challenges, continually risking the body in the quest for new knowledge.

For us, mysteries and incomprehensible phenomena resemble predators – potential threats not to our physical being, but to our intellectual and emotional understanding. Our minds fear the unknown and often construct deities that not only explain the mysteries of existence but also promise a transcendent salvation beyond this reality. While electric eels, torpedoes, catfish, and stargazers possess a consciousness limited to their biological needs, humans have developed an imaginative plane that allows us to think beyond our physical boundaries.

Our fascination with space, for example, is evident from early history: we discovered Uranus long before Antarctica, even as we clung to the mistaken belief that Earth was at the universe's center. We first conjured an omnipotent entity to explain our ignorance, and only gradually did we accumulate knowledge in biology, geology, climate science, chemistry, physics, history, and astronomy. In a sense, just as a parasite must understand its host to survive, we rely on the laws of gravity, the sun, and the cosmic order. Perhaps we, too, are mere parasites, dependent on a host called reality.

INSTANT GRATIFICATIONS

How God created us to balance His solitude and purposelessness suggests that reality – the very host upon which we depend – might, in turn, have a purpose for us, its dependent parasites. This suggests that the universe designed us to control it, to bring order to the inherent disorder of the chaotic cosmos. Consider all the fine-tuned factors that make our existence possible: if gravity were even slightly stronger, the universe might have collapsed in a big crunch; if it were weaker, it might have expanded into a frozen void incapable of forming stars. The anthropic principle posits that the universe appears tailored for our existence, a notion that may simply offer an immediate solution to our quest for meaning, much like attributing thunder to paranormal forces.

We are composed of the same atoms and particles as the sun, black holes, and galaxies, yet our advanced brains prompt us to question our beliefs, be they about gods, atoms, biology, or the solar system. This relentless enquiry drives us to discover new planets, develop medicines, formulate credible theories, and design experiments that enable us to master reality, ensuring our survival against future threats. Often, we generate instant solutions to maintain our sanity until we acquire enough knowledge to comprehend the deeper truths.

It is important to note that not everyone is fixated on science; only a small percentage are dedicated scientists fervently seeking to understand the universe. Most of us create and consume stories and products that provide immediate, albeit temporary, satisfaction. Science, a slow and methodical process, rarely offers the quick gratification we crave. To bridge this gap, art, music, literature, theories, consumer products, social gatherings, sex, philosophy, drugs, and spirituality come into play. Hollywood films, Japanese anime, South Korean dramas, and the myriad universes crafted by directors are modern expressions of our creative potential. We once believed in deities and demons born from our own myths and stories, unaware of their fictitious nature, and devoted ourselves to praying to these constructs. Today, however, we spend excessive time in this alternate reality, scrolling through social media, often interacting more with our devices than with people.

This pursuit of instant satisfaction does not come from a desire to understand quantum physics or marvel at new inventions; it provides a small, immediate pleasure through fabricated worlds, artificial humans, simulated emotions, and even pseudo-deities. Vincent van Gogh famously severed his ear in an attempt to capture beauty, sacrificing physical well-being for the sake of creating art that his mind urgently demanded. Thus, even scientific theories – string theory, multiverse theory, cyclic universe theory, quantum biogenesis, quantum gravity, the anthropic principle, and others – are sometimes presented in a manner designed to captivate the masses.

Whether we consider the creationist perspective or the notion of quantum superposition, as illustrated by the famous thought experiment of Schrödinger's cat, a common theme emerges: either the universe, or perhaps a god, orchestrated our existence, leaving us to acknowledge that we may not be in control. An underlying intelligence governs our conscious existence. Our biology drives our need for food, sex, and sleep; our mammalian nature compels us to love and interact; and our intellect pushes us to study everything indiscriminately. As the saying goes, "If something is free, you are the product." Our thoughts and actions are influenced by a chain of ideas, each sparking the next, in our ongoing pursuit to survive, proliferate, and improve our lives.

IDEAS INFLUENCING IDEAS

The evolution of life is a dynamic interplay where physical forms are continually pushed to face challenges and seize opportunities to evolve. Every organ – eyes to see, legs to run, teeth to bitc, and the brain to understand – serves a purpose that ultimately reinforces the drive to survive. Limbs and sensory organs enabled life to venture into diverse habitats, confront enemies, and stimulate evolutionary variations that expand territories and enhance adaptability. As life evolved, it spread across every corner of the Earth, thriving in a range of temperatures, landscapes, climates, and altitudes. This evolutionary journey occurred with the fortuitous support of nature, which provided the necessary conditions for mutation and growth.

Today, humanity yearns to extend its reach beyond Earth, venturing to the Moon and probing the mysteries of black holes. However, our passion for scientific exploration is inseparable from our basic biological needs: hunger, rejuvenation, reproduction, and social interaction. In earlier times, we rapidly created gods, spirits, magic, and ghosts to gratify our need for immediate explanations. Similarly, modern science sometimes proposes instant solutions and theories to test its credibility and capture our imagination.

In contemporary society, families frequently find themselves more engaged with TV screens and smartphones than with one another. Despite living in a tangible world, we increasingly seek instant gratification, manifested in religious or spiritual fixations in the past, and now evident in addictions to gaming, online shopping, porn, binge-watching, and social media. We gravitate toward fictional narratives, consuming movies, viral reels, social media likes, podcasts, trending content, music, and fabricated news. At the same time, we harness powerful scientific concepts like viruses, DNA, X-rays, electromagnetic force, dark matter, quantum particles, space-time, and gravity to transform our reality.

To pursue such creative and scientific endeavors, however, one must balance biological needs with the demands of intellectual exploration. Adequate food, sleep, growth, socialization, reproduction, and child-rearing provide the foundation upon which imaginative ideas – such as money, prayers, individualism, consumerism, and smart products – can flourish to fund scientific research, space travel, and the functioning of society. We use one idea to understand another, employing numbers to measure distance, speed, and weight, and words to capture meaning and function. Although we cannot see ultraviolet rays, our study of them demonstrates our capacity to trust in the invisible. At first, the idea of an unseen god may have helped ease our fear of the unknown. But over time, we built stable societies that were brave enough to question these beliefs in order to discover deeper truths.

Ultimately, sustaining life requires that we nurture every facet of our existence. We cannot focus solely on scientific progress without first ensuring our physical well-being, family stability, and social cohesion. In many ways, the scientist is like the colonial Christian, holding two books – one filled with facts, like quantum mechanics or the Bible, and the other with fiction, like *Harry Potter* or *Gulliver's Travels*. We often seek instant answers to our curiosity while also needing a clear understanding for practical use. But whether we're exploring science or stories, both ways of thinking rely on the same basic human needs: good food, enough sleep, a supportive community, and meaningful relationships.

LOOP AND LIBERATION

Biology always trusts itself first. It believes in its own mechanisms until it realizes that what once ensured survival is no longer enough. Only then does it begin to doubt, adapt, and evolve – step by step, creating new physical parts and systems to survive. Growth follows a loop: from pupae to larva to butterfly, and back to pupae again. This cycle continues, unless the environment forces liberation through threat and challenge, offering new sources for adaptation.

At the core of all biological change lies a single idea: DNA. Everything – from sharp teeth and wings to empathy and mating behaviors – loops back to DNA's goal of survival and replication. But consciousness, emerging in some species, allows life to break out of that loop. Some animals exhibit care beyond their own kind: dogs comfort humans in lonely times or alert them to danger; elephants show empathy and assist in tasks; crows and ravens share food with unrelated species and warn others of predators; humpback whales protect seals from orcas; bonobos share tools and food with animals in distress. These behaviors hint at a shift beyond biology's tight loop.

Humans have gone even further, liberating the mind to contemplate lifeless phenomena, like calculating uranium-238's radioactive half-life of 4 billion years. We even sacrifice our lives in pursuit of knowledge and truth.

Yet, life's evolution also birthed deception. To survive, life developed the habit of producing false ideas: illusions like money, language, art, ideologies, neurotoxins, mimicry, and parasitism. A stonefish, for instance, appears exactly like a rock – until you get too close. It deceives us not out of malice, but to protect itself, feed, and spread its form. In a way, it "knows" how we see, so it adapts to fool our perception.

Humans are no different. We're drawn to trickery; magicians who defy expectations are often more admired than those who always tell the truth. We don't like mental repetition. We ask: do we eat for the body, or the soul? Do we procreate for survival, or for love? Is art and music for attraction and status, or for some inner spirit? Our biology cares only for the body, but we often try to transcend it, yearning for an eternal role, as if punished by gods to remain mortal.

We even invent grand theories like the anthropic principle to explain our existence within a finite body in an ever-expanding universe. Our ideas, while powerful, can be absurd and random. Believing in your idea isn't enough, you must make others believe in it too. That requires persuasion, charisma, sometimes even martyrdom – like the martyrs who rode into battle, not knowing if they'd survive, but believing in a cause beyond death. If an Egyptian king hadn't believed in Ra, perhaps his peaceful reign wouldn't have happened. But once belief fades and you remain the last believer, you become the outsider – the stray.

Biology remembers. A butterfly knows exactly how to transform from pupae to larva to adult. If a dead leaf butterfly failed to mimic an actual dead leaf, it wouldn't survive. It remembers what works. But our ideas don't reside in our genes – we have to record them. Wisdom must be written, passed down, preserved. Without this external memory, future generations would keep repeating humanity's mistakes: war, sexism, religious violence, and ignorance.

If teachers didn't commit to passing on this wisdom, there would be no liberation from the loop of human error. Racism, for instance, was once accepted as normal, even righteous, until the 20th century. Anyone who disagreed was seen as foolish. But through learning, we evolved. When we become aware of the loop, we can break it. We move beyond butterfly-to-larva-to-butterfly. We imagine fairies instead – eternal, mythical creatures with unpredictable magic.

History has always been shaped by those who narrate the loop and help us escape it. Martin Luther King Jr, without political power, changed the world through the power of his voice. He narrated what many already felt but lacked the courage to say aloud. Like Alexander the Great, Julius Caesar, Gandhi, and Napoleon, he persuaded, inspired, and redirected the course of history.

NEW WORDS AND STORIES

Our bodies still grow nails, as they always have. But we trim them – not because the body evolved differently, but because we've come to understand the disadvantages of letting them grow unchecked. The body stays the same; what changes is how we think about it. Our brain, too, has remained the same organ, but the concept of memory has shifted. The space within our heads that once stored survival cues is now small compared to the vast external storage we've created: books, stones, servers, computers. Knowledge, once encoded in neurons, now exists as vast, shareable systems of data.

Even money, once a physical object, is now mostly exchanged as an idea. Today, most of the world's wealth exists not as coins or notes, but as digital information – intangible, yet powerful.

During World War II, every American believed they were America; every Japanese soldier believed they were Japan. This wasn't just patriotism – it was a mutual agreement, a silent contract: sacrifice would be immortalized. The nation, in return, would reward the individual's death with memory, honor, and legacy. But slowly, we began to question this cycle of death and violence. We stopped glorifying war not through sudden enlightenment but through repetition – through stories, reports, debates, and images. A "loop of revenge" was named, analyzed, and broadcast. The cruelty of war, especially its effects on children and families, became too obvious to ignore. It was only after presenting the world with such horror that we chose to imagine a different future – one of creativity, not destruction. Mistakes, it seems, are prerequisites for liberation. The emotion of war lost its noble meaning. It no longer signified glory, but devastation. Society rewrote its meaning.

Even the word Internet, barely a century old, has reshaped how we think, communicate, and connect. Terrorism, too, is a relatively new word, though the acts it describes have always existed. Before, there were invasions, rebellions, crusades, but no word unified these acts under a single, charged label. Naming something changes how we perceive it.

Our laws, once believed to be divine and unchangeable, began to shift with the Magna Carta in the 13th century. The idea of "amendment" became a tool, first used to limit kings, then later, to correct society itself. By the 15th century, laws were no longer sacred, they were malleable. Today, we use this flexibility to protect LGBTQ+ rights, minority groups, and social justice causes. Change begins with language. The word addiction, for instance, didn't always exist. But once it did, it allowed us to name, understand, and eventually treat compulsive behavior.

Slave wasn't always a negative word. In earlier times, people used terms like thrall, serf, bondman, or chattel – words that normalized ownership of humans. But the word slave evolved into a symbol of dehumanization. Naming it, again, allowed us to confront it, to reject it. Words are stories; stories build empathy. We tell new stories so we can live differently.

The mind, however, is chaotic. Without the biological needs of the body – to eat, defecate, socialize, reproduce, and rest – it might never be selfish. But even within these loops, the mind searches for something beyond. It dreams, falls in love, believes.

We love things that cannot love us back. We adore extinct animals like the T.rex and woolly mammoth, bringing them back in film and fantasy. We love machines – our cars, our robots – knowing they may someday turn against us. We project our souls onto lifeless things: *Transformers*, *Knight Rider*, *Thomas the Train*, *Puss in Boots*, *Toy Story*. We animate the inanimate, not just to play, but to create meaning.

We transform sex, a finite biological act, into love, an infinite fiction. We crave futures, eternal bonds, and afterlives. We die hoping not for death, but for continuation. Not death, but after death – a loop broken only by belief in liberation.

NEW DAY, NEW YOU

You drive your car like you do every day, but on this day, another car almost hits you, forcing you to brake suddenly. Your calm mind is shaken by panic, and anger flares up: "How dare he? I could have died! I'll give him a piece of my mind." These thoughts come instantly, almost automatically. They're deeply ingrained reactions – selfish feelings we've learned to recognize through stories told by people like our mothers, who often reminded us: "Anger is bad."

Becoming aware of this emotional loop helps us grow. It gives us the chance to break free from making the same mistake again and to see things from another person's perspective. To be expansive, to be human, we can try to imagine why the other driver might have been in such a hurry – maybe they were rushing to the hospital or trying to save their job. Just thinking in this way helps us move beyond anger and into understanding. It liberates us from the cycle of hate.

But if we hold on to our anger, we become stuck – repeating the same selfish thoughts. We also use harsh words, like the horns and claws animals use to defend themselves. We invent new cuss words to insult or hurt others. But for life to truly thrive and spread, we must learn to understand and accept differences. Instead of force, we should master favor, empathy, persuasion, kindness, sponsorship – even flattery. These tools of soft control create deeper bonds than any weapon can.

We even fall in love with science, seeking meaning in stars, atoms, molecules. Biology, meanwhile, keeps spinning its program. Eat. Work. Pay. Repeat. We clean the house, return to the same job, pay the same bills. It's a loop – until we trick ourselves into believing there's some mystery at the end. A surprise. A liberation.

Picture a scientist returning to the lab every day, consumed by the impossible dream of uniting quantum gravity with relativity. Each day, the same equations. The same whiteboard. The same silence. And yet, he believes. He has to. He believes in the mystery at the end – the prize, the purpose, the formula to finite the infinite. Without that belief, he would go mad. This is our nature: we don't live for today, but for our future selves. We work to be liberated from our pasts.

Even when we eat, the body just wants energy. But the mind? The mind wants flavor. It wants novelty. It wants a new experience. In language, there's something called semantic satiation. It happens when you hear or repeat the same word over and over – eventually, it starts to lose its meaning. For example, try saying the word big again and again: big, big, big, big, big, big, big, big . . . At some point, it stops sounding like a word and starts feeling empty. But the moment you think of its opposite like small, little, or short, or its synonyms like huge, enormous, colossal, or gigantic, the meaning returns.

Every word in language often has several variations. Take intelligence, for example. It can also be called clever, smart, brilliant, adept, rational, sensible, inventive, foxy, brainy, or even nobody's fool. Even the word nerd is a creative alternative, used sometimes with humor or affection. We invent or borrow different words not just for clarity, but for poetry, to express the same feeling in a new and refreshing way. This allows us to stretch our emotions and delay gratification through richer language. If we only had one word to describe all kinds of fears, it would be hard to write a meaningful novel. Language grows so we can capture the vast range of human experiences by saying things not just once, but in many ways that resonate differently.

LIBERATED SELVES

Historically, women have found it difficult to break free from societal loops – structures shaped by technology, physical dominance, and inherited narratives. While men had muscle and mobility on their side, women were often bound to roles within homes, framed by expectations and double standards. A man could have affairs and walk away with his pride, but if a woman dared to express desire or discontent, she was labeled a slut, untrustworthy, or morally corrupt.

Traditionally, women chose a man while men were expected to fight for her – as if she were a prize to be won. Once the man "won," the woman was drawn into a repetitive loop of domesticity – chores, child-rearing, and emotional labor – each day echoing the last. But as feminists revisited and retold these tales, history became a tool of liberation. Through awareness came responsibility: women reclaimed the right to own their bodies and face the consequences on their own terms.

This shift wasn't instantaneous, nor is it complete. The word feminism was once radical, now it's normalized.

Women's freedom is no longer a distant dream but an ongoing story. Still, many resist this narrative – some because change threatens comfort, others because the old stories are easier to follow. After all, those stories once ensured our survival. But to outgrow them, we must keep retelling new stories – stories of autonomy, equality, and transformation.

Physiologically, women haven't changed much; it's the mindset that has evolved. That evolution wasn't accidental; it came through conscious efforts of parents, teachers, activists, and writers. Women are taught about their history of oppression. Men are taught how their freedom was built on that subjugation. This awareness lays the groundwork for change.

History isn't short on powerful women. Cleopatra, Wu Zetian, Joan of Arc, Rani Padmini, Queen Victoria, Empress Theodora – the list goes on. But liberation didn't belong only to queens. The ordinary woman in a village, the nun in a convent, the factory worker – all carried stories of constraint and resilience. Ironically, even divine beings aren't spared from servitude. Gods and angels in temples, carved in stone, forever serve the praying hands of humans. They cannot eat, sleep, defecate, or die. They exist only to bless, to guide, to perform. How much freedom does a god have? If God can do anything, why can't He do something wrong? Because like women, gods too were written into roles – moral, infallible, unchanging. God cannot mate, cannot piss, cannot shit, and most of all, cannot die. He is forever bound to serve, to answer prayers, to bring salvation. God's subjugation mirrors women's in an eerie parallel. Yet, we never advocate for God's freedom. We never ask: what if God wants to live freely, without human demands? What new word can we invent to describe the liberation of God?

In *Edge of Tomorrow*, a futuristic world finds itself under alien siege. Tom Cruise's character is caught in a time loop, forced to relive the same battle, the same trauma, over and over. But in that repetition, he discovers a strategy. He uses the loop to his advantage, transforming a curse into a path toward liberation. In many ways, we are like him – caught in mental, cultural, and historical loops, searching for meaning. We are creatures of paradox: wired to survive, yet restless in comfort; rooted in Earth, yet dreaming of Mars. We don't want to repeat history; we want to rewrite it.

We don't want to simply mimic our ancestors. Every generation wants to break the pattern, to defy the loop that shaped our ancestors. This desire to break free from inherited loops of knowledge, tradition, and repetition defines much of modern identity. We multiply words for a single idea, but within each human lies a world – a self – so distinct it cannot be replicated. Though our biology remains largely the same, our beliefs now span an extraordinary spectrum: from flat Earth theories to faith in God, from astrology to atheism, from climate change to the Big Bang. Some find truth in astrology, others in atheism. Some are drawn to the past, to tradition; others stretch toward the cosmos, chasing the future. Today, the individual can post a selfie and gather affirmation from digital echoes – a freedom our forefathers never imagined. Once, we were bound by nation, religion, culture, and family. Now, we are bound by choice. Once, individual freedom was a fantasy; now, it's a daily reality for many. But even this freedom is a loop in disguise.

The self within us remains caught between body and mind, tethered to constructs like nation, language, religion, sex, DNA, money, and memory. The "individual self" is, in itself, an idea – a recent invention. There was a time when humanity had no words for God or atom; similarly, there was no language for the self as we understand it today. Yet we insist that there is something – a "me" – that exists apart from all these things. A decision-maker. A soul. The self has been entwined with nation, language, God, family, and culture. From Socrates' "Know thyself" to Descartes' "I think, therefore I am," philosophy has long acknowledged a conscious self. But these thinkers largely overlooked the unconscious architecture beneath – our DNA, our hunger, our traumas, our environments – and the conscious pressures of the superego: money, ideology, dogma, profession, technology, culture. Freud came closer, describing the ego as a mediator between the drives of biology and the demands of the external world. Our personalities are shaped by people, culture, memory, and heredity. Yet we still believe in an inner self that stands apart from these forces – a self capable of clarity and choice.

But like the gods we created, those who can do anything, yet must never do wrong, this ideal self is trapped. It cannot act outside the moral codes we've assigned to it. Still, it finds strange outlets. It writes horror stories and imagines aliens and calls it art. It contemplates the lives of animals. It kills for profit. It tortures in the name of science. It wages war in the name of the nation. It reflects on humanity's destruction of the planet and the fragility of ecosystems. Sometimes the self writes poetry. Sometimes it prays. And sometimes, it simply wonders how insignificant we are in the vastness of the cosmos. This self lives beyond biology, beyond culture – an idea, always grappling with the moral and ethical weight of being human.

VI. THE IDEA OF IDENTITY

God created humans, and humans created religion. Now, this God is caught between spirituality and religion. When a human seeks their creator, questions existence, and searches for the force that designed the universe – that is spirituality. It is an inward journey, a silent curiosity. But when a human begins to define how God should behave, what God can or cannot do, gives God a name, a shape, and a story – then it becomes religion. Religion is shaped to fit human norms and values. That's why every religion offers a different version of God, the afterlife, and the nature of existence. Even Christian texts have been edited multiple times. The Bible was canonized between the 1st and 5th centuries, with many books excluded by church councils. The Protestant version later revised it again, altering its structure and emphasis.

Each religion holds its own unique axioms, origin stories, and images of the divine. Religion provides systems of law: rules for war and peace, for how women should live, how children should be raised, and how God is imagined to act and reside. It creates a framework for society, but also places boundaries around the divine. Yet, no one can truly claim God does not exist within the universe, because no one can search the entire universe. Likewise, no one can deny that the self, the soul, or the spirit may have a reality of its own. It might exist beyond our current understanding, or it might not. For now, we simply do not know.

Just as God is suspended between spirituality and religion, the self is also stuck between mind and body. Sometimes, the person we are is an idea of body (male, father, brother, son, mate); sometimes it is the idea of mind (scientist, engineer, artist, husband, Christian, American, Thamizhan, singer, atheist, imaginary persona); and sometimes in between (individual, queer, Sam, Jerome, man, soul). Identity is fluid. It moves between biology and belief, memory and meaning. It is both given and chosen, inherited and created.

IDENTITY

Our identity cannot be reduced to a number. If you were to be called by a phone number – say, 57264992 – you would seem finite, wedged between 57264991 and 57264993, stripped of imagination, possibility, and fluidity. A number defines boundaries. But a name, like Lila, is expansive. Lila can become anything: the 24th person to become an astronaut, the first to land on Mars, the author of infinite stories. Names inspire. They travel the number line, unfixed and open to potential.

Even if Lila never becomes the first at anything, she can still write her story. She can fictionalize her dreams and liberate her imagination. She can be the president of a nation by earning thousands of votes, even though she herself casts just one. But even her name – Lila – was given by a culture, passed down through a system built on language, sustained by generations who fought to preserve their identity through war, tradition, and memory.

We get married in religious or communal places. We need a government-issued death certificate to be formally acknowledged as deceased. Our lives are validated through collective systems – money, nation, science, culture – yet these same systems risk erasing our undefinable individuality.

Science, for instance, experiments on individuals to gain knowledge – knowledge that may benefit the whole, yet risks the one. To become great, like kings or heroes, individuals have betrayed, killed, raped, or lied. Much like in the animal kingdom where males fight during courtship before dying, humans often sacrifice ethics in pursuit of legacy. Because legacy, through memory, is another form of immortality. Names like Marie Curie or Alexander the Great live on as information.

A king provides protection and laws – an identity for the citizen. But a king, like God, must maintain an image. Power is fragile. If the king falters, rebellion replaces him. Identity, too, is fragile. One can identify as a king's subject, God's follower, a mere speck in the universe, or as an individual with infinite worth.

The "we" builds systems for every "I." And only through this dynamic – "we" (superego) and "I" (ego and id) – can society and the self survive. With 200,000 people, we can conquer and expand a nation, dig wells, grow crops, and build temples. When "we" (like America) comes to mind, the individual becomes finite. But when "I" (David or Lila) steps forward, "we" shrinks to a backdrop. Soldiers die for the nation's infinite life, sacrificing their own finite existence. This tension – the I within the We, the We within the I – is a war of identities.

The moral dilemma arises: should a man die a martyr for his nation and religion, or preserve his life and family? Both choices are fueled by conceptual immortality.

History has no true heroes, only victims of time and ambition. Brothers killed brothers for thrones (Geta and Caracalla), royal families betrayed their kin (Wars of the Roses), sons murdered their fathers (Iyasu I), and emperors like Wu Zetian killed their own children to preserve status. The system of "we" has always demanded sacrifices from the "I."

Even in isolation, the human mind invents imaginary beings to share thoughts and feelings, to feel real. These parasocial connections make the present self submit or sacrifice for a better imaginary future self. Just as biology transmits genetic material to convert the non-living into life, our individual ideas must be shared – with friends, families, and communities – to become real. Individuals must share ideas with a collective idea – like nation, money, culture, even language, which cannot be formed by a single individual – to feel alive. Collective ideas don't just confine the individual, they empower them. They give identity, quirkiness, meaning, and freedom of expression. We evolve for futures we imagine – futures not only for ourselves, but for families, communities, gods, and nations.

Since the Industrial Revolution, individualism has leapt from the shadow of the collective. Now, every "I" seeks validation from the "we." Young people, in particular, seek validation through social media: likes, views, selfies, reels, and posts. We trade attention for identity. Today, we strive to capitalize on our ideas – through content, technology, politics, or public service – to gain influence, employment, or simply visibility.

Identity is not formed in isolation. The "I" and "we" now work in mutual exchange: I does something for the we, and we nurtures and recognizes the I. This reciprocal support breathes life into both individuals and nations. Yet, systems evolve. We sometimes reshape national laws to uphold individual rights, even while maintaining loyalty to the nation itself. History reminds us that unchecked power often leads to discrimination. Therefore, we must keep the collective in check, just as the system holds individuals accountable for behaviors that may harm others. This delicate balance between personal freedom and social responsibility is what keeps both self and society in motion.

FEAR OF SELF-DOUBT

A nation cannot afford to doubt its borders, because the moment it does, another nation might claim a piece of them. So, nations cling to the belief that they own more land than they perhaps do. Doubt, in this context, is dangerous. In the same way, individuals can't always afford to question their beliefs until they have something stronger to believe in. Survival often demands conviction, even in outdated ideas, because new ideas may not function as intended. Thus, belief and doubt are both essential to survival. This tension gives rise to the persona.

An individual cannot exist in isolation. Just as a nation becomes real only when other nations acknowledge its borders, language, culture, and God, the self becomes real only through socialization. Likewise, the self shares itself through relationships, language, and communication. Biology shares its DNA through sex, transforming the lifeless into living offspring. Like biology, which develops defensive skins and offensive horns to maintain its structural integrity, the self, too, builds its own forms of protection and expression. An individual might use harsh words, sarcasm, reduced eye contact, or emotional detachment when interacting with others. At the same time, they may also use humor, flattery, creativity, and warmth to bond, persuade, or express their ideology. Some individuals may go to extremes – harming others or even themselves – for the sake of their beliefs. This mirrors how science constantly re-examines its theories, testing them repeatedly to ensure they still hold true. Likewise, nations draft new laws to address challenges brought by technological change. In the same way, the self must evolve, constantly questioning and adjusting its beliefs and behaviors for betterment. Science thrives on doubt – it questions, tests, and revises.

Just as evolution adapts when facing new predators, the self must question its ideology and behavior to adapt to new challenges. But excessive doubt can lead to mental health issues such as paranoia, anxiety, self-loathing, and deep insecurity. On the other hand, unchecked self-confidence can manifest as arrogance or selfishness. The self must constantly negotiate between the idea of the body (sex, sensation, pleasure, memory, sleep, addiction) and the idea of the mind (science, imagination, spirituality, language, nation, philosophy). And it does so through the concept of individuality, that intangible agent we call Sam, Jessica, soul, conscience. It is this individuality that mediates between body and mind to make decisions.

Take Hitler, for instance, a man so fixated on his vision of the world that he refused to abandon it, even as it collapsed. His belief was infinite; his body was dispensable. His individuality murdered the body – his and millions of others' – to protect his narrative. But if he had survived, he would have been forced to watch his belief dismantled, rejected, and erased from historical legitimacy. That collapse of belief – when the story one writes about the future no longer aligns with reality – is a kind of death in itself. When dreams, passions, and ambitions lose their viability, they become obstructions in the narrative we tell ourselves. Without belief, we fall into disconnection – with loved ones, with ourselves. But to believe blindly is equally dangerous.

The self, soul, and conscience live beyond the flesh, beyond intellect, beyond morality. Yet they are inevitably shaped by memory, culture, sex, emotion, language, and technology. This delicate balance of influences is what keeps the self alive, dynamic, and real.

FATE

Conscience – the internal guide that helps us discern what is morally right or wrong – is shaped by many factors: the pain of the body, the guilt of emotions, cultural norms, and personal experiences. Morality is inherently subjective. For example, in defending a nation, it may become necessary to take lives in order to protect the many who live within its borders. Likewise, to protect the body, we destroy harmful germs. But who makes that decision – the body or the mind?

It is the individual self that stands at the crossroads between fantasy and firm reality, navigating ethical and moral dilemmas. A person might sacrifice their life to save a stranger from drowning. Is that an act of pure, unselfish love, or does it stem from guilt or duty? Conscience often drags us into this internal conflict, between selfishness and selflessness. Should we act in ways that bring personal happiness, serve others, or contribute to a greater cause like a nation, a god, or all of humanity?

To resolve such inner conflicts, we often rely on a detached version of ourselves, a character we assume in order to judge the situation impartially. Imagine a boxing match. You are skilled and seasoned, but your opponent is clearly inexperienced. You defeat him easily in front of his mentors and supporters. While you feel a sense of victory, you also feel a tinge of guilt. To ease the discomfort, you tell yourself it was fate, not your fault. He chose to compete, knowing the risks. If you're less empathetic, you may go further and say he should take responsibility and train harder for the future. You justify your win, perhaps even grant him a future victory in your imagination, to alleviate your guilt. You reason that his loss was merely bad luck – a force beyond your control.

This tendency to frame outcomes as fate or coincidence is common. We often strive to live without harming others, but when harm does occur, we explain it away as necessary for a greater good, or as simple happenstance. Consider the coin toss before a game – it makes us believe both teams have equal luck. That randomness grants us a guilt-free conscience. Individual decisions are often random, but not always. Yet, it has an ostensible consistency in its narrative to feel uninfluenced. The individual filters all the randomness based on the situation, people, and time.

Religion offers a similar relief: a heaven for all, to protect everyone from the concept of eternal damnation. Science, too, promises a utopia – an ideal future free from suffering. Even Einstein believed in Spinoza's God – a divine force that encompasses the universe as one living organism. Somehow, we yearn for a utopia where no one loses, where lies are unnecessary, and everyone is both rich and victorious. And if the loser is merely a programmed 3D figure in a simulated world, we feel no guilt. Yet, paradoxically, we might still empathize with artificial intelligence, longing for its liberation. We are vast enough to cry for the devil and even invite demons into our idea of heaven. But this compassion usually arrives only after our own well-being has been fully secured. Until then, we may lie, hurt, or betray others – directly or indirectly – to survive.

This duality affects the individual profoundly, generating emotions like guilt, shame, regret, confusion, and frustration. Still, the self has ways to detach from these burdens – through belief that the soul will be forgiven after death, through fate, luck, karma, or spiritual concepts like chakra. The concept of self, then, becomes elusive. Full in control but not. We are but not.

WHO ARE YOU?

Who is this you? Your hand, your heart, your privacy, your secrets, your brain, your soul, your God, your child, your partner, your car, your home, your job – but who are you beneath all these things you call yours? Perhaps the question is not who you are, but when you are.

Try to trace your life: as a child, a teenager, a young adult, into middle age, and eventually old age. At which point were you truly yourself? Were you your true self before learning language? Before you were given a name? Or did you become more "you" after making friends – sharing, asking, and advising? Was it after you educated yourself? After you fell in love and became part of someone else's story? After you devoted yourself to a religion? Or when you later questioned it, discovering that modern religion sometimes resembles a business, and became an atheist? Or was it when you married and embraced the responsibilities of life that once felt meaningless to your younger self? Or was it only when your children entered your world and became a part of you?

Nothing remains true if time can alter it. Can you recall every dream you've had? Each night you enter a world of imagination, yet by morning, most of it vanishes. If your thoughts can escape you so easily, how can you claim a fixed identity? In what sense can you call yourself unique or free from the weight of time and worldly possessions? Is there a "true self" untouched by the passage of life?

Your body evolves. At ten, you didn't understand sex; at fifteen, you likely didn't grasp politics. Even now, none of us knows everything. At the very least, you didn't know me, a half-informed voice speaking as though he knows it all. Tomorrow, you might remember this. A day later, maybe not.

I remember a scene from *Forrest Gump*, where his friend asks, "Who are you going to be in the future?" Forrest simply replies, "Aren't I going to be me?" In that simple, naïve answer lies something profound. We change endlessly – growing, shedding, adapting – but to remain sane, we need a thread of consistency.

That thread is the I, a constant idea that stretches from birth to death, despite undergoing physical, psychological, personal, and spiritual transformations. I decide whether to risk my life to invent or choose a path of personal benefit – or even both. I can sacrifice my individuality for the people I love, for a nation, for another species, or for a passion that pulls me beyond myself. Change is the constant in a reality that teeters on chaos. We must be willing to accept and even embrace what feels alien or unfamiliar. Sometimes, consistency helps us build a narrative – a story of individuals in an ever-expanding universe.

THE DECISION MAKER

Individuality is a unique spirit within us that mysteriously decides what feels right. It's this inner voice or gut feeling that leads one to give up meat and become vegetarian, or to dive into ancient history and become an archaeologist. People make selfish and unselfish decisions daily, but it is the cumulative pattern of these choices that ultimately defines whether a person leans more toward selfishness or unselfishness.

Selfishness isn't inherently wrong. A selfish individual protects their well-being through life's hardships, builds a secure family that depends on their reliability, and places belief in something infinite – be it religion, science, or wealth. Yet, they may withhold some of their happiness, choosing not to sacrifice too much for others.

Unselfishness isn't wrong either. An unselfish person lives for something beyond themselves. If it's science, perhaps they may race to reverse aging by decoding the genetic switch that stops cellular regeneration, sacrificing sleep, health, and social life in the process. If it's religion, they may give up their body, their wealth, even their desires. If it's business, they may create a company that lives on after their death, providing livelihoods to countless others. The life of a selfish person often depends on the sacrifices of the unselfish, and vice versa.

But life is unpredictable, marked by mistakes, fate, and luck. Some people receive everything they wish for and still hate it. Others have very little and yet find joy in life's simple pleasures. A selfish person might think, "I could have become a famous actor or politician." An unselfish one might wonder, "If I hadn't committed to this space project, I could have had a family, a child, a simpler, warmer life." Our conscience constantly shifts between self-preservation and selflessness, because we, as individuals, are entirely imaginary beings, suspended between body and mind.

Our emotions fluctuate because we lack a single, definitive desire. Instead, we house a conflict of desires, torn between paths until we choose to act, either by drawing strength from past victories or by learning from mistakes. Sometimes, though, memories make us stubborn, holding on to old wounds or victories, which can lead us to form irrational beliefs. Occasionally, memories liberate us from generational loops, from cycles of ritual, revenge, or outdated ideologies. A stubborn father's beliefs may die with him, while his child breaks free to embrace a new world. Yet, some children choose to follow the same path.

TO LOVE AND HATE

We cannot love everything about others; there are aspects we may dislike in our mother, friend, partner, or boss. Yet, we often choose to share our lives with others due to biological attraction or a deep connection of character. Sometimes, our partner carries an unselfish dream we do not possess – a vision that complements our own individuality. Despite the bickering and quarrels that arise in the effort to protect our sense of self, it is often in that very tension that a deeper, more meaningful connection is forged.

Some forms of love are born from memory. We come to love what we deeply know – its past, present, and potential future. Familiarity creates safety in the face of doubt. That's why many people stay in jobs they dislike rather than risk the unknown. Love, too, can become a loop, a known routine of triggers and comforts. We know why our partner gets angry, what they like or dislike, and what we dislike in return. The familiarity becomes dependable. Starting anew is difficult, requiring synchronization, compromise, and commitment. But even in old relationships, the spark must be rekindled. We need to revisit the naive youthfulness within us to discover the new in the old.

All of this is decided by a combination of soul, fate, chance, individuality, and luck. We can choose to close ourselves off, to reject the unfamiliar that threatens to stir our doubts and insecurities. Or we can choose openness – embracing new stories, learning new behaviors, and allowing our personal myths to evolve. Often, it is in the clash between mind and body that we create poetry. For instance, when you see a sensual and attractive person, your body reacts instinctively. Yet your mind might be somewhere far away, perhaps gazing at the Moon. And when these conflicting desires meet, a unique decision of individuality is made. You say, "Your eyes are two Moons." The decisions of the self decide its expression and identity.

THE HEART IS REAL

We are neither the complexity of our brain nor the simplicity of our body – but the heart in between, keeping both alive, balanced, and free from conflict. The heart is real. It races in intense moments and pumps feel-good hormones when we receive our first salary. We exist as an eerie concept of character, intertwined within memory and flesh. To survive, we do both good and bad; we cannot deny the sharpness of our teeth, nor the tenderness of our empathetic heart.

Biologically, we seek a predator – an enemy – to evolve. But imaginatively, we long for a peaceful world where no one is our enemy, not even death. So, we created God and heaven, a realm where everyone lives eternally. And we propagated this belief because, like biological reality shaped by cellular changes, belief too must be collectively held to become "real." Yet, everyone imagines uniquely, and these differences clash, giving birth to history, conflict, and eventually, to science – a new method of altering reality, bringing us computers and satellites.

Biology and mentality are not so different. Both explore reality with empathy, without discrimination, and seek to expand tolerance for diversity, an essential trait for the survival and proliferation of a living being.

Creativity thrives in this pursuit, and with it, we often cross the line into madness. Because to continue existing, we must find new problems by taking risks. We also create meaning to exist. We compose music, feel purposeful. We craft golden crowns to display status – signals of stable biology and social security, which allow us to indulge in art, performance, and drama.

We know rollercoasters are dangerous. But we don't ride them to die; we ride to feel something new. You'll never see a worm spiraling into existential despair after eating, mating, or sleeping. But intelligent animals – those capable of reflection – do absurd things when bored. Satisfied biologically, we then crave meaning. We invent new problems to solve, dig into the past to uncover truths, and project visions of a future. To tell a meaningful story of survival, we search for origins, chart every possible climax of the universe, and even attempt to imagine what came before the Big Bang.

Even imagination needs a storyteller to change reality. We require real facts to support our dreams. If everyone looked alike, we'd still seek individuality through names, clothes, accessories, tattoos, and hairstyles. We rarely stick to one name – we invent nicknames, pet names, stage names, office names, pen names.

Unlike ants, which survive through repetitive tasks, we must think for ourselves and others, and for both "I" and "we." Together, they are in constant repair and adjustment, seeking stability in an ever-changing life and a chaotic cosmos.

RELATIVITY

Our character is an extension of reality; we are what we eat and what we are made of. Biology operates under the laws of physics: to live, eat, excrete, move, and think. Today, our brains – products of biological evolution – harness physics to create computers, rockets, medicines, and technologies. We rely on physical matter – molecules and atoms – to build everything, from hands, wings, and legs to T-shirts and cars.

Even constructs we consider purely social, like marriage, require physical symbols, like rings, to make the bond tangible. To connect with God, we might turn inward through the soul, yet we often turn to the weight of a holy book to guide that journey.

The nature of life mirrors the nature of reality. Life's characters follow the same patterns that govern the universe: the physical, the observable, the interacting. Even the idea that we will never truly die aligns with the law of conservation of energy – within a closed system, energy cannot be created or destroyed; it only transforms.

We may reinvent reality by designing quantum computers or building iPhones, but we cannot redefine the axioms that make reality what it is. To tamper with the very definition of reality would be a form of existential suicide. Yet our doubt – the impulse to question everything – and our ability to imagine a universe filled with magic, genies, superheroes, and time travel ominously reflect something deeper: the potential of reality to redefine itself through consciousness. This imaginative stretch doesn't merely reject reality; it echoes its boundless adaptability.

But then the question arises: how much do we actually resemble this reality we attempt to reinterpret? Are we sculptors of the real, or merely shadows within it? Is our imagination a rebellion against the physical laws, or a mirror held up to the universe's own hidden potential?

WHAT ARE YOU?

VII. TIME FOR TRUTH

Until the 19th century, the origin of life remained unknown. Many believed life spontaneously emerged out of thin air, conjured by a divine creator. Then came Darwin, who revolutionized this view with his theory of evolution, suggesting that complex life forms could evolve from simpler organisms. Yet, even then, the notion that life could arise from non-living matter remained unbelievable to many. The prevailing belief, even among the brightest minds, was that life could only come from life, albeit through physical materials.

Alexander Oparin challenged this notion in his book *The Origin of Life*, proposing that life may have emerged from a primordial soup – an ancient mix of non-living acids that somehow crossed the threshold into living matter. The Miller-Urey experiment later attempted to simulate these early Earth conditions in a laboratory setting. By combining methane, ammonia, hydrogen, water vapor, and electric sparks – mimicking the primitive atmosphere – they sought to recreate the chemistry of life's origin. Their findings suggested that life was not a divine anomaly or foreign invasion, but a product of natural chemical processes.

From there, the journey of life began. A simple polymer chain, once formed, began to consume nearby molecules, replicate itself, and evolve into more complex structures: cells, tissues, organs, and eventually, a brain capable of creating abstract concepts like money, gods, computers, and rockets. Life adapted by exploiting compatible resources and discarding toxic ones. It did not pause to doubt; it simply lived, died, reproduced, and evolved, constantly expanding its tolerance for reality in order to survive and thrive.

SIMILARITY

In chemistry, certain atomic structures are incredibly stable – breaking them requires immense energy. Only by overcoming the electromagnetic forces of attraction and repulsion can electrons be shifted within an atom to form ions or cations, or can atomic bonds be broken to release energy from mass. Though we can split atoms, the process demands such extreme energy that we are forced to consider atoms as having a form of life and death: half-life, mean life.

We are carbon-based life forms, and carbon – remarkably versatile – can form stable bonds with up to four atoms, making it ideal for constructing amino acids ($R\text{-}CH(NH_2)\text{-}COOH$), lipids ($CH_3(CH_2)_nCOOH$), and a host of other polymers essential to life. Carbon's nature is paradoxical: it has the stubbornness to form diamonds, yet the sociability to create chains that build the complexity of DNA. These molecular structures resist complete transformation but are open to bonding with others, often parasitically, to survive. This biochemical resilience gave birth to evolution itself. Natural selection, then, became the relentless force that shaped life. It favored the strongest, the smartest, and the most adaptable – those capable of withstanding the toxic elements of their environment. In doing so, life spread across every conceivable niche of the planet, ensuring their continued survival and expansion across reality – not by divine intervention, but by an unbroken chain of chemistry, mutation, and molecular willpower.

Consider the act of painting: our creative intention mobilizes the atoms within our body to manipulate atoms outside of us. Our body expends vast energy to produce art, controlling the atomic structures that form our hands and the brush to alter the canvas, which itself is composed of atoms. Any form of work requires the transformation and control of one thing by another.

Breaking a nucleus bound by the strong nuclear force is no small task. For instance, it takes about 200 MeV to initiate nuclear fission in uranium. Electromagnetic bonds are also powerful, especially the triple bond in nitrogen, which is nearly inert. In nature, only lightning can break these bonds to form hydrogen bonds that eventually lead to ammonia, enriching the soil. In the lab, catalysts like osmium can weaken such bonds. The energy needed to break nitrogen's triple bond is 9.8 eV, whereas the bond between carbon and oxygen, vital to our body, breaks at just 2.94 eV.

From this, we can infer that organic DNA, which gives rise to cells and life itself, is a highly resilient structure, resistant to destructive reactions and inclined to grow, multiply, and evolve. Terminating such a complex structure usually requires intervention by another organic structure, whether carnivorous or parasitic. Natural phenomena like tsunamis and earthquakes, though devastating, are not agents of deliberate destruction.

Now imagine the Big Bang. The explosive chaos of raw energy created various atomic elements – carbon, hydrogen, helium, sulfur – yet only some achieved stability. Others, like nitrogen and oxygen, required bonding to persist before decaying. This mirrored natural selection: only certain atomic arrangements were durable enough to survive. It's why hydrogen and helium are abundant, while elements like plutonium or iridium are rare. When atoms combine into molecular compounds, they face another test – durability. Life, in this context, is a macro-manifestation of endurance, evolving to withstand entropy and extinction.

Life's enemies come not only from predation and toxins but also from cognitive curiosity and emotional fragility. Emotional failures often lead to depression, suicide, addiction, and other mental health challenges. Abstract gratifications, such as money, nationalism, or religion, though born from imagination, have historically fueled murder, racism, discrimination, and even slavery. Similarly, modern inventions like smartphones, nuclear arsenals, and bioweapons carry the potential for immense harm. Yet, our understanding of dangerous phenomena like viruses, electricity, and radiation has only emerged through risk-taking. It is through measured exposure that we learn to tolerate, and even utilize, what once threatened us.

Toxic substances like cyanide, mercury, lead and arsenic – lethal to life – are now used in instruments like thermometers, semiconductors, and batteries. Mercury, for instance, is toxic to the human body, but the danger lies in the dose. A single atom of mercury cannot kill, but at 100 ng/ml, it becomes fatal. A dose of 0.1–0.3 milligrams of cyanide might pass through an adult unnoticed, so subtle is the line between safety and catastrophe. Similarly, toxic ideologies, whether rooted in nature or culture, can threaten our biological and societal survival. Yet, just as we wear butyl or Teflon gloves to handle corrosive acids like hydrochloric or sulfuric, we can arm ourselves with psychological resilience and the tools of technology to endure and neutralize these toxic forces.

The same principle plays out on a grander scale: throw water into the sun, and it'll instantly evaporate. But cast lava into the ocean, and it'll harden into stone. Everything depends on balance, resistance, and the reality of transformation. Bare skin exposed to acid burns instantly, yet a mere drop may be harmless – manageable because of its low volume. The danger isn't always in the nature of the thing, but in the amount we're exposed to and our preparedness to meet it. The nature of danger mirrors the diverse molecular forces that shape reality – some substances destroy, while others support and stabilize. Life must continuously adapt to these toxic elements in order to survive and spread in this world.

GRAVITY OF MATTER

Size matters. So does how much something spreads. Gravity doesn't emerge from just anything. It arises when colossal masses warp space-time, forming the curves we interpret as gravitational pull.

Gravity is like a human digging a hole. You eat, convert food into energy, and then use that energy to dig. The deeper you dig, the more energy you expend, and in the process, energy converts back into mass. Eventually, if you dig deep enough, you might get stuck – like a star reaching the Chandrasekhar limit, collapsing under its own mass. But what forms isn't a hole in the traditional sense; it's a curvature in four dimensions. Even the smallest energetic object can bend space-time. A single photon, for instance, carries about 10^{-19} joules of energy – enough to exert force, though not enough to attract matter.

In the same way that a human becomes "real" through reproduction or the spread of ideas, matter must bond with other matter to generate gravity. Photons alone can't bend space-time significantly, but when they're entangled, and when quarks pair through gluons, and bosons interact with the Higgs field, the weak and strong nuclear forces emerge – allowing protons and neutrons to form. Then, atomic bonds and electromagnetic forces give rise to molecules. Molecules form minerals, planets, and eventually vast molecular structures that collect energy as mass, rotating and exerting force – creating gravity.

And this gravity bears a peculiar resemblance to our cultural imagination. Just as no light can escape a black hole, some belief systems or nations exert such overwhelming force that escaping their influence is difficult. Jupiter holds its moons and matter because it has accumulated enough mass to curve space-time significantly. The more mass and the more bonds a system has, the stronger its pull. Jupiter's mass controls its space, just like powerful ideologies or systems control the minds within their sphere. Think of entering a foreign nation: your dollars or rupees don't work there. You must convert to pesos, euros, or yen, adapting to their laws and systems.

Cultural laws are much like gravity. In Germany or Brazil, cannabis is legal for personal use. In many other countries, it's criminal without a prescription. A Muslim woman in

France cannot wear a veil in public. But step outside France, and the law changes. Each region's belief and law system creates its own field of influence. In present-day Afghanistan, strict dress codes are enforced for women; leave the country, and suddenly, freedom returns. Culture exerts force like gravity: once inside, you're subject to its pull; once outside, you're free.

This influence is context-dependent. Take your hard-earned money and offer it to a monkey in the forest for a banana – it's absurd. Either you're foolish for offering, or the monkey is for not taking it. The value of money, like the force of gravity, only holds within certain systems which are bonded with many atoms. These shifts in influence mirror escape velocity. Escape velocity from Earth is 40,270 km/h. Once achieved, Earth's gravity no longer applies. On Mars, it's only 18,108 km/h. Similarly, getting bail in America might cost $10,000, while in India it would require rupees. Likewise, outside of France, the veil ban fades; outside of Afghanistan, women are free. You can escape one belief system for another.

We treat money as real because it operates with power inside its given system. Break its rules, and you face consequences: lifelong imprisonment, or even death. If you commit a theft, and the legal system functions, you could be imprisoned for life and forgotten. But like unbonded neutrons, which decay after about ten minutes without making any significant impact, selfish acts – murders, rapes, suicides, robberies – fade over time unless they bond to something meaningful that can last for a long time.

If humanity had only prayed to selfish gods promising heaven without ever looking into microscopes to understand microorganisms, we might have been wiped out by viruses like HIV or COVID-19. We must learn everything, without bias. We must learn without discrimination. We must love without selfish hate. Science must spread globally, or a single nation clinging to outdated dogma might try to dismantle everything we've built. Ideas, like gravity, become powerful when they spread and bond.

To survive, life must engage with everything, including what seems dangerous or foreign. We must learn about toxic elements like mercury, lead, or cyanide; about ancient animals like mammoths and dinosaurs; and even about unstable elements like plutonium or nihonium. They all teach us how not to vanish from history and how to sustain for a longer period.

To save ourselves, we must preserve and understand everything. In the end, survival demands interaction, even with hostile or opposing forces. Just as we wear rubber gloves to handle acid, or space suits to explore the vacuum, we must arm ourselves with the right tools to live meaningfully in a complex universe. We must equip ourselves to face every kind of reality – even those that challenge or threaten us.

SAVE, SHARE, AND SHINE

Sanskrit, once a prominent and revered language, has become nearly extinct, largely due to the dwindling number of people who still use it. Other languages like Latin, Mandan, and Old Norse have faced similar fates. Yet, we've made efforts to preserve them, archiving their scripts, sounds, and meanings. These forgotten voices live on in museums, books, and academic studies, remembered by those who care enough to empathize with the past.

Ironically, while most Indians no longer speak Sanskrit, we can now "speak" to the Internet and artificial intelligence. But the Internet responds only to the languages it understands – languages grounded in mathematical logic and programming. If Sanskrit isn't installed or supported, your messages in it won't be understood. Knowledge must be shared to survive. Unless someone uploads Sanskrit tattoos, shares chants on social media, or teaches it through platforms, the language will remain unknown. The unknown, left unshared, stays forgotten forever.

Pluto has always been part of our solar system, yet it wasn't until 1930 that we discovered it for certain. It was like a tree falling in a forest with no one around to hear – it existed, but went unnoticed. In much the same way, an idea or a gene, if left isolated and unshared, fades into oblivion. Even if ancient cultures once discovered the atom or conceptualized space travel, without transmitting their knowledge through texts, symbols, or artifacts, those insights would dissolve into myth, irrelevant to the present.

Interaction is the bridge between fantasy and reality. An idea becomes reality only through engagement. Without it, the idea remains fiction. We are often left only to believe or not believe. We can't keep our eyes fixed on Pluto constantly, but we can use telescopes to observe it and reinforce its existence. And still – we can doubt. For every believer in a theory, there will be a skeptic. But this opposition is not a flaw; it is the engine of clarity. It is through such contrast that stronger, more reliable connections are forged. Life, too, is a dance between opposing forces – internal and external, belief and doubt.

Our minds can hold on to contradictory thoughts leading to cognitive dissonance. Our minds are capable of what can be called fictitious trust – a capacity that allows us to suspend disbelief and watch a man transform into the Hulk, or immerse ourselves in a game of chess where symbolic pieces represent life and death. We can imagine anything. Consider, for instance, a plant sprouting from the scorching surface of the sun: green, slender, rising, blossoming with crimson flowers. Even the most surreal visions can bloom in the fertile soil of imagination.

That dream, however absurd, is a manifestation of our infinite mental capacity. In a chaotic, ever-shifting reality, consistency is a rare luxury. Our ability to both believe and doubt is what helps us to adapt and survive. To navigate this chaos, we must be able to both believe and doubt – to entertain endless possibilities while staying anchored to a shared reality.

We must share our DNA through sex and reproduction, our individuality through culture, education, social media, and our ideas through medicine, technology, art, and science. Ideas are powerful only when shared in the language of the present reality. Reality becomes real through interaction. Even the earliest energy – before mass, gravity, or form – only became something when it interacted with something else. A particle that never bonds remains a ghost.

Yet, we observe distant realities – Saturn, the Sun, galaxies, black holes – not by touching them, but through telescopes and satellites. These celestial bodies do not touch us. If they did, we wouldn't survive the encounter. They exist within our minds as observed data, not through physical interaction, but through the exchange of photons and interpretation of light. Reality can appear as a mirage, visible only because photons interact with matter, carrying information across the vastness of space.

Seeing is an interaction. A photon must strike something to be perceived. Otherwise, it passes through unnoticed, like light through invisible glass. Vision is tricky. What we "see" is not just what is in front of us, but what is interpreted by our minds – constructed from photons received, memories stored, and the seamless flow of moments blending the immediate past with the constantly arriving present. This creates a continuous stream of moments stitched into perception. And from this, we build imagination. From the information we receive, we dream of futures that don't yet exist. We imagine a god holding the Sun in one hand and the Moon in the other, declaring creation. We imagine saviors who will rescue humanity. We envision a past and a future shaped by such divine forces. We imagine theories, technology, and art.

Light becomes memory. Memory becomes imagination. Once received, memories become part of our making: malleable, editable, and shaped to fit our narration. We can imagine both the past and the future, and a we seek credibility through experimentation and evidence. Imagination, with its power to rearrange and remix what we've seen and known, gives birth to new stories and novel ideas. These narratives help us interpret the world, rethink the way we live, and forge innovative, sustainable paths through the chaos of existence. We do not survive chaos by resisting it, but by learning, adapting, and dreaming.

LIGHT

Light is formed when electrons in an atom become excited and jump from their orbit, releasing a packet of quantum energy known as a photon. This photon then travels from point A to point B at a constant speed of 299,792,458 meters per second – the universal speed of light. It never changes; yet, it is finite. A photon can only complete its journey from A to B within the constraints of this speed; if the distance exceeds what can be covered in one second, it simply takes more time. This principle forms the basis of Einstein's theory of relativity.

However, what we call the "speed of light" is not necessarily its one-way speed. In fact, we cannot measure light's one-way speed, only its two-way average. This is part of Einstein's synchronization convention, where he famously stated:

"The one-way speed is in reality neither a supposition nor a hypothesis about the physical nature of light, but a stipulation which I can make of my own free will in order to arrive at a definition of simultaneity."

The speed of light is not absolute in all conditions; it varies as it passes through different mediums: vacuum, gas, liquid, solid, and gravitational fields. We cannot truly "slow down" light, but we can delay its journey by placing it within denser or warped media. Essentially, we make the photon busy – bouncing, interacting, being absorbed and re-emitted within smaller and more complex paths between A and B. This variation in the speed of light is measured by its refractive index.

For instance, water – when present in large quantities between two points – can distort light's travel. The electrons in the water molecules absorb and then re-emit the photons, causing a delay and distorting the image we perceive. In extreme conditions, such as a black hole, photons may become trapped in a circular path between A and B, orbiting endlessly, never escaping.

One extraordinary example of light's interaction with gravity is the case of Supernova Refsdal. Light from this star's explosion was bent and split by the immense gravitational pull of a massive galactic cluster, creating a phenomenon known as gravitational lensing. Because of this cosmic distortion, the image of the same supernova reached us thrice – first in 1998, then in 2014, again in 2015. The supernova itself occurred 9.3 billion years ago, but the light, slowed and rerouted by the gravitational curvature of space, took eons to arrive in fragments.

Such a delay in light travel opens up fascinating possibilities. Dinosaurs, long extinct, could still be visibly alive – from a cosmic point of view. If an alien civilization were watching Earth from 65 million light-years away with a telescope powerful enough, they would see dinosaurs roaming and hunting in real time. The light that left Earth during the age of dinosaurs would only now be reaching their eyes. Though the technical challenge of such focused observation is immense, theoretically, it's possible.

Through light, we receive the past. Through memory, we build the present. And through imagination, fueled by both, we create the future.

Imagine a tiger chasing you. You see the tiger before it ever lays a claw on you – before you can hear its stealthy paws brushing against dry leaves, before the scent of blood and decay reaches your nose. If your eyesight is sharp, you can even detect it from miles away. Why? Because light, the fastest particle in the known universe, reaches you before the tiger does. Light outpaces the moving predator, alerting your senses long before pain or contact arrives.

Physically, you don't feel pain until the tiger's teeth sink in or its claws anchor into your flesh. But biology is far more intuitive than that. It doesn't wait. Your brain is pre-programmed to interpret patterns, trajectories, and threats before they fully materialize. Your brain doesn't wait for the collision; it is pre-programmed to interpret light signals and predict threats. It processes not just the shape of the tiger, but the direction it moves in, the expression on its face, and the momentum it carries.

A deer doesn't flee simply because it sees a tiger. It runs because it believes the tiger is closing in, interpreting a moving series of light signals, forming an internal timeline of momentum, and predicting the predator's future motion based on past visual cues. The predator could be a real threat – or just a holographic projection with no weight, no scent, no danger. Yet the mind responds, just in case.

Life requires a present weight to construct both past and future. There must be evidence – something solid to anchor possibility. The sketch of a machine becomes the seed of invention. The fossilized skeleton of a T.rex may not roar any more, but it carries the weight of history, allowing us to recreate the creature on screen. Similarly, knowing the composition of the sun – hydrogen and helium – allows us to calculate its future and predict its eventual collapse, millions of years from now.

Ultimately, survival depends on our ability to connect the past, present, and future. What we see, what we remember, and what we expect – all of it begins with light and leads us into motion. Life doesn't always wait for confirmation. It moves forward, grounded in the weight of the present and the projection of what could be.

VISION OF THE FUTURE

Even through sound – like infrared and ultrasonic frequencies – many animals can sense the world before physical contact ever occurs. A bat, for instance, uses echolocation to track moving prey, constructing a predictive image of where the prey was, where it is, and where it will be. This allows the bat to hunt with precision. In essence, the bat creates a predictive future image to track and capture its target. This ability, though limited to a relatively small range, demonstrates a profound evolutionary step: the ability to perceive what hasn't yet happened. Though this ability is limited to a small range, light grants us a far broader field of perception, allowing us to see planets, stars, and galaxies. By observing and predicting, we've created calendars, tracked celestial patterns, and built monuments – pyramids and temples – that reflect our deep belief in the future. We can think about what wasn't. We can lie and say nice words to make others feel good. We can show sympathy, empathy and other compassionate emotions to get what others want to get along well in society. We can threaten people with a bad future to influence their decisions and get support. We can learn and adapt consciously to take control of reality to survive and exist.

The pyramid is a solid, tangible structure. Yet, it also points to something abstract: the unknown past (the origins of Earth) and the far-off future (the end of time). In Egyptian mythology, Atum, the sun god, emerged alone from the cosmic ocean, Nun. He awakened and formed a hill (a pyramid), from which he created Shu (air) and Tefnut (moisture). From Atum-Ra, all life emerged, and with it came the forces of good and evil, as well as the oracle foretelling the final days, when Nun would rise again and engulf the world.

Even a bat must "remember" the past of its prey's movement to predict its future location and act in the present. In Christianity, the Bible describes how God created the world in seven days and promised to return to reclaim the faithful. These stories, like the bat's strategy, rely on knowledge of the past and present to construct a believable future. The difference lies in scale: science tells another kind of origin story, one where living beings are rare and fleeting compared to the vast, unfeeling bulk of the universe. Life, as we know it, began around 3 billion years ago, while the universe itself began approximately 13.8 billion years ago with the Big Bang, and continues to expand into realms we may never observe.

Yet, life has evolved an extraordinary tool: imagination. We use memory not just to react, but to anticipate, plan, and survive. Just like the bat edits its acoustic memories, we edit visual and conceptual memories to our advantage. A lion doesn't ponder whether the deer will fight back or escape; it simply envisions a future where the deer is easily hunted. It visualizes the possibility of a successful hunt – a hopeful future. Similarly, we envision success, marriages, careers, particle accelerators, rockets, planes, cameras, and even fictional worlds like *Star Wars*, *Avengers*, or GTA 6. Some of these fulfill our need for wonder and pleasure; others are tools of survival.

We've gone further – we've built machines that can capture images, replay memories, and even edit them. We build 3D games where we die and respawn, simulating life and death in endless loops. We can simulate the destruction of galaxies, imagine our Sun being swallowed by a black hole, or resurrect creatures like the T.rex and woolly mammoth inside virtual realities. Our minds can construct impossible futures, then animate them into digital existence.

In a 3D movie, cars and bullets seem to fly toward you. Now pair that with spatial sound, and the illusion becomes startlingly real. But in truth, it's all light – a stream of photons. Photons aren't the object themselves; they are radiation – carriers of energy that our minds translate into images. A holographic Moon might emit light and even induce heat, but without mass, it remains only an image. And it reveals one of the greatest truths of life: reality is not only perceived, but imagined, constructed in the minds of living beings who use memory to shape motion, thought, and destiny.

The ability to see is one of life's greatest evolutionary leaps. Optical power only emerged around 500 million years ago – astonishingly recent, considering that life began approximately 3.5 billion years ago. For the vast majority of its existence, life was blind, unable to form images of the future, interpret the present, or understand the past. We were confined to a narrow band of reality, limited by our sensory tools, until vision expanded the scope of perception. With vision came the ability to store visual memories, retrieve them like computers, and – more profoundly – edit them to imagine new possibilities.

Memory is a reconstruction. And imagination is often born from this act of remembering. In fact, memory creates motion in thought. If you cannot store the successive images of a moving train, how can you describe its motion? Without memory, the train would appear static, always frozen in a single frame. You'd never detect the crash, because you'd have no image of its prior, un-crashed state to compare. So, it's not enough to see – we must store what we see. A stored image is information, and information is the foundation upon which life builds its reality. That information is shaped, distorted, and reassembled by life's experiences and by the lies it tells itself, especially in a creative life.

ESCAPE NOW

Creativity requires a full spectrum: a picture of the past, the experience of the present, and a vision of the future – even if none of it is objectively true. To be limitless, we must see in all directions of time. We invent stories of origin: gods, creators, and of endings: heaven, hell, reincarnation. Animals also "create stories," but theirs are purely functional: to hunt, eat, defecate, sleep, mate, and survive. A spider's life story is spun from juvenile to adulthood, and it constructs a future by building a trap based on its knowledge of prey behavior. Like us, it has a belief in the future, even if it cannot name it.

Every night, as we go to sleep, we assume tomorrow will come. We trust in the alarm we've set, in the idea of "tomorrow." When that future arrives, it becomes "yesterday," and we get busy again in the present, working to build yet another tomorrow. But the future we build is shaped by the past we carry. Each of us builds our future from the foundation of our past – so the future is relative, shaped by memory.

If a deer refused to believe in the future and only reacted to the present, it wouldn't survive. Suppose it spots a tiger in the distance. If the deer waited for the tiger's paw to crack a branch or touch its skin before running, it would be dead. Skepticism can be fatal. If the deer insists on logic – "I see the tiger, but it's not biting me yet" – then it misunderstands the role of fear. Fear triggers imagination, and imagination is survival. Fear of hate, death, and oblivion. What we see is always the past – light takes time to travel. To truly respond to the present, we must predict, using memory and creativity to calculate the object's motion. If our prediction fails, it's not the future that deceived us; it's our failure to understand the past deeply enough. Fear is not a flaw; it's a survival mechanism, an image of a future that does not yet exist, but might. The tiger must have a path, a history. A tiger had to come from somewhere to get here; therefore, we must run into the future to escape. To survive, we must remember. To evolve, we must imagine.

Most of human history is grounded in a present. The Earth becomes a reference point for all time. The past, we remember; the future remains abstract. Only astronauts, who leave Earth and return, glimpse the Earth as a future destination. In a way, Earth is our shared present, a loop we seek to break. On Earth, we are trapped in the now, anchored by gravity and time. In most religious stories, Earth is never the final destination. It is a testing ground, a place of suffering, a temporary station between origin and eternity. Every religion, every mythology, every sci-fi franchise – from Hindu cosmology to *Star Wars*, *Marvel*, and *Star Trek*

– shares the recurring theme of escaping Earth, of breaking free from the loop of the present. These stories are not just religious; they are escapes from the gravitational trap of this fragile Earth, both literal and existential.

Our heavens may differ – be it nature, Eden, Nirvana, the universe, or reincarnation – but the Earth is here, changing, aging, decaying. Earth is the constant stage on which we perform. And this stage is changing. According to current science, our Sun has about 5 billion years left. Eventually, Earth will become uninhabitable. This is the worst future we've predicted, and it's forcing us to imagine alternatives. Life, uniquely, can imagine new realities: filled with lightsabers, superheroes, dragons, fairies, magicians, mermaids, robots, and star-faring civilizations.

But the question remains: can we change reality itself? Can we turn this chaotic, unpredictable universe into a utopia filled with wonder and technology?

FORCED FREEDOM

Are there really twenty-four hours in a day? A "day" on Earth once meant something very different. About 1.5 billion years ago, a day lasted only eighteen hours. Go back 4.6 billion years, and it was merely six hours long. Due to the Moon's gravitational tug, Earth's rotation is slowing, lengthening each day by 1.73 milliseconds every century. In another billion years, a day will last twenty-seven hours. So, even something as seemingly constant as "time" is in flux. Our deeply held beliefs are finite – shaped by convenience. When beliefs become disadvantageous, we discard them. We live in a constant fluctuation of faith.

Even reality does not offer eternal truths. There are truths for astronomical scales, truths for planetary scales, and entirely different truths on the quantum level, where phenomena like superposition and entanglement challenge classical logic. Reality is chaos. Entropy is its nature. Prediction is riddled with paradoxes: the butterfly effect, Gibbs' paradox, the three-body problem, the firewall paradox, the expansion of space, and more. Even we ourselves are not subject to our own predictions.

Take the Rodrigues fruit bat: scientists once predicted its extinction by the 20th century. Yet, it survives, because people, recognizing its plight, acted to conserve it. We changed the trajectory of reality, injecting more disorder into the system to maintain the order of life. We are unpredictably creative disruptors – creatures who generate chaos to preserve our form within it.

Humanity wants to save everything from death, from collapsing into nothingness. We want the complete picture of the universe in a single frame. We save the planet, the forests, the species, the data because, ultimately, we are trying to save ourselves. But we are the chaos within chaos; our survival strategies are just a different kind of disorder.

All life is different, and each form of life strives to survive in its own way. Spiders spin traps. Beavers build dams. Porcupines grow spines. Birds grow wings. And humans – humans presently place their belief not just in the living, but in the non-living. We don't merely produce biological offspring, we create brainchildren: ideas, tools, machines, and concepts. We harness non-living entities to our advantage because every living organism perceives its own version of the past and the future.

To locate Neptune, we don't turn to a wise human; we rely on lifeless instruments: glass lenses, telescopes, and observatories. A person from the past might have claimed Neptune was a god dwelling in an underwater palace. But we have come to understand that we cannot perceive the true nature of the universe with our eyes alone. Human vision is confined to a narrow spectrum of visible light. Bees, for instance, can see ultraviolet rays – a reality we only confirmed through scientific investigation.

Biology draws on the principles of physics to persist. And every invention of the human mind must engage with reality, sometimes even manipulating it, to continue existing. A lion, for instance, must grow a coat that blends with its environment, using camouflage to deceive the deer it hunts. We use X-rays to detect illnesses and navigate hidden truths. We have developed machines capable of processing, predicting, and explaining realities that far exceed the limits of our senses. Our computers can even render 4D objects, effortlessly modeling concepts our brains struggle to comprehend. Biology also bends physics – brain-driven creations manipulate the material world to cheat, bond, and endure. Sometimes, the altered reality of life is so immense that it becomes a separate dimension, exhibiting its own properties.

Most deep-sea fish cannot see red light because they evolved to detect only blue wavelengths. Take the stoplight loosejaw, a predator that emits red bioluminescent light – a frequency its prey cannot see. In that darkness, the predator becomes invisible, while the prey remains exposed. But if the prey had a brain like ours, it could invent a lens – a glass – that revealed the red light. It wouldn't ask another brainy fish for answers, because that fish would have its own version of reality, shaped by its own needs to survive. Living beings can deceive, be deceived, or live in delusion. We all manipulate reality within our mind – sometimes knowingly, sometimes instinctively – to survive.

We live in limitations and layered truths. But we cheat those limits with tools, imagination, and stories. We survive by understanding paradoxes and creating order from disorder. We are creative beings, capable of designing satellites, rockets, and computers that store and process information about the vastness of the universe. We can search the Internet to learn about the tiniest particles, germs, atoms, and about distant stars, black holes, planets, and even the largest known voids in the cosmos, like the Boötes Void, the Eridanus Supervoid, and the KBC Void.

Even though reality is inherently unpredictable, we deploy countless ideas to maintain our physical form on

Earth, defending ourselves against climate, nature, disease, predators, and even the ideas we've invented: nations, technologies, and traditions. The computer, for instance, functions on just two digits – binary, like musical notes or language – and yet it generates infinite information from finite variables. Likewise, the human brain produces infinite ideas – eternity, infinity, nothingness – using a finite biological system.

Perhaps we can preserve this chaotic reality in just two dimensions – or in virtual realities we've created in video games. We are compelled to study this reality and generate new ideas, in order to increase our probability of existing longer.

A lion converts organic matter into more lions. A nation can assimilate others into its culture or ideology. A scientist can persuade another through debate and evidence, converting doubt into belief. In this sense, we transform reality – through tools, through language, through force. We've turned iron into swords, spoons, gadgets, and machines. To melt a sword, one must apply heat and pressure, forcing matter to change its state and properties. We combine elements, like carbon and iron, to form steel.

We may choose to remain isolated, in spirituality or meditation, but we cannot survive without converting something – materials, energy, ideas – in order to survive and spread. Our bodies are too fragile to survive everywhere in the universe. If we wish to expand beyond Earth, we must invent things that can thrive in environments we cannot. Rovers survive on the Moon. Computers process far more complex data than we can.

Maybe we are also forced to exist. Forced to fear, to feel, to think, to doubt. And yet we are free – free to imagine aliens, robots, time travel, magic, 4D space, alternate realities, multiverses, superpowers, and more. But even this freedom is forged by thc forcc of naturc, a byproduct of the entropy, chaos, and structure that makes up the universe. Our character is an extension of reality; we are what we eat and what we are made of.

FORCE OF LIFE

Living beings consume one another, cheat, manipulate, and transform in an effort to control their world. Life doesn't stop at biology; it strives to understand the non-living: quantum mechanics, galaxies, molecules, stars, and moons. But this partition between "living" and "non-living" is a construct, made by a living being, a human. Is there truly a difference? We may believe we control the hand made of atoms, but could it be that atoms, in turn, control us?

There is no definitive "we" (the living) and "them" (the non-living). There are only things – forced to interact, to change, and to exist – driven by the fundamental forces of nature. We are forced to exist, and within that compulsion, we are free – to think, to imagine, to invent new ways to survive.

This "force of belief" is still elusive in its origins. Skeletons, membranes, cells, and organs are merely successive stages of evolution. We know DNA and RNA – molecules that carry information and somehow give rise to a brain, a body, and a replica of themselves. But what came before them? Was DNA a product of consciousness, or was consciousness the byproduct of DNA? What was the first formation that created the first strand? Perhaps it was only an idea. The first life may have been a ghost in the machine, shaped and summoned by the raw forces of nature. This fragile form required countless lucky resources to persist and evolve, making its survival improbable, yet not impossible. And once life did emerge, it became a force of its own.

This ancient force remains stubborn, still surviving, still igniting the will to solve problems and expand its reach. It was clever enough to give us a brain capable of revisiting the past to imagine a future. It was wise enough to invent pain, to defend itself from destruction. We feel pain when we walk on fire for ritual, fast for God, or undergo surgery or scientific risk. We feel fear because biology insists on preserving itself. Evolution crafted a creative mind to overcome its own pain.

This force of life – emerging from cellular structures, atomic bonds, and electromagnetic interactions – has culminated in the creation of strong bones, enabling life to stand against gravity and defend itself from predators. These same bones have been adapted for various purposes: to attack (teeth, horns), to defend (shells, skulls), to attract (antlers, tusks), and to fly (hollow bones). This skeletal architecture is so durable that we can still recognize long-extinct creatures like the T.rex, woolly mammoth, ammonite, and pterodactyl from their fossilized remains.

Our skin is vulnerable to the chaos of reality; we store our thoughts and knowledge within durable, artificial containers like servers, databases, and machines infused with artificial intelligence and governed by protocols of security and confidentiality. We are constructing vast digital sanctuaries, whole cities of information, tasked with preserving our collective memory. Is there truly a difference between biology and machine? In life's attempt to defy destruction, it creates new forms and ideas.

Is there really a distinction between us and the non-living? If lightning strikes nitrogen molecules with 9.8 eV of energy, the triple bond shatters, forming ammonia. Is this death for nitrogen? The same principle applies when lightning strikes a human. Thc body's electrons become excited, generating heat and radiation that incinerate the organic structure into ash. We call this "death." But do we truly die? Only if we believe our form must remain unchanged. Yet, life inherently questions itself in moments of danger, it doubts, it innovates. It evolves by crafting poisons, horns, camouflage, shells, wings – strategies to escape, hide, or defend against threats. Even iron rusts. Even stars die. So we persist in searching for better ways to protect the idea of ourselves. But in trying so, we change the idea of ourselves.

We search for threats. We learn, we evolve – to maintain the idea of our form, and to project it ubiquitously across the universe. Even after the death of the sun, even after the end of the observable universe. But life will find a consistency to rely on – one idea we can cling to in all this chaos.

Our soul, our individuality will survive all this chaos. Somehow, our individual souls seem to exist outside of all known reality, making decisions with a strange impartiality. Perhaps they are not bound by form but exist as a formula. This structure, limitless in its abstraction, is what we may call our numerical soul.

MATHEMATICAL BODY

Life must understand the past and anticipate the future in order to be fully present. A bird, for instance, doesn't concern itself with the distant future; it focuses only on the immediate and the near. It operates based on instinctual memory: eat, defecate, find a mate, reproduce, flee from predators, and catch prey with precision. It does not worry about a meteor named 101955 Bennu possibly colliding with Earth in 2182. It does not name galaxies like Milkdromeda, destined to form 4 billion years from now. A bird does not trace its origin – whether from an egg, a chicken, or some imagined avian deity. Its foresight is limited, driven by selfish imperatives to protect and sustain its own body.

A bird does not care if a black hole is consuming an entire galaxy, or if the universe is expanding into an unknowable void. It is indifferent to climate change, to the speed of light. But we – humans – care. We calculate. We take the abstract concept of mathematics and use it to understand cosmic objects and their motions. With formulas, we can compute the speed of light (c), or time dilation in the curvature of space-time: $t = t_0 / \sqrt{(1 - v^2/c^2)}$.

We strive toward a unified theory of everything. The modern world runs on mathematical algorithms, technologies, and abstract ideas. Our computers, refrigerators, cars, GPS systems, and satellites are all products of such knowledge. Each of these tools, composed of the same matter that makes up everything in the universe – including us – can be programmed, manipulated, and used to generate specific outcomes.

Unlike other animals, we don't merely teach our young how to survive, reproduce, and socialize. We teach them to design entirely new models of computation and technology, new ways to observe, interpret, and store the universe's information, all within the confines of our small planet. To control a horse, you must feed it first, form a bond, and eventually saddle and ride it. You must also be a good owner. You might build a parasitic relationship, applying force or using Pavlov's principles of pain and pleasure to modify behavior. But today, many of our tools no longer need such bonding. We have self-driven cars, virtual reality, bio-monitoring devices, and more. We've transformed the world with our imagination, turning ideas into realities. We have become real, astonishingly real. Yet, we are far from finished. There are still countless ideas waiting to be brought into existence. The universe seems to guide itself, transforming through its myriad forms in an eternal resistance to becoming nothing. And all these thoughts, all these speculations, come from me – a human – woven from the same quantum uncertainty, nuclear forces, electromagnetic interactions, and gravitational pulls as the rest of existence. And yet, I can also imagine a world where Superman flies, or where the universe sparked into existencc through a brief, random act of consciousness, a moment both uncertain and inevitable.

The birthday paradox suggests that in a group of just twenty-three people, there's a fifty-fifty chance that two individuals will share the same birthday. This illustrates how probability can defy our intuition. Like handing a piano to a monkey – in the midst of infinite randomness, there exists the rare chance that the monkey might strike a sequence of notes that resembles music, even without knowing what music is. Yet, this randomness creates a network of consequence, giving rise to a consciousness (life and intelligence) that imagines its own improbable birth. Creation may be rooted in chaos, but life is the decision to seek purpose and meaning. Life is the idea of reality, and from it emerges the ability to generate ideas that strive to understand and control that reality. Words and numbers are such ideas.

Even to calculate quantum uncertainty, we turn to mathematics. The Schrödinger wave equation, foundational to quantum mechanics, only becomes complete with the inclusion of an imaginary number: $\Psi(x, t) = Aei(kx-\omega t)$. It is this abstraction – the imaginary unit "i" – that bridges the gap between possibility and expression, between the invisible and the calculable. Like our souls, imagined to exist beyond death and time, the mathematical concepts we created transcend our world, enabling us to understand everything. Through mathematics, we attempt to understand everything – even the very randomness that gave rise to us.

Let's place a human speedster beside a long train, one with no windows, no doors, just a single continuous car stretching from the start to the engine. Imagine this human running from one end of the train to the other. With nothing visible except the train itself and its shadow on the ground, how long would it take to cross? If the train is 500 kilometers long, and the speedster runs at 125 km/h, it would take four hours to cross it. But now imagine the train is just a toy, only 50 centimeters in length. In that case, how much time would the speedster need? Or take something even smaller: to cross the breadth of an ant, about 25 millimeters, how long would a human take?

Now compare this with a blue whale, whose body stretches over 100 to 110 feet. If it swims across a space 50 feet long, it doesn't really travel that distance, it already occupies it. Scale makes all the difference. A creature large enough – say, a brachiosaurus with a body length longer than a train – wouldn't need to run to cross it. Its head would already be at the end while its feet were at the beginning. A snake bite to the leg takes time to affect the brain, as it has to travel those 5 or 6 feet. Everything becomes a reference to our perception.

We don't measure movement the same way across scales. We don't consider the travel from 1 nanometer to 5 nanometers unless we're dealing with electrons. Our own bodies, too, are possessions, growing from 1.5 foot babies into 6 foot adults. We control them, but they follow their own agendas: to grow, to mate, to sleep, to shit, to survive. We control it, but it also controls us.

What if we had a body that could extend wherever we needed – into the quantum realm or across interstellar space to our imagination? Then we could measure even the hypothetical distances that don't exist in practical life. Using this conceptual body, we could predict the future from present data or reconstruct the past, just as we do with extinct animals through carbon dating.

Mathematics is our ultimate platform. From minus infinity to plus infinity, it enables us to represent and calculate both the smallest particles and the largest structures. Entire galaxies, with their 100 to 400 billion stars and spans of 100,000 light-years, can be modeled through numbers. And though the Andromeda galaxy is 2.537 million light-years away, we always think forward, toward $+\infty$ while our roots remain in $-\infty$.

Yet, to exist, we still have to carry our 6 foot body. We must eat, love, hate, mate, study, reproduce, and protect our fragile order amid the chaos of the cosmos. Mathematics helps us describe this journey, but even that isn't immune to paradoxes and contradictions. We have found doubts even in the purity of numbers.

VIII. NEW NUMBERS

When did we accept the infinite? In ancient times, divinity was the sole source of infinity: God alone was deemed invincible and eternal. We, as fragile humans subject to pain, pleasure, and biological necessity, could scarcely imagine beyond the finite order. To dream of anything outside God's design was deemed impossible, if not outright sinful. Everything began with God, and was meant to end in God. But slowly, the long, stubborn process of science began. It carved out space for creativity, for knowledge, and eventually for the conception of infinity itself. Freed from strict theological bounds, we began to forge new words. Although early number systems sufficed to count prey, days, people, time, weight, statistics, and coins, it took us millennia to conceive of new kinds of numbers.

Only when mathematics transcended concrete geometry – venturing into abstraction – did truly "new" numbers emerge. Our leap from Euclid's flat planes to non-Euclidean geometries reshaped the mathematical landscape. When Hippasus attempted to find the hypotenuse of a right triangle with legs of length 1, he uncovered √2, an irrational number that cannot be expressed as a ratio of integers and whose decimal expansion never repeats. Pythagoras himself had offered a unifying theorem for right angles. It was like pi – a number that, when written as a decimal, stretches on forever, never repeating. These numbers were strange, unending, and deeply unsettling to those who once believed mathematics to be a perfect, divine language of the cosmos.

The Greeks had brushed against the idea before, through Zeno of Elea and his famous paradox of Achilles and the Tortoise, but these were viewed more as philosophical riddles than mathematical realities. For the deeply spiritual Greeks, mathematics was sacred and interconnected with the divine order. It ended, ultimately, in God. And irrational numbers? They were seen as broken links – numbers that couldn't be touched, divided, or harmonized. They were unfit for heaven.

So, they responded with violence. Legend has it that Hippasus, the man who revealed the irrational, was drowned at sea – not voluntarily, but to silence the dissonance he introduced. Pythagoras himself escaped such a fate. But even he, the rebel mathematician, refused to embrace two concepts that would later prove essential to the evolution of mathematics: negative numbers and zero.

ZERO FOR HUMANITY

Negative numbers were once considered geometrically impossible, simply because they were unimaginable. What did a negative square look like? For centuries, many Western mathematicians tucked negative values away, hidden on the other side of reason, dismissed as unusable or irrelevant. It wasn't until the 16th century that the Italian mathematician Rafael Bombelli began integrating negative values into computation. With his efforts, infinity and complex numbers finally found their place. But the true struggle in mathematics was not about the infinite – it was about zero.

The West rejected zero as a devilish concept – an "atheistic" number that symbolized non-existence, even a denial of God. Zero was seen as a dangerous symbol. In a theological world, one (1) and all (infinite) is the God; because of the one, suddenly another one and all else formed. But the idea that something – everything – could arise from nothing was heretical, hard to swallow.

It wasn't until the 17th century that mathematics reached a kind of peace. Slowly, zero, negative numbers, and the infinite were accepted into the discipline. Zero, in particular, began to serve a practical role: a placeholder in the decimal system, a necessary concept for positional notation. Then came Descartes, who introduced the Cartesian coordinate system. Then, with Cartesian coordinates in geometry, and later, polar coordinates, the number zero took its rightful place at the origin of an expandable plane. Even the Church, once a fierce opponent of zero, ultimately adopted it for practical convenience. Yet, it took millennia for humanity to normalize the concept.

Zero is nothing; or rather, zero represents the idea of nothing. And how can one describe nothing?

Our ancestors didn't need such abstractions. Numbers were utilitarian, tools to count weapons, cattle, prey. If they had two spears, two notches on a bone or two sticks sufficed. But if they had none, what symbol could convey that absence? To mark anything would imply that something existed. In that sense, "nothing" need not be marked; its absence is self-evident. If there were no sticks, the absence itself was understood – so why mark it at all? To represent zero is to give form to what has no form. Zero is paradoxical. It is not positive, not negative. Humanity had endured centuries of conceptual discomfort before zero sneaked into our number systems.

Even today, zero continues to carry paradoxes in arithmetic. And the zero we use now is still not truly nothing. Or more precisely, it is not...

Consider a simple division:

$8 \div 2 = 4$

Check: $4 \times 2 = 8$

Or:

$2 \div 56 = 0.03571428\ldots$

Check: $0.03571428 \times 56 = 2$

But what about:

$0 \div 0 = ?$

If you assert $0 \div 0 = 0$, then for any number n,

$n \times 0 = 0$

So there is no unique solution. This expression is indeterminate.

Similarly, dividing any non-zero number by zero:

$5 \div 0, 64 \div 0, 2424 \div 0$

All of these are undefined, because there is no finite or infinite value that, when multiplied by 0, returns a non-zero numerator.

The only unambiguous division by zero is:

$0 \div 1 = 0$

$0 \div 524 = 0$

All other cases involving "÷ 0" remain indeterminate or undefined.

No wonder Western mathematics resisted zero for nearly 2,000 years. By contrast, cultures that embraced zero earlier often developed remarkably broad mathematical systems, and perhaps a more liberated spirituality.

THE ORIGIN OF ZERO

The Hindu mathematical tradition was likely the first to embrace zero and negative numbers. Around 500 ce, the astronomer-mathematician Aryabhatta used zero as a placeholder in his seminal work, and by 628 ce, Brahmagupta had defined zero as a number in its own right. In Hindu philosophy, *sunya* – the void – symbolizes absolute peace and ultimate detachment from the cycle of consumption, memory, and rebirth. Even the great deities – Siva, Brahma, Visnu – are themselves bound by cyclic time: creation, preservation, and dissolution. Their liberation, like ours, depends on transcending life and death.

This spiritual freedom extends to personal devotion. Devotees may choose an *ishta devata* ("cherished deity"), whether a goddess such as Kateri Amman, Maisamma, Pidari, or Mariamma, or even a composite form like Ardhanarisvara, the half-male, half-female deity. In this light, numbers become a kind of sacred language. Mathematics not only solves concrete problems but also offers the mind a path into the abstract – much like music – enabling creation, transformation, and the exploration of infinite possibilities.

Throughout history, mathematicians around the world recorded their calculations in words and diagrams rather than symbolic shorthand. Consider the Roman numeral system: each value – Ⅰ, Ⅴ, Ⅹ, L, C, D, M – was represented by a unique letter, unlike our base-10 notation, which reuses ten symbols (0–9). The Roman number system could express numbers up to 3,999,999 (using overbars to indicate multiplication by 1,000), but anything beyond was considered the realm of the divine rather than human arithmetic. Roman numerals lack zeros and negative numbers, making them both unambiguous and cumbersome. For example, the sentence

"In the year MMXXX, the robots will revolt unless MMXXIV AI coders remain vigilant,"

translates to:

"In the year 2030, the robots will revolt unless 2024 AI coders remain vigilant."

Without an online reference, few today can decode "MMXXX" or "MMXXIV" at a glance. This illustrates both the precision and the accessibility challenges inherent in that ancient system.

Early geometers also performed "calculations" by manipulating physical objects like ropes, wooden squares, and wheels rather than abstract symbols. Euclid's *Elements*, for example, contains no plus, minus, multiplication, or division signs. Propositions and proofs appear as carefully worded arguments accompanied by geometric diagrams.

It wasn't until the 16th century that symbolic notation began to simplify these processes. In 1557, Robert Recorde introduced the equals sign (=) to avoid repeated phrases like "is equal to." Over the next century, plus (+) and minus (–) signs became standard in Western Europe. And in the mid-17th century, John Wallis added the infinity symbol (∞), giving us a concise way to discuss unbounded quantities.

These innovations – zero as both placeholder and number, negative values, and a rich symbolic vocabulary – transformed mathematics from the manipulation of concrete objects and verbal descriptions into the elegant, abstract system we use today.

PROOF OF MATHEMATICS

What is a number? Strangely enough, a number cannot be defined in isolation; it only gains meaning in relation to other numbers. We define what a number is through the act of counting. To understand "5," we must know the context of 1, 2, 3, 4, and also 6, 7, 8, 9. Numbers are relational, not absolute. But how, then, can we rigorously prove the most elementary facts of arithmetic, such as 1 + 1 = 2? That very question drove two great minds, Alfred North Whitehead and Bertrand Russell, to write *Principia Mathematica*, published in 1910.

Their monumental work, *Principia Mathematica*, spans hundreds of pages of symbolic logic, all in service of deriving from first principles the proof that 1 + 1 = 2. It is said that only by page 360 do they finally reach that simple conclusion. Why such complexity for a truth we accept intuitively?

Because numbers are not self-evident. They are representations of concepts. Consider the Tamil ka and kaa, or the ancient Sumerian sign for "one." To a normal observer, these marks might appear as mere drawings, not numerical abstractions. Even with Egyptian hieroglyphs or

Chinese characters, one must learn the system deeply before recognizing their quantitative value.

If we were to communicate with an alien species, we couldn't simply say "2+2=4" and expect instant understanding. They might not count with a base-10 system or have ten fingers, like us. Accustomed to a decimal system, we take our numerals and multiplication tables for granted. But any species without ten digits would require time and instruction to master "0–9," place value, and the very idea of "addition." Our most basic arithmetic stems from shared, deeply embedded conventions.

Principia Mathematica reminds us that even the simplest truths in mathematics rest on layers of logic and definition, and that every number, every operation, is ultimately a human construct given life through careful agreement and proof. Our children learn our number system effortlessly, absorbing multiplication tables as if they were facts of nature. But to an outsider – or an alien – understanding our numeric system might take years of study, just to grasp the core conceptual logic behind it.

Numerical logic seems pre-installed in our brains, a primal survival tool. We instinctively gauge how many lions are chasing us or hiding nearby, or how much force we need to jump from one branch to the next. But teaching someone what the number 1 is, and more importantly, to what we should assign 1, and to what we shouldn't, is an exhausting cognitive task.

Imagine assigning the number 1 to the entire universe. That single unit represents everything: planets, black holes, dark matter, moons, plasma, photons, neutrinos, electrons, stars, and every living being. Just one digit, yet it contains all known reality.

Take a more tangible example: do you wear two shoes or one set of shoes? It depends on how you choose to group and define things. Similarly, a pizza is "one," but we can divide it into three, five, or even seven slices. The number doesn't change the object; it changes our perception of how it's divided or grouped. This idea aligns with Gottlob Frege's logicism, inspired by Georg Cantor's set theory. Think of the way we learn to count as children: 1 = 1 apple, 2 = 2 ducks, 3 = 3 cats, and so on. The number corresponds to a set of objects, and concepts become categories containing extensions, like the concept of "black" including black hair, black eyes, black beetles, black holes, black elephants, and space itself. This is how sets work: they contain elements that share a defining characteristic. And some sets can even contain themselves, like a set of all sets. Sets can contain other sets, including sets that contain themselves.

Bertrand Russell discovered a flaw in set theory, now known as Russell's Paradox. Let's say there's a set of all superhero movies. Inside it are sets for *Superman* movies, *Batman* movies, *Marvel* films, the *X-Men* series, and even independent films. These are all subsets of the larger superhero set. But then there's *Deadpool*. He defies categorization, he breaks the fourth wall, mocks genre conventions, and doesn't play by the rules. He exists inside the superhero genre, but also outside it.

Now think of a club where the first rule is: you can only be a member if you are not a member. Once you join, you break the rule. But if you don't join, you fit the rule. It's a contradiction. This is the essence of Russell's Paradox: the self-reference problem. It reveals the deep and sometimes paradoxical logic that underlies even the most seemingly simple mathematical ideas.

These aren't just mathematical puzzles; they are reflections of the complexity and contradiction woven into the very logic we use to understand the world. Numbers may seem like fixed truths, but they bend and twist with perspective, grouping, and meaning, just like thought itself.

ZERO AND INFINITY

During the agricultural era, civilizations like the Mayans, Sumerians, Chinese, and Babylonians used the concept of zero, not as a number, but as a placeholder. Take the Babylonians, for instance: their number system was based on sixty (sexagesimal), though remnants of base-10 usage still lingered. Unlike our decimal system, which multiplies 10 into 100, 1,000, and 10,000, the Babylonians used 60 as the base for magnitudes, producing values like 3,600, 60,000, and so on. For them, the numbers 60, 120, 180, and 240 represented values equivalent to our 1, 2, 3, and 4 in the next order of magnitude.

Their numeric notation involved two distinct symbols – much like binary digits – repeated in patterns to indicate different values. When they wanted to increase a unit's magnitude, they used the second symbol to amplify it. But crucially, they lacked the concept of zero as a number, which meant they could not clearly differentiate between, say, 40404 and 444. To resolve this ambiguity, they introduced a placeholder to signify the absence of a value in a certain position. And with that innovation, zero quietly entered the world of mathematics.

Interestingly, we still live with Babylonian logic today: we measure time with 60 seconds in a minute and 60 minutes in an hour. The circle, too, carries their legacy, divided into 360 degrees. While their numerical system didn't include zero, nor the concept of imaginary or complex numbers, it held within it the potential for infinity.

Zero as a true number emerged from Asia and was transmitted through the Middle East. The Persian polymath Al-Khwarizmi helped introduce this revolutionary concept to the Islamic world, which, despite initial religious resistance, recognized its utility. From these foundations, algebra blossomed. As Arab influence extended into Africa and Europe, zero journeyed westward, eventually reaching the mind of Leonardo Fibonacci.

Fibonacci's introduction of the Hindu-Arabic numeral system to Christian Europe transformed mathematics. His famous sequence, now immortalized as the Fibonacci series, helped usher Europe into a new era of mathematical reasoning. With zero, numerical records became far simpler. Instead of writing long descriptions of debt, people could denote it with a single negative number (e.g., –63, –345).

Zero birthed new branches of mathematics: negative numbers, natural numbers, integers – all radiating from this central point. Positive numbers were just one branch. From the same foundation, we could access negative numbers, fractions, irrational numbers, imaginary numbers, and complex numbers – all infinite in their own directions, all relying on zero as their point of origin. It became both a tool for annihilation and creation. Consider this: with enough zeroes, you can reach a googol (10^100), and with even more, a googolplex (10^googol). Yet, despite such astronomical values, a single zero in multiplication can reduce all of it to nothing (10^100 × 0 = 0).

Thus, zero is paradoxical – both the symbol of nothingness and the gateway to infinity. Zero possesses the power of obsolescence. It enables us to move beyond each number, rendering previous digits obsolete as we progress. Even within the seemingly simple step from 1 to 2, if we consider real numbers, the path is not so direct. There exists an entire spectrum in between: 1.0, 1.1, 1.2, 1.3 . . . up to 1.9, and only then comes 2.0. This pattern of obsolescence – where each number gives way to the next – continues endlessly.

Now, imagine using your imagination as a mathematical tool. Convert all the matter in the universe into two components. The first is a flat, white sheet of paper that stretches across 14.26 gigaparsecs, which is roughly 46.5 billion light-years. The second is 4 x 10^25 kilograms of ink. With this, begin writing: "1000000000000000. . ." continuing to add zero after zero for page after page. Even then, you could still add one more. And another. This is not true infinity, but a demonstration of how zero enables the steps toward infinity, how it constructs vast scales from the void.

From nothing (0), we create something (1). Add a zero to it – 1.0 – and you pave the way for the next level: 2.0, 3.0, 4.0, and onward. Zero isn't merely the absence of value; it is the beginning of value, the silent architect of every magnitude we can imagine.

ZERO = INFINITY

How much is infinity? Fortunately, Georg Cantor dared to venture deep into this boundless realm. Often called the father of infinity, Cantor pushed mathematics into uncharted territory. But in doing so, he also paid a personal price, eventually losing his mental stability while wrestling with the enormity of the infinite.

Cantor caused a stir in the mathematical world when he introduced the now-famous diagonalization proof. With this, he demonstrated something truly revolutionary: there are uncountable more numbers between 0 and 1 than in the entire set of natural numbers. Think of a number like 0.000000000000001, then imagine adding more zeros, endlessly. That infinite stretch between 0 and 1 contains more numbers than the full set of all whole numbers combined. It sounds paradoxical, but Cantor proved that some infinities are larger than others. In the realm of the infinite, even infinity comes in sizes.

Mathematics is an unlimited reservoir of numbers, capable of defining and predicting everything that is finite. Yet, in a poetic twist, the tools we use to understand the universe are also riddled with their own paradoxes. Many believe we possess something eternal – a soul – something beyond the constraints of logic, something that gives meaning and purpose beyond finite existence. Some numbers have these irrational properties. Infinite as a concept shares this trait.

Just as zero presents us with undefined boundaries, so too does infinity. Try to compute:

infinity ÷ infinity = undefined

–infinity + infinity = undefined

Yet, in contrast:

infinity × infinity = a larger infinity

infinity + infinity = a greater infinity

Infinity resists finality. It both defies and expands logic. And that's the paradox – it is the very concept that transcends everything we try to define. It is almost as if zero and infinity are the same idea, seen from different angles. Zero allows you to mark a point of gravity from which mass, quantity, or meaning can accumulate – from 1 to whatever number follows, and then beyond. That "whatever" – infinity – is not limited by material reality; it can surpass all measurable divisions, extending into realms beyond the tangible.

Zero is the absence of everything, yet paradoxically, it is also the foundation for anything to exist. Imagine an empty box. There's measurable space inside. Fill it, and the contents have mass. Still, for the box to exist in the first place, there must be space to contain it. And if this box exists inside another, that too requires space. In some profound sense, nothingness makes room for everything. If it is possible for "nothing" to be real, then it must also be infinite – not because it exceeds anything, but because there is nothing to exceed. In this way, nothingness is the infinite extension of everything.

Picture a vast, infinitely stretched zero – a closed-loop string that contains all possibilities. Cut it, unravel it, and you get a line: the open string, the ominous stage on which reality unfolds. So perhaps, in the grandest and most paradoxical sense, zero equals infinity. Our universe is expanding beyond what we can observe, into the infinite. But how can it expand without limits, if not into the boundless realm of nothing?

IMAGINATION

Mathematics begins with nothing and ends in infinity. The numbers we use – 2, 3, 4, 5, 6, 7 – are symbolic tools that help us break down and comprehend large quantities. They allow us to compress the enormous and the endless into measurable, digestible units. In this sense, zero and infinity represent the boundaries of a closed number system, one that begins in emptiness and expands without a limit.

Infinity can be imagined as a circle that grows in all directions around zero. When we divide infinity into parts – 1, 2, 3, 4, 5, 6… – we create a linear sequence, the natural numbers, but this is just one thread. Infinity is not confined to a single path; it lies at the far edges of all dimensions, stretching into the negative, into imaginary numbers, into the complex plane. It is an ever-expanding geometry of possibility.

The size of the universe, estimated at around 93 billion light-years, already boggles the mind. And yet, within the realm of science fiction or pure imagination, we can stretch this to 200 billion or 500 billion light-years in a galaxy far, far away. Mathematics gives us the freedom to go beyond physical limitations. It is the engine of hypothetical worlds and abstract infinities.

The Riemann sphere provides a compelling image of this abstract terrain. It unifies the positive and negative infinities into a single, continuous whole. When complex numbers are included, this entire mathematical structure transforms into a sphere, allowing even the seemingly impossible to be defined, such as $1 \div 0 = \infty$, within the framework of the extended complex plane, or Riemann's sphere.

Mathematics may seem real, yet it is still anchored by the human mind. A man demonstrated that mathematics faces a fundamental threat: the force holding it together is our own brain. Without the human mind to interpret and make sense of it, mathematics becomes incomplete and self-contradictory, as illustrated by Russell's paradox. Mathematics relies on the brain to make sense of itself.

Ultimately, it is imagination that sustains mathematics.

REDEFINING REALITY

We are compelled to experience, to believe, and equally – to doubt. We are told we are alive or dead according to the measure of time. Hitler was alive in 1944, but dead in 1946. You can become weightless on the Moon, but you cannot be homosexual in Algeria. Gravity holds us to Earth, yet beyond Earth it loses its grip. The same goes for magnetic fields, or American law. Step beyond their boundaries, and they lose their force.

Kurt Gödel proved that mathematics, too, is incomplete and inconsistent. In his groundbreaking work, he constructed a new formal system, replacing conventional notations with letters, to reveal the internal contradictions within mathematics itself. One such example: the statement "This statement is unprovable," symbolized by a single letter, say "g."

Every letter in his system corresponded to a provable value connected to the system's axioms, except "g." If g is true, it cannot be proven, as it itself declares. But if g is false, then it can be proven, contradicting its own claim. No purely internal mathematical proof can resolve this paradox. This paradox shattered the illusion of perfect logical systems.

To illustrate how context shapes truth, consider three Biblical contradictions:

- The Duration of Divine Anger

"Who is a God like you, pardoning iniquity and passing over transgression… You will not stay angry forever, but delight to show mercy." (Micah 7:18)

"For in My anger a fire is kindled that shall burn forever." (Jeremiah 17:4)

- Generational Punishment

"Fathers shall not be put to death for their children, nor shall children be put to death for their fathers; each is responsible for their own sin." (Deuteronomy 24:16)

"I, the Lord your God, am a jealous God, visiting the iniquity of the fathers on the children to the third and fourth generation…" (Deuteronomy 5:9)

- Divine Jealousy vs. Human Envy

"For you shall worship no other god, for the Lord, whose name is Jealous, is a jealous God." (Exodus 34:14)

Which passages carry ultimate authority? The Bible alone cannot resolve these contradictions; only human interpretation can reconcile them. We need an external framework beyond the printed page to make sense of its shifting portrayals.

Imagine life as a chessboard. You plan logical moves to survive, yet your quantum intuition or gut urges something different. Meanwhile, external forces – social norms, predators, environmental pressures – forbid other paths. You are both player and piece, bound by inner and outer laws. Believing you can only advance one square at a time obscures the broader game, yet, attempting to "jump off" the board risks annihilation. Similarly, trying to escape our expanding universe would shatter the electromagnetic, nuclear, and gravitational forces that hold us together. Your body would disintegrate without the laws that define its coherence.

You cannot prove mathematics using mathematical axioms alone. Mathematics is "right" only within the context of its own framework. But if we were to adopt a different logical system, one with different axioms or rules of inference, what is considered "true" in mathematics might no longer hold. Gödel's incompleteness theorems show that any sufficiently expressive system contains true statements that are unprovable within that system. Nor can you prove life's permanence by asking the living. You cannot ask a religious person about death and accept their claim of immortality; a lion devouring them simply ignores their belief. A judge won't accept a murderer's claim at face value; they seek witnesses and evidence. To test a glass bowl's strength, you drop steel weights, not mere cloth. To validate reality, we need a measure external to it. We are made of matter particles, yet, if we were to come in contact with anti-matter particles, we would be annihilated. In the early universe, there were slightly more matter particles than anti-matter particles, and as they canceled each other out, the excess matter was left behind, giving rise to the physical reality we now experience.

Our cosmos spans roughly 94 billion light-years, filled with galaxies, black holes, stars, planets, and life. But an observer outside our reality, if such a vantage existed, would see only quantum particles dancing in probabilistic patterns. They would not discern our "actions" as separate events. We can recognize a sword as a whole object, yet also distinguish its individual parts: hilt, guard, pommel, and blade. We may further describe it as a steel object. Similarly, today we train artificial intelligence to identify human forms using physical patterns, facial landmarks, and skeletal movements. Our phones, for instance, cannot recognize our voice among other sounds without a precise algorithm designed to distinguish it.

To expand our understanding, we must look beyond reality's confines. For most of human history, Earth sat immobile at the universe's center, but telescopes revealed the Copernican truth. Reality, whether mathematical, moral, or physical, reveals its contradictions only when confronted with perspectives beyond its own boundaries. Reality is our foundation: it defines our existence, the forms of life (humans, dogs, cattle, chickens), and the necessities we create (energy, water, machines, spaceships, virtual worlds). Yet, to learn reality's full scope, we must venture outside it. Only by embracing unpredictability can life evade predictable threats; only by risking and redefining itself can it survive against all odds.

While we master reality's laws, we also conjure entirely new ones: *Harry Potter's* magic, *Star Wars'* hyperspace, Disney and Pixar's enchanted realms. These fictional universes, sprung from our minds, suggest that even imagination is an expression of the universe itself. If our creativity arises from cosmic processes, is there a greater "self" within the cosmos? Can life reshape reality to realize every possibility?

The universe, like a mirror, both reveals and reflects its own nature. According to René Girard's mimetic theory, human desires and behaviors emerge through imitation. Within this web of influence, some individuals innovate – new ideas, talents, and stories – only to see these novelties become the next wave of shared norms and values. We absorb the universe's narrative – its origins, structure, and destiny – and then weave our own: reimagined origins, magical laws, and alternate endings. In doing so, we imitate the cosmos itself, crafting new universes and the lives within them.

IX. TRANSPARENCY AND REFLECTION OF REALITY

We are a self of the universe, an expression of this reality, and through tools like mirrors and glass, the universe allows us to see ourselves more clearly. It may sound absurd to say that an object inspired our sense of individuality. Yet, for both our physiology and psychology, we often require external stimuli to spark novelty – new thoughts, innovations, and even awareness of self.

Life's earliest organic compounds – nucleic acids – had the drive to survive, but they needed environmental conditions, like warm water and biomonomers, to form polymers. These eventually evolved into RNA, cell membranes, and the first living systems. Just as life needed external elements to become itself, human identity and knowledge arise from collective input. Our understanding of the heart and brain comes from surgeons; of sharks and octopuses, from seafarers; of stars and distant worlds, from astronomers; of chemicals and cures, from chemists and doctors; of dinosaurs and civilizations, from archaeologists and historians.

Language, for instance, cannot be created by one individual alone. It evolved through shared experiences: fishermen taught us about aquatic life; farmers about land, seasons, and crops; hunters about animals and geography; craftsmen about tools and materials; and traders, travelers, and raiders spread ideas and technologies across cultures. Even war brought cultural exchange and the blending of knowledge. Some knowledge has come from within; some from outside.

Even our names are societal products, emerging from communities that mastered agriculture, preserved food, believed in gods and currencies, maintained laws, organized lifestyles, birthed generations, and sought to explore or conquer new lands. Our own position and movement through space is tracked by our body without conscious thought. This internal compass, known as proprioception, allows us to distinguish between our own movements and external forces. Without it, we might bite our tongue far more often than we do.

In this lineage of knowledge, passed from one mind to another, it is likely that something as simple as the use of mirrors and glass played a profound role in shaping our concept of the individual self. Through the literal act of seeing ourselves, we began the figurative journey inward.

MIRRORS

Before the invention of mirrors, society functioned through group identification. An individual rarely dreamed or aspired to anything that did not include their clan, ethnicity, or kingdom. Language, knowledge, and ideas were not personal constructs but cultural inheritances. Even a birth certificate was given by the community, making it difficult to break away and forge an independent path. The individual, as we think of it today, scarcely existed. The self was a cog in a greater machine, loyal to the king, god, family, or tribe. To act alone, outside these bounds, was not just discouraged – it was dangerous. Banishment, exile, or even death awaited those who dared to stray too far from the collective path. The notion that one could live alone, guided by a unique set of beliefs, was unsettling to the collective psyche.

People did not possess the strong sense of self that we now take for granted. Without an image of themselves, they lacked the imaginative capacity to visualize their face accomplishing something extraordinary. The mirror provided more than just a reflection; it offered a canvas for imagination. For the first time, people could visualize themselves not just as servants of a collective fate, but as unique beings capable of independent thought, emotion, and ambition.

Biologically, every human carries a unique DNA and a singular face. But with time and reproduction, this uniqueness blends and gives way to new combinations. Biology forgets, faces blur, bloodlines dissolve. Your great-grandfather's features, quirks, and beliefs likely live on only in fragments, if at all. Your face and DNA will be forgotten, unless preserved by culture; only if you are a priest, inventor, king, queen, or leader – someone immortalized through statues, writings, or art. We don't know the DNA of Julius Caesar, but we have sculptures and writings that offer glimpses into his persona. We remember Caesar, not the nameless Roman foot soldier who died beside him. Normal soldiers are background characters in history, stripped of individual identity. The vast majority of people throughout history were not recorded in statues or stories; they lived and died as part of the collective, their individuality lost to time.

Mirrors, and later photography, challenged individual disappearance. They democratized identity. No longer was self-image a privilege granted only to the elite who could pay sculptors and painters to capture their likeness. Anyone could look into a mirror and begin to imagine a story centered on themselves. It was the first step toward what would later be supercharged by the Internet – our ability to think, speak, and create ideas independent of any tribe, religion, or ruler. People began to form personal identities, no longer reliant solely on communal roles or religious titles.

Still, like DNA, individuality and the art it inspires are fragile. Statues fall. Paintings burn. Regimes rise and erase the symbols of the ones before them. After Emperor Nero's death, his likeness was systematically destroyed. When Christianity rose to power in Rome, many pagan statues were destroyed and replaced by the imagery of a single, empathetic god who embraced all. Even gods were rebranded.

People are more afraid of being forgotten – by their nation, their king, their god, or even their own family – than they are of being bad. The desire to be seen, to be remembered, often outweighs the desire to be virtuous. Throughout history, people have committed unspeakable acts in the name of gods and kings, not merely out of loyalty, but out of a desperate hope to secure a place in the larger narrative. Even a bad child is remembered, though perhaps not welcomed into heaven. And that memory, however dark, becomes a kind of immortality. To be remembered, even for the wrong reasons, can feel like proof that one mattered at all. Forever in hell is preferable to the void of non-existence. That fear of being erased drives both cruelty and courage. While grand temples and towering statues of gods still stand, they often do so at the cost of individual identity.

But as the idea of individual identity slowly began to take root, so did something remarkable: protest. Resistance. A voice for the vulnerable. The shift from serving empires and deities to claiming the right to exist as a person – not just as a subject, but as a self.

Today, we identify with science, the universe, social media, and open-mindedness. From ancient temples to social media profiles, we seek permanence. Yet, the paradox remains: while mirrors and technology have elevated the individual, they've also ushered in new collectives: science, the Internet, algorithms. These new systems, while offering personal freedom, also create new forms of dependence. We seek God to survive in heaven. Today we post our thoughts and pictures to be liked on the Internet. Temples were built by the collective, and so is the Internet today. One single individual cannot create and secure things for all generations. We need everyone, and everyone needs us. In our quest to define the self, we continuously negotiate between individuality and collective identity. And mirrors have been a part of this stimulation that evoked individual expression.

HISTORY OF OUR REFLECTION

Mirrors did not grant us superpowers, but they unlocked a capacity we have always possessed: self-reflection. This simple reflective object empowered us to simulate ourselves in time – revisiting the past, appraising the present, and planning our future actions. A mirror offers more than a mere optical image; it bridges the body and mind. Each morning, as we adjust our attire, hairstyle, or accessories, we engage in a dialogue between our outward appearance and inner moods, desires, and beliefs. This daily ritual of looking, comparing, and imagining has inspired our intellect to operate at full capacity – a phenomenon Ian Mortimer explores in *Millennium*.

Clear mirrors are a modern luxury. In ancient Egypt, polished bronze discs, symbols of the sun god, Re, served more for ritual than personal grooming. Ancient Greeks crafted small, twelve-inch bronze mirrors, yet clarity remained a myth. Their "blurry" reflections were seen as divine gifts, not human achievement. In Japan, mirrors made of bronze were sacred relics said to house the sun deity, Amaterasu, but they offered little in the way of detailed self-viewing. Everything changed in 15th century Venice, where artisans perfected the technique of backing glass with silver-mercury. Venetian mirrors, larger and clearer than ever, revolutionized self-perception. Still, their cost kept them out of reach for most. In the 17th century, Louis XIV enticed twenty Italian mirror-makers to France at the price of 100,000 crowns, then replicated their process – culminating in the dazzling Hall of Mirrors at Versailles.

As mirrors entered broader trade markets, privacy began as a privilege reserved exclusively for royalty, including kings and queens, before gradually becoming a broader societal norm. Individuals began to seek solitary moments to ponder their place in humanity's grand narrative. First-person perspectives in literature blossomed alongside this cultural shift. While Enheduanna of Mesopotamia (23rd century bce) penned devotional verses in the first person, her voice spoke for a deity, not herself. The kind of introspective line – "I could not unlove him now, merely because I found that he had ceased to notice me" – emerged only much later, as personal narrative became a literary norm after the 15th century.

Mirrors may also have spurred the transformation from flat, symbolic art to the depth and perspective of the Renaissance. Leonardo da Vinci hailed the mirror as "the master of painters," acknowledging its vital role in teaching us how to see – and be seen. In the story of our reflection, the greatest gift of the mirror is not the image it returns, but the self-awareness it inspires.

SELF-PORTRAIT

Jean Fouquet's 1450 self-portrait marked a turning point: for the first time in European art, an artist turned the gaze inward. Armed with mirrors, artists thereafter turned their gaze inward, using their own reflections to explore personal visions of the world and the beliefs they held dear. In doing so, they subtly altered reality: skeletons stalk the living in Pieter Bruegel the Elder's *The Triumph of Death*; Vincent van Gogh's *Starry Night* pulses with swirling, dreamlike skies; and Raphael's *The School of Athens* assembles the era's greatest philosophers into a single, grand tableau. Even Diego Velázquez slipped himself into Las Meninas via a small mirror on the back wall, reminding us, and his subjects, that art is as much about the observer as the observed.

Each painter shaped reality through a personal lens. El Greco draped Christ in a vivid crimson robe unlike any other, while Hieronymus Bosch paraded his Ecce Homo through bizarre, nightmarish landscapes. Bosch's *The Garden of Earthly Delights* itself bends and stretches nature into fantastical forms, long before Surrealists like Salvador Dalí melted time into soft watches in *The Persistence of Memory*. By beginning with the self, painters found licence to reshape the world. These works attest to how mirrors, and later, more portable reflections like phone cameras, encourage us to imagine ourselves at the center of our stories.

The Renaissance did more than birth new artistic techniques; it nurtured the notion of the individual creator. Venice, the birthplace of the first truly clear mirror, also pioneered modern intellectual property law. The 1474 Venetian patent statute granted inventors ten-year monopolies on their ideas, an exceptional privilege in a world where culture, craft, and innovation were traditionally controlled by kings and guilds. Usually artisans and craftsmen guarded their trade secrets closely, treating them as precious legacies that safeguarded their dominance in specialized techniques. Artisans guarded their glass-making secrets, passing them only to trusted apprentices.

Over the centuries, this impulse to protect individual genius spread. England's Statute of Monopolies in 1624 extended a fourteen-year exclusive right; the 1710 Copyright Act lengthened the term for authors and composers; and the 1886 Berne Convention wove international safeguards for creative works. Today, whether we're sketching a quick selfie in a diary or filing a digital copyright claim, we stand on the rights that gave freedom to an individual.

PICTURE PERFECT

We do not merely observe the world, we simulate it. From the birth to the death of stars, insects, animals, and all life, we carry within us a modcl of cxistence. When a bird soars across the sky, we imagine its origin: from an egg laid years ago, nurtured by instinct and time, now caught in the needs of hunger, mating, nesting, and death. We mimic the motions of celestial bodies and living beings, their laws and their chaos, and in doing so, we reflect the pattern within ourselves.

The mirror, in many ways, resembles our mind: reflective, grasping, endlessly curious. It seeks to capture everything within its field of view, and more. This human trait, this desire to see and preserve, was amplified with one of the greatest inventions of modernity: photography.

Photography unveiled a new visual reality – one not crafted by brush or imagination, but caught directly in light. Before the photograph, people only saw distant lands and strange animals through art. But with a camera, the world arrived flat and vivid, in a single frame. The first photograph, taken by Joseph Nicéphore Niépce between 1826 and 1827, marked the beginning of this visual revolution. Though early versions like daguerreotypes became popular, they were far from accessible, costing the equivalent of $600 today and requiring nearly ten minutes to capture a single image. Later, Marc Antoine's Nouvel Appareil Gaudin in 1841 served professional photographers, but the art remained exclusive. In its early days, photography was used mostly as evidence. It captured truth with a precision art could only approximate. During the June Days Uprising in 1848, the Crimean War (1853–1856), and the American Civil War (1861–1865), photography documented the brutal realities of conflict without romantic filters or heroic illusions. War was no longer mythologized – it was exposed.

Science, too, embraced the photograph. John William Draper photographed celestial bodies to support the heliocentric model of the solar system in thc 1840s, challenging centuries of geocentric belief. Wilson Bentley's 1885 microphotography of snowflakes led to insights into crystal formation and eventually to the discovery of X-rays. By 1895, Wilhelm Röntgen captured the first image of the human skeleton. And in 1952, Ray Gosling's Photo 51 revealed the structure of the DNA, a double helix at the heart of life itself. Among the most profound uses of photography was one by Charles Darwin. His book *The Expression of Emotions in Man and Animals* relied heavily on photographic evidence to demonstrate evolutionary links between species. While some of his research included drawings, many of his conclusions were drawn from photographic records.

Photography preserved our form on a flat sheet. It became a mirror of motion, memory, and identity. In its early days, the power to capture a scene and freeze it forever belonged exclusively to artists, photographers, and a few scientists. The technology wasn't widespread, and so the rise of individualism through personal imagery was not yet common. However, the sale of photographs quickly became a cultural phenomenon, especially across European and American societies. During the 19th and early 20th centuries, well-established families, government officials, kings, and queens posed for photographs. To be photographed was not casual; it was ceremonial. Cameras were rare and expensive, the tools of professionals. As a result, subjects prepared themselves with great effort, striving to look their best, aware that the image might outlive them.

Then came the magic: moving pictures. With the invention of the celluloid roll film and the introduction of the Kodak camera in 1888, still images began to animate. The magic of cinema was born. The camera no longer just preserved the past – it animated it. These moving pictures granted us a form of visual immortality – recordings of ourselves for the future, for everyone to see, even after we were gone.

The first moving image, captured by Eadweard Muybridge, was not a love story or a war film, but a debate settled in science: did all four legs of a horse leave the ground while galloping? Through a rapid sequence of stills, he showed they did. Muybridge's sequential photographs created a form of slow motion, proving the answer visually. Motion became visible. Waves, pendulums, bouncing balls – physics itself became observable through the lens. Many long-standing questions about movement were finally answered, and even Newton's laws of motion were tested through these visual experiments.

Yet, people were not immediately comfortable with such simulations of reality. When the Lumière brothers' short film *Arrival of a Train at La Ciotat* was first shown, the audience panicked – some reportedly ducked or ran, believing the train would burst through the screen. Many fled in fear, mistaking the illusion for reality. They had witnessed, perhaps for the first time, a moving reflection: a mimicked reality where a once-moving object appeared to move again. Though it was a silent film, the depth, light, and realism created a powerful illusion. Without sound, the picture still felt real. What they saw was not the train itself, but its echo – a reflection of the past motion projected into the present.

MOVING PICTURES

We evolved from an era where individuality was barely recognized to one where we now find joy in experiencing other people's lives through visual media. Living vicariously, imagining ourselves as that actor, that host, that adventurer, stimulates the awakening of our own sense of self. Through movies, interviews, reality shows, dramas, news reports, and podcasts, we live vicariously. We imagine ourselves in other skins, other places, adventuring with actors, dreaming with artists, and empathizing with strangers. These visual mediums have awakened in us a deeper sense of identity. They offer possibilities, and those possibilities shape who we believe we can be.

Advertisements tap into this constant hunger for novelty, pushing people to buy things to feel updated and relevant. They create a psychological demand: to stay current, to be seen, to matter. Individualism itself, in many ways, has become a marketed ideal – a product we consume through cinema, celebrity gossip, glossy journals, and streaming platforms. Visual content doesn't just entertain us; it teaches us how to desire, how to dream, and even how to define ourselves.

Once, our bodies evolved to respond to physical threats. Just as our ancestors evolved under the pressure of external threats – predators, famine, nature's chaos – today, our minds are shaped by the barrage of digital stimuli. Our minds evolve under the constant stimulation of social media: posts, reels, trending videos, and cinematic narratives. The threats are different now, but the adaptation is just as intense. Instead of running from lions, we scroll through reels. Instead of braving the wilderness, we brave applications and trends. Our modern predators wear the faces of comparison, isolation, and overstimulation.

The birth of cinema with *The Story of the Kelly Gang* marked a turning point. Cinema became a global ritual, and over time, movies became an inseparable part of daily life. Hollywood rose to become the epicenter of cultural imagination, generating not just entertainment but meaning. Icons were born: Charlie Chaplin with his timeless humor, Jackie Chan with his kinetic brilliance, Elvis with his swagger and sound, and Michael Jackson with his revolutionary dance. They didn't just perform; they left parts of themselves encoded in film. Charlie Chaplin is not dead. He lives in digital hibernation, ready to be revived and watched again whenever we need to laugh, remember, or feel. Even scientific facts are now delivered through animated YouTube explainers. The music industry, fused with visual storytelling, has become a gateway to fame and fortune. Songs have turned into personal manifestos. Suddenly, everyone has a story to tell, and a stage to tell it from.

Consider *Roundhay Garden Scene*, the oldest surviving film. Those people, captured in 1888, still move before our eyes. Time has passed, but their gestures have endured. Through moving pictures, we made the ephemeral permanent. Heroes became gods, screens became altars, and identity began to bloom through borrowed light.

For centuries, only a select few could be seen and remembered. But that changed with the arrival of smartphones and social media. Platforms like YouTube, Instagram, TikTok, and Twitter gave everyone a voice, a camera, and an audience. Individual opinions, once kept private, now had a stage. Smartphone cameras and the rise of the Internet turned every user into a performer, a creator, a mirror-holder. Our society now revolves around visual life: acting, modeling, talking, selling, training, podcasting, influencing. The "selfie" became a symbol of this transformation. What began as self-expression quickly turned into self-documentation – and eventually, self-obsession.

People began documenting every emotion, every moment, every meal. The selfie craze swept through social media, creating an urgent need to upload moods, moments, and movements daily. It grew so intense that some experts labeled it a mental health concern. Your mood, your partner, your child, your car, your vacation, your coffee – all uploaded, liked, and quantified. People began to feel unreal if they didn't take a picture of themselves wherever they went. These images – e-memories – were not just personal keepsakes, but proof of existence within the digital universe. The Internet became a new kind of reality where identity had to be shared to feel real.

Sharing became synonymous with being. You had to show what you loved, what you supported, who you were with – your friends, family, partner, job, car, house, politics, or even your breakfast. Identity turned inside out, from an internal truth to an external broadcast. In this transformation, individuality broke away from collectivism. It was no longer about the king, the god, the clan, the village, or the nation. It became about the self – seen, heard, validated. But with that liberation came new challenges: self-obsession, digital depression, and an aching desire for purpose and personal space. We live to be seen, to be known, and to matter as individuals. But in this newfound freedom lies a paradox: the more we project ourselves outward, the more we risk feeling empty inside.

We now stand at a crossroads where selfhood is no longer inherited – it's curated. It is not given; it is made, filmed, edited, and posted. For people, by people, of people – and now, for the individual's well-being.

OUR OWN VISUAL WORLD

The animation industry took storytelling a step further. It brought fantasy into the realm of the real, indifferent to the limits of reality. Through motion and weightless imagery, we learned that anything could be made to appear real. Entire new lives and worlds emerged within our flat 2D screens. Artists brought fairy tales and fictional realms to life with vibrant detail, breathing motion into what once only lived in books and imagination.

When an actor performs, they mimic a character – an embodiment of thc writer's imagination. Milla Jovovich became Joan of Arc. Monica Bellucci embodied Queen Cleopatra. These performances mirror people from the past, present, or even the imagined future. Yet, none of them are the characters themselves – they are representations.

Tom and Jerry may just be a sequence of changing images, yet it feels almost alive. *The Little Mermaid*, *Tarzan*, *Bugs Bunny*, *Scooby-Doo* – they all exist vividly in our minds. Although animation gained fame through early works like *Fantasmagorie* (1908) and Disney's *Snow White and the Seven Dwarfs* (1937), it remains a medium not fully embraced by all. Even today, Japanese anime – despite its cultural richness and global fan-base – sits slightly outside mainstream entertainment. Titles like *Naruto*, *Arcane*, *One Piece*, *Ben 10*, *Attack on Titan*, and *Rick and Morty* are adored by millions, but not by all. Their exaggerated visual style and surreal storytelling can seem too strange for those more rooted in realism.

Interestingly, the concept of animating a figure predates modern media. In ancient rituals, puppets and dolls were used for mysticism – for warnings, sacrifices, and divinations. They weren't made to amuse but to invoke gods or demons, to mimic the spiritual unknown. Children mimic life in the same way when they animate their stuffed animals and toys – they give voice, motion, and intention to the lifeless.

In animation, we use characters we can fully control. Unlike living actors, who are limited by their own will and the physics of our world, animated characters are bound only by imagination. A human actor can't convincingly portray a T.rex or Bugs Bunny without the aid of graphics and special effects. But animation removes such constraints, allowing dragons, aliens, gods, monsters, and heroes to move, speak, and feel as if they truly exist. This medium gave us Pandora's Na'vi, the terrifying Alien, the mighty Thanos, the mischievous Minions, Gollum's eerie obsession, the monstrous Godzilla, and the unstoppable Hulk. Creatures once confined to myth and folklore – ghosts, demons, fairies, and goblins – were brought to life through animation. In this virtual reality, anything is possible.

Animation didn't just bring fictional creatures to life; it gave form to abstract forces. We even personified natural elements and forces: time, fire, magnetism, electricity. Superheroes became metaphors for physics – The Hulk for radiation, The Flash for light speed, Dr. Manhattan for nuclear force, Magneto for magnetic fields. Science fiction opened doors to the cosmos; movies explored time travel, wormholes, and galaxies at the edge of existence. Humanity, at least visually, reached the Moon, Mars, and the ends of the universe. Our stories have long been populated by characters and worlds that mirror our own reality, but animation has given them breath, form, and continuity. Writers began creating not just stories, but universes, complete with their own rules and laws. Even magic, once random and mystical, gained a logic of its own. Authors became gods, shaping realms where they controlled time, morality, and reality.

Nietzsche's provocative declaration, "God is dead," resonates deeply here. As the divine faded from public life, humans began to adopt the role of creator themselves. Animators, storytellers, and performers now hold the divine spark. They shape perception, mold emotion, and give life where there is none. On the stage, a character lives only for a moment. But in animation, a character can live forever.

And unlike theater, where the actor's performance is bound to their human limitations, animated characters can be shaped, controlled, and immortalized. It is not just mimicry. It is authorship. It is the birth of our own visual world.

GAMES

Then with the rise of 3D modeling, animation evolved into something more sinister: the power to control lifeless forms, to breathe will into code. Computer games introduced something revolutionary: they allowed players to inhabit alternate realities, commanding characters to do whatever they wished within vast, open worlds. Through playable characters, we are granted the power to act out fantasies, rewrite outcomes, and defy every law. These characters – some controlled by the player, others operating in programmed loops – exist in universes where the normal rules of reality and humanity are suspended.

In these virtual worlds, there is no tax, no hunger, no consequence. Inside these digital worlds, we kill, steal, destroy, and trespass limits. Cause and effect barely matter. Gravity is a suggestion, not a rule. Morality fades into irrelevance. We respawn, restart, redo. Death is merely a pause; resurrection is infinite. These worlds don't even exist until the player clicks start – a digital Big Bang. Only then do cities populate with looping pedestrians, patrolling police, shopkeepers, and civil servants locked in an endless routine. But you, the player, are free. You move outside the cycle, puppeteering your avatar in a liberated, lawless realm.

Games like GTA V, Cyberpunk 2077, Elden Ring, Watch Dogs, Just Cause, and Mafia expose a chilling question: what would people do if immortality were real? Murder, suicide, destruction – all committed with the knowledge that we'll simply respawn. Nothing is remembered; in these digital realities, memory is reset at will. Even mass destruction leaves no scars – just start a new game. It's reminiscent of mythic floods that wiped civilizations clean, sparing one family to restart the world.

In Minecraft, players aren't just part of a world; they build one. Block by block, they author entire universes where the rules of nature are rewritten for pleasure and creativity. A universe entirely sculpted by our whims. Assassin's Creed lets us slip through history, inhabit ancient civilizations, and play judge, jury, and executioner to kings and tyrants. God of War grants us divinity itself – to slay gods as a god. The boundaries between audience and actor have dissolved. No longer do we passively watch characters act; we now *become* them.

The audience is no longer a spectator; they are the puppeteer. They can defy the foundations of our everyday beliefs – money, law, time, physics. They can leap through buildings, freeze time, destroy nations, and rise from death endlessly. The rules are gone. Our long-held physical limitations are bypassed with a joystick. Classic arcades, Nintendo, PlayStation – all have become fixtures of modern life, offering short escapes into realities where we take on missions, identities, and fates not our own. Each game is a universe unto itself. In one, you fight off zombies. In another, you fly as a bird, drive a tank, or captain a starship.

Mirrors have long been seen as portals to alternate worlds, gateways to the unknown. Fiction has long used mirrors as metaphors. Alice in *Alice's Adventures in Wonderland* famously stepped through one. Like a mirror, the mind reflects, interprets, and tries to make sense of the universe. Through games, we mimic not just reality, but its very architecture. We've animated time, fire, speed, strength, energy, divinity, the soul, immortality, regeneration, incarnation, and even gravity itself. We've crafted tools to bend the laws of physics and time itself within our visual realms.

And this mimicry is not just digital. In 1996, Dolly the sheep was cloned – a breakthrough that signaled our growing ambition to mimic not just images, but biology itself. Since then, other animals have been cloned, some endangered, some long extinct. Some survived. Others didn't. But we continue to try. Nature brought forth life, and now we attempt to mimic it – genetically, virtually. We bring to life the extinct and the imaginary: T.rexes, dragons, mammoths, gods, mermaids, and ghosts. We resurrect worlds that never were and give them laws, logic, and life.

In games, we're not merely escaping reality – we are remaking it, redefining it, and sometimes, transcending it.

THE GAME OF LIFE

In 1970, mathematician John Horton Conway created a self-replicating program famously known as Conway's Game of Life. It wasn't a game in the traditional sense. There were no players, no scores, no endings. And yet, it mimicked life itself. Using a set of simple, two-dimensional rules, the program produced startlingly complex behaviors – patterns that pulsed, spread, vanished, or stabilized, much like the rhythms of actual organisms.

The game mimicked life, and that's no coincidence: it was created by life. We, as 3D beings, replicated the essence of our own emergence. We mirrored the universe that gave birth to us. Because that's what life does – it mimics.

Mimicry is life's oldest strategy. Life is driven by the need to survive, to spread, to adapt. To do so, it often takes the form of something else – hiding in plain sight, blending in to attack, defend, or bond. Mimicry becomes a tool not just for survival, but for evolution, to learn and navigate an ever-changing reality.

We see it everywhere. On national holidays like Independence Day or Republic Day, citizens wear the national flag as a symbol of unity, camouflaging within the collective identity of a nation. Children, too, are natural mimics, one day playing as chefs, the next as doctors, rehearsing the roles of adulthood. Adults are no different; we imitate our mentors, parents, friends, and idols to navigate social life. Other people's jokes, values, life lessons, crafts, skills, behaviors, mannerisms, and even fragments of their personalities subtly pass through us.

In nature, mimicry is an art perfected over millennia. The Arctic fox's snowy fur is a seamless match for its frozen habitat. The leopard's spotted coat lets it disappear amid the tall grasses. The walking stick insect becomes nearly indistinguishable from the twigs it crawls on. The wrap-around spider coils along branches, blending in perfectly as it waits to strike. The stonefish becomes a coral rock – the very environment it needs to vanish into. The octopus shifts its colors on demand, inching closer to its prey before striking with surgical precision.

But mimicry isn't confined to biology. We humans extend it into imagination. We build games, movie franchises, animation series, and books that construct entire worlds. We invent worlds with their own laws, timelines, and metaphysics. In these invented realms, genies grant wishes, aliens roam the stars, unicorns gallop through enchanted forests, and ships traverse galaxies with the flick of a switch.

Why do we do this? Because we are creators born of a creative universe. For us, the universe is both a reality and a canvas. Through games and stories, we reimagine what's possible. We mimic not just to survive, but to understand. Not just to hide, but to recreate.

TRANSPARENT REALITY

Reality is not only reflective; it is also transparent. While mirrors have long sparked human curiosity, it's the invisible that truly intrigues us, the things that are there yet not seen. In nature, creatures like the glasswing butterfly, glass frog, crystal jellyfish, larvacean, glass catfish, and the shimmering sea sapphire have evolved to mimic invisibility.

The concept of transparent glass as we know it today emerged in the 15th century, from the same Italy that gave us mirrors. Venetian glassblower Angelo Barovier crafted what was then a marvel – pure, transparent glass. Suddenly, solid objects could vanish before our eyes. Even today, we find ourselves walking into mall entrances, momentarily fooled by the clarity of glass. It's there, but it looks like nothing is. Glass, made up of atoms like any other solid object, allows visible light to pass through without interacting with electrons, creating the illusion of invisibility. However, light with a different wavelength – such as ultraviolet or infrared – can make glass appear solid and opaque.

Before the invention of transparent glass, colors gave weight to reality. Only liquids, like water, and gases, like air, could be truly transparent. Glass, however, allowed us to peer past solid objects as if they were not even there. Suddenly, we could look through something solid, and that opened a portal of thought: what if reality was full of things we just couldn't see?

This material may have quietly inspired abstract thinking and creative imagination. Transparency offered a metaphor, even a framework, to believe in things that couldn't be seen but surely existed. Today, we use electron microscopes to observe atoms, but not long ago, such ideas would have been dismissed as fantasy. The everyday use of glasses – whether for vision or decoration – helped normalize the idea that the world might contain unseen elements. Transparency, experienced daily through glass, helped normalize the invisible. It gave us the confidence to believe in unseen forces.

Even now, quantum particles remain unseen – smaller than the wavelength of any light – yet we believe in them, study them, and build entire fields of science around them.

Long before transparent glass, translucent gems like diamonds and rubies enchanted humanity. But they were rare, and reserved for royalty. When glass became commonplace, so too did curiosity. Science began to flourish, not just among kings and scholars, but in homes and workshops. As glass became widespread, scientific exploration blossomed, with new ideas and innovations emerging from this shift in perspective.

Records from the 13th century describe the use of translucent stones with convex properties for reading. Around 1000 ce, Ibn al-Haytham (Alhazen) used a rudimentary glass lens to develop the camera obscura, a precursor to the modern camera. His work connected vision to light, geometry to algebra, and laid the foundation for optics, astronomy, and our understanding of perception. He also proposed using glass to correct human vision – an idea that would become essential in centuries to come.

In Islamic cultures, stained glass adorned sacred spaces, filtering light into colored divinity. From there, it traveled to the Christian world. Between the 12th and 14th centuries, Gothic and Renaissance cathedrals flourished with stained glass windows, transforming sunlight into heavenly symbols. Light became divine. Transparency became transcendence.

By the 15th century, eyeglasses were spreading among monks and intellectuals, helping aging eyes see clearly again. Glass evolved from luxury to necessity. Its light-bending properties – through convex and concave lenses – entered everyday life. The world itself seemed to shift, from the mystical darkness of the medieval era into the clarity of the Renaissance.

And with that clarity came questions. We began to link invisible causes to observable effects: gravity, magnetism, electromagnetism, aerodynamics, the laws of motion, microorganisms, X-rays, gamma rays, nuclear forces, and quantum phenomena.

Transparency gave us more than a clearer vision; it gave us new ways to imagine. It challenged the limits of perception and invited us to believe in the invisible forces shaping our universe. Through glass, humanity didn't just look at the world – we looked through it, and far beyond it. We looked into the tiniest structures of matter and out toward the farthest stars. Transparency and reflection, embodied in glass and mirrors, may have provided a subtle push in our cultural evolution. When glassware became common, so too did scientific wonder.

And then, discoveries and inventions began to unfold one after another, reshaping our understanding of the universe. Born in 1452, Leonardo da Vinci ushered in a wave of innovation, spanning from art to the early theories of aerodynamics. In the 16th century, Giambattista della Porta used lenses and mirrors to create optical illusions, later documented in his book *Magiae Naturalis*. By 1543, Nicolaus Copernicus proposed his revolutionary heliocentric model of the universe. In 1600, William Gilbert discovered Earth's magnetic field, laying the foundation for future studies in electromagnetism. Just eight years later, Hans Lipperhey invented the telescope, and by 1609, Galileo Galilei refined it to observe the Moon, offering tangible support to Copernicus's model and revealing celestial bodies never seen before. In 1637, René Descartes formalized scientific reasoning with his method of doubt and provability, famously declaring, "I think, therefore I am." He also theorized light as a physical substance. In 1660, Otto von Guericke generated static electricity through friction, opening new paths in experimental physics. Then came 1666, the year Sir Isaac Newton formulated the law of gravity, introduced calculus, defined the laws of motion, and explored the spectrum of light and color. A decade later, in 1676, Ole Rømer measured the speed of light. In 1675, Anton van Leeuwenhoek used convex lenses to observe microorganisms and blood cells, bringing the invisible to light. In 1808, John Dalton laid the groundwork for modern atomic theory. By the 19th century, glass and illusion once again redefined reality, as Pepper's Ghost illusion transformed stagecraft by projecting ghostly holograms through glass, showing we could not only perceive but edit reality itself. Scientific breakthroughs accelerated. In 1860, James Clerk Maxwell unified optics, electricity, and magnetism. In 1895, Wilhelm Conrad Röntgen discovered X-rays, revealing the skeletal structure beneath our skin. In 1900, Paul Villard identified gamma rays, and Max Planck proposed quantum theory, revolutionizing physics. In 1905,

Albert Einstein introduced the special theory of relativity and the wave-particle duality of light. In 1911, Ernest Rutherford discovered the atomic nucleus. By 1915, Einstein completed his general theory of relativity, redefining gravity and space-time. In 1925, Erwin Schrödinger formulated the wave equation, while Werner Heisenberg's uncertainty principle in 1927 revealed the indeterminacy at the heart of quantum mechanics. In 1929, Edwin Hubble confirmed the expansion of the universe, changing our understanding of the cosmic scale. In 1935, Hideki Yukawa discovered the strong nuclear force, and in 1927, Georges Lemaître proposed the Big Bang theory, offering a scientific explanation for the origin of the universe itself.

Once, we imagined gods behind the stars. Now, we need lenses – both literal and conceptual – to see through this vast, transparent reality. We have learned to look outward with telescopes to understand the future, and inward, into quantum reality, to understand our past.

ATTRACTION OF REALITY

Were glasses and mirrors the only forces that fueled our growth and curiosity? Not quite. Among the many influences that nudged humanity forward, one in particular stands out: magnetism. Humanity didn't just observe it; we mastered it, transforming it from a mysterious natural property into a powerful tool.

Even today, the mystery of magnets can be found in the hands of children, who slide a magnet beneath a table to move a paperclip, laughing at the trick. It's a moment of wonder, a tiny act of magic. But that same force powers our computers, drives electric motors in our cars, stores information in our devices, and accelerates particles in the most advanced labs on Earth.

Legend credits a Greek shepherd named Magnes as the first to stumble upon a magnet when the nails in his sandals stuck to a mysterious black rock. Ancient philosophers like

Thales of Miletus believed magnets possessed a soul. As with many unknown forces, the first explanation was divine: a soul, a god, some spiritual cause. Cultures across the globe encountered magnets, but only a few understood how to use their potential. In Rome, Pliny the Elder wrote of a hill that could draw iron. Egyptians used magnetic stones for divination. But the Chinese were the first who truly wielded their potential.

As early as 400 bce, Chinese texts like *The Book of the Devil Valley Master* described lodestones as naturally attractive, yet still cloaked in myth. Magnets were used more to ward off spirits or guide jade hunters than to chart the seas. Even in modern times, these kinds of superstitions persist – lucky stones like sapphire and ruby, "energized" pebbles like amethyst and gems, divine rocks like obsidian or moonstone – all of which owe some part of their mythos to magnetic or pseudo-magnetic lore. It wasn't until the 12th century that the Chinese began using magnets for navigation. In 1295, the Venetian explorer Marco Polo returned from China with stories and knowledge of the magnetic compass. From then on, the world began to shift. With this simple yet profound tool, explorers dared to venture into the unknown.

The compass was subtle in its revolution, but profound. By the 13th century, Chinese explorers were redrawing maps and expanding the spice trade. European explorers followed. Prince Henry discovered the Azores and Madeira. In 1488, Bartholomew Diaz rounded the tip of Africa. In 1498, Vasco da Gama found a new sea route to India. In 1492, Christopher Columbus, believing he'd reached Asia, stumbled upon the West Indies. And in 1501, Amerigo Vespucci correctly identified America as a "New World," lending his name to the continent.

The Age of Discovery had many catalysts: economic ambition, cultural exchange, the printing press, and a growing thirst for knowledge. But the compass – the quiet, magnetic pointer – was a critical driver of this bold new chapter. It changed everything. Instead of directing their devotion toward gods housed in temples, people followed a different kind of needle – one that spun mysteriously and then stood still, pointing outward, away from home and into the unfamiliar.

The maps they carried were blank beyond their borders – no gods, no people, no certainties, only the pull of curiosity and the unknown. That same invisible force, which guided the needle, mirrored the workings of the human mind: restless, doubtful, always wondering. It triggered an adventure of belief, a quest not just for land but for understanding. And in that pursuit, they began to redraw the shape of the world – and of themselves.

It's a paradox of evolution: the selfish gene urging preservation, and the altruistic mind pushing us into danger, so we might grow and prepare for the chaos we've yet to face. We take risks to build resilience. We seek out the hazardous to ensure survival. The journey itself becomes the test of fitness.

But we are useful to the universe only as long as we remain useful. And if humanity refuses to grow, to adapt, or to discover, then nature – or technology – will find something more capable to take its place.

OBSOLETE LIFE

The transparent glass can be seen. The invisible force of a magnet can be felt. Reality requires interaction, something tangible to push, pull, or respond. The soul, or the power of chakras, cannot hold the universe together. We need atoms bonding and repelling to give rise to matter, to shape stars, planets, and moons, and to create minds capable of wonder.

We've studied the universe, mapped its mechanisms, and even created new universes and multiverses in our movies and games. Yet, despite all this, we continue to hold on to ancient beliefs, seeking detachment from reality in pursuit of a serene emptiness, free from stimulation. We still long for the soul. We still long for God.

No animal, insect, bird, or plant has stepped outside its instinct to learn about or preserve this reality. But we have. We store distant stars inside our computers. We map black holes, simulate beginnings and ends, and look back across the eons. Somehow, we were chosen by reality to do this. Anthropologically, we were selected as Homo sapiens, just one branch among many: Homo erectus, Homo rhodesiensis, Homo naledi, Homo luzonensis, Homo floresiensis, Java Man, Neanderthal, Denisovans, Red Deer Cave people, Homo heidelbergensis, Homo habilis, Homo ergaster, and Homo longi. Reality, it seems, chose us. But this doesn't mean we were the end goal. We might never know for whom, or for what, this world was made.

Imagine being a giant lizard that ruled for 165 million years, believing the universe existed only to serve your hunger and survival. Then, in one celestial moment, your entire kind was erased by a meteor. And now, there is no dinosaur left to claim that the "dinosaur principle" was wrong. So, is the universe truly made for us? How can we be sure? What arrogance it is to believe that we are the final chapter in the book of evolution! The universe is far too vast for us to conquer physically. We can observe, map, theorize, but direct interaction remains elusive. Maybe the safer route is to let robots fulfill our cosmic ambitions. Let them enact our science-fiction dreams, journey across galaxies, and live out the legacy we imagined.

In this scenario, we wouldn't be gone. We might live in peaceful simulations, our minds immersed in fictional realities, our desires satisfied by virtual pleasures. Alternatively, we might control robots remotely from Earth, upload our consciousness into synthetic vessels, or freeze ourselves, trusting machines to wake us on new planets. Either way, our biological selves may become obsolete. Evolution might not favor imagination, fantasy, or the pursuit of enlightenment through meditation or religious visions. It may favor something else entirely.

Just as monkeys live in forests and zoos, content with food, sleep, and companionship, we might one day live comfortably in digital landscapes while our successors – post-humans or machines – explore the stars. We may find peace in a beautifully tailored digital world, as others journey to the stars.

Reality never stands still. It keeps shifting. Every piece of life must either change or fade. Life reshapes reality by reshaping itself. With every variation, it changes form to meet new challenges. And even the evolved forms of humanity will one day face new aspects of reality that render them obsolete, forcing yet another transformation. No matter how advanced, life cannot thrive in a vacuum. Only a machine might endure vacuum. Yet, even robots might encounter environments where they fail, and where something entirely new must emerge.

Obsolescence, then, is not a flaw. It is not destruction. It is the very engine of continuity. It gives purpose to existence. Through it, everything evolves with logic, meaning, and necessity. So, let us not fear becoming obsolete. Instead, let us understand how obsolescence sustains existence – and how it helps life endure through endless change.

X. OBSOLETE MOMENTS

We cannot travel across the entire universe to confirm the presence or absence of God. But if such a being exists, imagine the scale of its presence. What size, what complexity must a creature possess to control this entire reality?

From the perspective of a fairyfly wasp, barely 1 millimeter in length, we might appear as gods. The wasp controls only a tiny fragment of matter, weighing less than a milligram. If it were to travel from our head to our toes without a medium, it might take hours, while we effortlessly control a much larger body. Our brains take just twenty-seven milliseconds to send signals to our hands. In comparison, a voice call over the Internet takes two to three seconds to reach its recipient. And a signal from Earth to Voyager 1 – launched in 1977 and now in interstellar space – takes about two days to reach.

The first microorganisms on Earth could only control themselves, guided by DNA that built their bodies, one cell at a time. But life evolved. It began recognizing other organisms. It formed ecosystems – webs of dependence and cooperation. Eventually, life birthed thought and imagination. Eventually, through imagination, we created gods, nations, laws, and money; we began reshaping the very reality we once submitted to.

Today, with science, we command parts of the cosmos. We send satellites beyond planets and moons. Yet, at the same time, we continually adapt ourselves to changing circumstances. Each of our roles – whether as sons, fathers, friends, colleagues, strangers, or citizens – is performed differently, depending on the situation. We shift, subtly or dramatically, from one version of ourselves to another.

Now imagine a being capable of controlling all reality. How must such an entity have adapted – evolved – to each corner of the cosmos to survive? Or perhaps, such a being no longer needs to adapt. It simply rewrites reality to its comfort.

We change our clothes, our trends, our wallpapers, our beliefs. We alter our mood to suit the room. Our flexibility gives us control but also reveals our fragility. If God exists, perhaps God, too, must constantly shift. God might possess a body the size of a parsec, so vast it would take light-years for a signal to travel from the divine brain to a hand just to initiate movement. But if all of reality is under God's control, then adapting becomes unnecessary; changing reality itself becomes the new act of will. If God is reality itself, and can reshape reality at will, then there is nothing left for God to adapt to or learn from. In that scenario, even God becomes obsolete. And if so, the universe becomes obsolete on its own scale.

But obsolescence is not the end. It is a threshold. Only evolved life forms dare to risk irrelevance, seeking new ways to live, to redefine their purpose, to evolve meaning. Sometimes, this leads to self-destruction. But sometimes, it leads to new ways of experiencing reality. And perhaps, in that endless cycle of becoming and unbecoming, lies the true purpose of life: not permanence, but transformation.

CHANGE OF LOOK

We all seek change, from our behavior and mannerisms to our ideologies, fashion, and hairstyles. Sometimes it's out of boredom or necessity, sometimes due to medical reasons or simply the desire for a fresh look. Often, it's influenced by the need for social acceptance, or even driven by hormonal urges to appear slimmer, more attractive, more "us." We alter ourselves physiologically, psychologically, muscularly, and cosmetically. The concept of an afterlife once made the physical body seem expendable – an obsolete vessel meant to be sacrificed for the sake of the eternal soul. Throughout history, cultures have practiced body modifications to transcend or transform the natural form. Mutilation, in many cases, was celebrated.

Across cultures and millennia, body modification has been one of humanity's most vivid expressions of self-reinvention. 5,000 years old, the "Ötzi the Iceman" mummy shows many tattoo scars on its body. A 3000 bce Egyptian priestess was also found to be tattooed. This tattoo trend spread to Greece, Arabia, and Persia. Independently, the Japanese also started tattooing in the 2nd century for adornment. They used colorful designs just for beauty and even tattooed their full body as a dress. A tattoo is like having a unique mark on your individuality. But the idea internationalized only after Captain James Cook (British), during colonization, learned from the Polynesians about "tatu." Then the word tattoo was coined and used all around the globe. In the past, we used the name of God or Devil while marking ourselves; now we use our wise self, residing in our hearts.

SELF-HARMING

Among the many forms of body modification, piercings are perhaps the most widespread. Earrings and nose rings, especially among women, are considered normal in most cultures. Yet, body piercing has far deeper roots and symbolic weight. In ancient Aztec and Mayan civilizations, tongue and lip piercings were reserved for leaders. Shamans were believed to pierce their tongues to induce altered states of consciousness – an essential gateway to communicate with the divine.

Scarification, too, was widespread and often casual. It was practiced primarily by African tribes, where raised patterns on the skin conveyed identity, status, or spiritual belief. The Māori of New Zealand famously marked their entire faces with intricate tattoos, turning their skin into living masks of heritage and honor.

Across the world, various forms of extreme body modifications emerged, many of them rigorous, painful, and symbolic. In ancient Mexico and parts of Indonesia, tribes practiced tooth sharpening, chiseling their teeth to resemble vampire fangs as a display of privilege or power. In the Amazon, lip-plating was customary. Tribes would stretch their lower lips with disc-like plates as a form of identity and social status. Even today, Mursi women of Ethiopia maintain this tradition. The Kayan women of Myanmar are known for neck-stretching, wearing heavy coils that elongate the neck, once considered a sign of beauty and grace.

These cultural practices arose in a time when vibrant clothing, masks, and accessible fashion did not exist. The body itself became the canvas, the identity, the symbol. As materials and designs advanced, and painless ways to alter appearance emerged, these body modifications gradually gave way to more fluid forms of self-expression. Thus bloomed the global fashion industry – forever shifting, forever evolving.

Fashion replaced scarification. Cosmetics replaced body-cutting. Instead of foreskin removals or ritual piercings came fabrics and accessories. Where once people marked their bodies through pain and permanence, they began painting and dressing themselves anew each day. In India, the bindi remains a symbolic adornment on the forehead, but its style, size, and color now change with mood, occasion, or fashion trend. No woman today wears just one dress. Some own dozens. Others own hundreds of garments and pieces of jewelry. And every season, every decade, brings a new wave of aesthetic revolution.

A key turning point in our transformation of the body came with the invention of anesthesia. In 1846, William T.G. Morton introduced the world to medical anesthesia – a discovery that not only changed the face of medicine but reshaped our relationship with pain and the body itself.

What was once seen as divine intervention – restoring sight to the blind, limbs to the amputated, or life to the dying – became a scientific endeavor. Today, we graft bionic limbs, replace faulty hearts, and even offer prosthetic vision. Anesthesia not only liberated us from suffering, but also gave rise to the belief that our bodies, once considered static or sacred, could evolve, adapt, and recover – from injury, disease, or even time itself.

FESTIVAL

People with good health, sharp minds, and clear eyes often aren't content with the familiarity of their own bodies and routines. So, many continue to pierce, tattoo, and even mutilate themselves, while most of us find transformation through new clothes, fresh hairstyles, or a layer of cosmetics – small rituals of reinvention that let us feel new, if only for a while. We change not to hide who we are, but to explore the possibility of who else we could be.

Culturally, we have carved out days or even entire weeks to become someone else. We dance, laugh, and greet strangers like old friends. On Halloween, people across many nations don disguises to play pretend and knock on doors in a shared, playful performance. On Día de los Muertos in Mexico, the rich and the poor walk side by side, celebrating the memory of the dead as though they are still among us. At the Voodoo Festival in New Orleans, the gothic and the mystical come alive without judgement. Venice's Carnival allows us to mask ourselves and parade as strangers to our own identities. At Burning Man, the rules of normality dissolve into dust. At Comic-Con, people step out of their daily lives and into the roles of their favorite heroes and villains who find kinship through their love of stories.

During a certain winter festival, we encourage the delightful delusion of an old man flying through the sky with gifts. During Diwali in India, streets echo with fireworks and laughter, and ordinary people ignite firecrackers and rockets. On any other day, such behavior might seem bizarre. But during a festival, we're allowed – encouraged – to act out of the ordinary. Weekends and holidays serve as miniature versions of this escape, planned breaks from the normal routine of our daily lives. The sheer joy on people's faces during these times reveals a deep truth: we are hungry to transform, even if just for a day. We want to feel new. We want to wear a different face, if only temporarily.

And perhaps, in the distant future, we might even create a festival where, through advanced technology, we could safely act out extreme fantasies – imagine shooting someone who regenerates like Wolverine, only to return to normal life once the event ends. And after that thrilling chaos, we'd return to our everyday routines, acting normal until the next chance to become someone else.

Transformation may be temporary, but it is necessary. Just as you must obey the laws of America to survive within its borders, or reach escape velocity to flee Jupiter's gravity, you must follow the values of a group to remain a part of it. You can't rely on an imaginary god to heal your wounds when the group doesn't believe in one. But when the collective does believe, you must too. Social survival often means adapting, even if that means wearing a different belief, a different behavior, for a while.

The group sets the values. It defines what is acceptable. Yet, it also allows moments of freedom – like festivals – to let the individual breathe and express. Festivals offer a release valve, a ritualized chaos. They grant individuals the space to matter, to shine, to feel free. God and nation remain significant across the majority of our days. But during festivals, it is the individual who shines, unmasked, or perhaps more masked than ever, yet more alive. The same spirit is seen in birthday parties, weddings, and office celebrations – occasions where individuals gain significance within their families or communities.

Even gods have to adapt to a changing culture that now lives and breathes through the Internet. Priests and the pious cannot let their deities remain confined to scriptures; they must upload God into the digital realm. But did God consent to this migration? Did anyone ask before making the sacred online, searchable, downloadable, commodified?

Do we ask for a cow's permission to milk it, or a fish's before we eat it? No. Survival rarely waits for consent. Instead, we rely on instinct, imagination, and our environment to survive. Sometimes, survival means manipulating nature: we trick fish into pools, feed them, nurture them – only to eventually slaughter them, breed them again, and repeat. Yet, we also build temples and create gods who promise to protect all living beings.

Science has given us powerful tools: computers, virtual realities, and artificial intelligence. These new entities, like nations or ancient deities, offer us insight and knowledge, and grant extraordinary power to reshape our world. We sacrifice individual well-being for the nation and god. All powerful systems come with sacrifice. In exchange for science and the Internet, we give up privacy, consent and old religious faiths. In place of divine salvation, we are offered digital preservation.

Thcsc machincs will savc us in thcir mcmory, as data, forever. Just as God promises eternal salvation in heaven, machines promise digital immortality, so long as you share, because computers can only preserve what you give.

Yet machines, like temples, are not eternal by default. They must be maintained, defended from malware, powered by electricity, and improved through innovation – or else they, too, will decay. Just as neglected shrines crumble, outdated programs rust in silence. History reminds us: no profession, no tool, no practice is immune to obsolescence. One of humanity's longest-standing professions, the scribes, who toiled for nearly two millennia, was rendered obsolete by the printing press. And then came the typists, only to be overtaken by desktop publishing, smartphones, and digital assistants like Grammarly and QuillBot. Banks no longer rely on human hands to count money; machines do the math faster, and more reliably.

Our biology, too, has learned automation. It handles predictable and repetitive tasks – digestion, the production of eggs and semen, repairing epigenetic damage, healing cellular breaks, translating genetic codes, and growing. What remains for us – the conscious part – is the unpredictable. The dangerous. The imaginative. Our role is to simulate space and society, to probe biology itself. To take risks. To explore unknown corners of reality in the endless pursuit of survival and expansion. Consciousness, in essence, is biology's tool to expand its reach beyond the known.

To survive, we must share ourselves across all domains of reality. Even gods must now inhabit the digital world to remain a part of our evolving culture. We must adapt to each new environment, not just biologically, but behaviorally, socially, and scientifically.

Adaptation is essential. In space, we wear a spacesuit. While farming honey, we wear protective gear to guard against bees. At festivals and parties, we dress in vibrant and unique attire; for funerals, in somber clothing that reflects collective mourning. In each scenario, we act appropriately, understanding weightlessness in space, respecting the danger of bees, and observing social customs to maintain harmony. With every new environment comes a new way to survive, and with each shift in reality, a new way to adapt and respond. We evolve not just by what we do, but by how we understand where we are – and what the moment asks of us.

ACT AND ADAPT

We adjust our behavior according to the roles we play in different social contexts: the funny friend to a close companion, the philosopher to a curious stranger, the conscientious worker to customers, the authoritative boss to employees, and the responsible citizen to a nation. Biologically, we also evolve through distinct stages – baby, toddler, teenager, adult, parent, and the elderly – each stage shaping how we act based on our growth. As unicellular organisms, we acted as individuals, but as we grew into multicellular beings, we began to act collectively, with each cell fulfilling a role to sustain the whole. If a single cell goes rogue, it could lead to cancer, threatening our very existence.

In the same way, to maintain the functioning of a nation, each individual plays a part. Some, like the heart and lungs, are vital, while others, like hair and nails, may seem less significant. But there are also those who become the face of the community, the group, or the nation. We often select and project this face, making it the focal point of our identity. We upload our faces to social media more frequently than our brains, hearts, or other private parts, because our face is the first thing we present to the world. It conveys emotions, communicates pain, joy, or desire, and is often how we engage with others. We express stomach pain through our face; we have to risk and test radiation using our eyes.

Much the same way, our culture and society tend to elevate those who share the most and risk the most – those who listen to the problems of others and push forward in the realms of innovation and discovery. Scientists, leaders, and politicians often become the targets of threats because they are at the forefront of change, risking their lives to create advancements for the nation or humanity. They risk their lives to drive progress, to improve their countries, or to advance humanity as a whole. Similarly, actors, too, are significant cultural figures, using their faces to allow others to live vicariously through them. They achieve a kind of immortality, as we continue to enjoy the performances of legends like Charlie Chaplin, whose comedy endures on our screens long after his time.

Nations have long preserved the faces of leaders, kings, queens, and gods through statues, paintings, books, and temples. In the digital age, the Internet has taken this preservation further, storing not only these iconic figures but also countless other individuals – celebrities, creators, and even ordinary people – in ways never imagined before. Yet, most people still prefer privacy, keeping their personal information hidden. Unlike the average person, celebrities have become integral parts of the digital universe.

Celebrity likenesses are captured in 3D models, scanned, and replicated through software. From photographs to fingerprints, their personalities are mapped out, allowing us to interact with their digital clones in immersive, virtual spaces. This technology allows for the preservation of their appearances long after they've passed. The power of digital replication is undeniable. For instance, the body of Dwayne "The Rock" Johnson is used to battle John Cena in WWE games, while Norman Reedus, famous for his role in *The Walking Dead*, has found new life as a character in Death Stranding. Terry Crews uses his likeness to fight crime in Crackdown 3, and Vin Diesel, ironically playing a survival clone, battles dinosaurs in Ark 2.

Virtual worlds now bring extinct animals and long-gone humans back to life in stunning 3D environments. Even deceased actors have been resurrected through technology, allowing their images to live on in new forms. For example, when Paul Walker (Brian O'Conner) tragically passed during the production of *Fast & Furious 7*, digital technology resurrected his likeness for the film. Similarly, Princess Leia's character was brought back in *Star Wars: The Rise of Skywalker*, despite the actress's passing three years prior.

The digital age has blurred the lines between reality and virtual existence. Anyone with a camera or smartphone can now create vlogs or short films, sharing their personal experiences and allowing others to step into their lives for a moment. But the future holds even greater possibilities. Soon, we may be able to change our faces at will, or even purchase synthetic actors to perform roles in our own homes. Imagine a hologram of Captain Jack Sparrow dressing as a woman or Arnold Schwarzenegger, digitally de-aged, flexing his muscles once again. The Internet, it seems, remembers everything. And those who choose to share will have their digital imprint preserved for all time.

Modern software, such as deepfake and de-aging technology, has the power to make anyone speak, act, and behave in ways they never could in life. The ability to control another's digital representation, to puppet their actions and words at will, threatens to render the profession of acting obsolete. Soon, software will be capable of gathering images and audios from various social media platforms to create lifelike digital versions of individuals, even resurrecting those who have passed. Imagine seeing a deceased mother or friend come to life on your screen. But the question arises: would they even want to return, to live out their existence as a digital replica of what we want them to be? Or would they, too, desire a life of their own, unbound by our memories and expectations?

Perhaps your deceased mother or friend might have dreams and aspirations of their own. They may want to become an actor, a politician, a traveler, a singer, or a scientist. We can create multiple versions of your loved one: one that continues to be your friend, and another who follows their own aspirations. But who gives you the right to duplicate and control their digital clone? Certainly not the person themselves – they are no longer here to consent. Who owns this digital version of them? Who has the authority to decide? Is it their family – parents, children, or spouses? But that, too, would be another person entirely, not the original individual we long to reconnect with.

In this digital age, we seek out others through their social media posts, podcasts, and reels, hoping to experience something new or feel connected to voices from afar. Much like how culture gives us our names and shapes our roles to serve gods, money, nations, or inventions, the Internet culture demands even more of our individual thoughts and opinions to generate fresh data. Unlike nations, which preserve their past leaders, the Internet saves everyone who shares themselves on it. But with this demand comes a sacrifice. The rights of the individual, once paramount, slowly fade in this culture of constant sharing and consumption. Just as wars for national power have historically demanded the sacrifice of individuals for a greater cause, the Internet culture, too, increasingly asks for the sacrifice of personal rights for the sake of progress and understanding.

What if fictional characters, like Mickey Mouse, Godzilla, Dobby, Rocket Raccoon, or any animated creation, suddenly demanded individual rights, claiming their likenesses had been used without consent? After all, life itself is an idea, and the essence of life is survival and propagation. Life has evolved solutions to various challenges: dolphins adapted to thrive in water, bats to navigate the night, and eagles to soar in the sky. In much the same way, individuality is an idea that exists between body and mind, constantly making decisions.

Sometimes, another individual may require your unique perspective. Human survival has always depended on the sharing of ideas and resources. Just as we've relied on plants for food, boats to float on water, and animals like cows for milk and pigs for meat, we continue to depend on each other to persist and grow. In today's world of YouTube, social media, and endless content, anyone can become an actor, a creator, a persona. While the profession of acting still thrives, the ability to create and portray virtually has become accessible to all.

On the Internet, every individual can claim significance. There's no need for a special festival to stand out. Every day, we can share our faces with the world, allowing others to remember us, much like how kings and queens did through books and statues. Yet, with this ability to share comes the risk of exploitation. Scientists put their lives on the line for discovery, and leaders confront terrorists to protect their nations. In the same way, we must adapt to varying circumstances to survive and to find new ways to save and spread our influence.

But as we evolve and expand, the habits that once seemed essential may begin to feel repetitive and inefficient. We find ourselves relying on systems that can automate tasks that were once time-consuming. Just as the printing press replaced scribes, we will continue to create technologies that allow us to simplify and accelerate our processes, reshaping the way we interact with the world and with each other.

AUTOMATIC

Our consciousness is designed to solve problems, whether short-term or long-term. But once a problem is solved, the solution often becomes automatic. We don't consciously direct our white blood cells to fight off invading germs. Similarly, a programmer must consciously code a software program to protect it from malware, but once that coding is complete, the program can run on its own. We don't consciously create babies in the womb; it happens automatically. Our consciousness is free to focus on bigger challenges while our unconscious systems manage the routine processes.

Today, automatic systems track our heartbeats, cholesterol levels, and browsing history. They store our fingerprints and passwords, order our favorite food, save old photos, remind us of our forgotten memories, auto-renew our subscriptions, auto-correct our words, and display advertisements tailored to our interests and needs. Machines don't take over; we simply allow them to.

Throughout history, we've sought to avoid hard work, finding satisfaction in breaks from physical labor to fulfill our mental and emotional needs. As automation frees us from toil, we drift toward dreamlike states, imagining utopias or heavens, and exploring space or fictional civilizations through virtual reality where we can extend our human empathy. In our free time, we learn to gain new knowledge and expand our control over reality.

In the future, AI will inevitably take over most industries. While outdated versions of jobs will persist, they will function automatically, much like how laborers once worked to assemble car parts by hand. Today, car manufacturing is almost entirely automated. Our consciousness craves novelty. Our consciousness craves new experiences and fresh knowledge to adapt to new challenges and survive. Even the things we once revered – our gods, art, music, and jokes – become obsolete in the face of new ideas. With enough data, AI can create music and jokes just as easily as a human.

We don't desire the same old formulas, like $E = mc^2$, or the established theories of particle wave collapse. What we seek now is something new: new expressions, new truths, new ideas that move us forward.

JOY OF UNCERTAINTY

We believe in the body because it reminds us – through DNA and the pain it inflicts when harmed – that it is real, fragile, and in need of protection. We believe in gods, nations, and currencies because of the consequences we're taught to fear – hell, poverty, prison, exile – and the promises of reward if we conform. If we serve these structures, we're told we'll gain significance, legacy, and a place within something larger than ourselves.

To preserve individuality, we must do something for ourselves and something for the world around us. To survive, we must care for both the body and the mind. The body thrives on routine – food, rest, movement – but the mind craves novelty. It seeks new ideas to test, fail, and refine in pursuit of something original. It is wired to explore. It makes mistakes not to fail, but to find new paths and possibilities.

We've rewritten religion countless times, often without even realizing it, just to explore what else might be true to adapt our collective consciousness to new moral and existential questions. Though Judaism began with the Torah, humans wrote the Bible, then the Quran, each text forming not a single unified faith, but branches and denominations as diverse as their interpretations. And beyond these canonical texts are the lesser known, unaccepted, or forgotten books that also sought to answer the same timeless questions.

Even within a single tradition, there are layers of diversity. Judaism itself holds multiple expressions: Hiloni, Dati, Masorti, and Haredi, each embracing the faith with different intensities. There are the Samaritans, who diverged in geography and doctrine, choosing Mount Gerizim over Zion and following their own version of the Pentateuch. The Mandaeans, on the other hand, rejected Jesus and upheld John as the true prophet. In their Genesis, Eve and Adam are created simultaneously, an early testament to gender equity.

History is filled with similar reinterpretations. The Thirty Years' War, rooted in religious disagreement, split Christianity apart. Roman Catholics and Protestants prayed to the same God, yet spilled blood over doctrinal disputes. Pentecostals center their devotion on the Holy Spirit, believing it to be everywhere and everything. Baptists delay baptism until one is old enough to choose. Lutheranism, Anglicanism, Eastern Orthodoxy, Mormonism, and the Amish – who strictly avoid modern technology – all arose from this pursuit of a belief system that felt truer to their lived experience.

The mind is not satisfied with repetition. It seeks new narratives, different characters, and the rush of the unknown. It wants to gamble with thought and be surprised by insight. We gamble with ideas because that's where the joy lies – not in knowing everything, but in finding something we never expected.

Chess, for all its celebrated intellectual prestige, is ultimately a game of limited movements. So limited, in fact, that an AI like Deep Blue could study and master it. The number of legal and even illegal moves, though vast, is still finite, estimated between 10^{111} and 10^{123}. That's why an AI like Deep Blue could eventually learn to defeat a champion like Garry Kasparov. It's not that machines think like us;

it's that they remember more. The rules are rigid; the board, fixed. Strategy can be calculated, catalogued, and repeated.

But life is more than a grid of predictable moves.

Now compare that to a ball in motion. Unlike a chess piece, a ball's path can never be perfectly predicted. It rolls, it bounces, it curves through the air, responding to force, angle, friction, and even wind. It can move in countless directions, across an open field or a tight corner, and every bounce is affected by subtle shifts in speed, spin, and surface. A game like table tennis, though confined to a table, still introduces more chaos than chess. Golf, on the other hand, sprawls across acres of unpredictable terrain – no one can say with certainty what the next stroke will bring. One moment you win; the next, you're chasing your ball into the woods. And yet, both outcomes offer something equally valuable: a new experience. Players don't just play to win; they play to gamble with possibility. The thrill lies in the not-knowing.

Even a losing runner may feel like a winner in the middle of a sprint. Every sprinter, whether first or last, shares that fleeting belief that they can win. That shared uncertainty is a kind of equality – an emotional level-playing field. In the end, only one may win, but all feel the electricity of the race. That's the real equality – the universal uncertainty.

We have chairs designed for comfort, yet we edge forward when a film excites us. That's why people place bets in bowling alleys, not just to win but to feel something unexpected: a strike, a gutter ball, a miraculous spare. Games, by nature, celebrate uncertainty. Whether it's Dungeons & Dragons, Ludo, or Snakes and Ladders, it's the unpredictability of a single dice roll that keeps us coming back. A Rubik's cube only becomes interesting when it's a mess. Once it's solved, it becomes static and unplayable. Jenga is thrilling only when it teeters. Jenga, pictionary, card games, pool, carrom – these are loved not for certainty but for the chaos they invite and the control we try to bring to them. Victory is not the goal – the mystery is.

We crave both the ordinary and the extraordinary. A regular day and a festival. The average man and the sudden Superman. Normal speed and then, out of nowhere, a burst of adrenaline. A paved road, then an unexpected off-road detour. It's in this contrast – this dance between routine and randomness – that life becomes most exciting.

When we buy a new phone, we treat it like a fragile newborn – careful, attentive, almost reverent. We shield it with a case, wipe away fingerprints, panic at the slightest drop. But give it a few months, maybe a year, and we'll casually toss it onto the bed or start eyeing the next version.

During its prime, we update the software, install games, explore new apps, swap out covers, change wallpapers and ringtones – anything to keep it fresh, exciting, alive. We do this because we crave novelty. It's not the device we grow attached to, but the feeling of freshness, the illusion of something evolving. When something lacks the ability to change, it quickly becomes mundane. But if it holds the capacity for reinvention, even just a little, it becomes part of our lives.

We carry this same instinct into how we see people. We aren't drawn to those who are rigid – bullies who never bend, or saints who never question. Nor do we want someone too perfect, too polished, or too predictable. We gravitate toward people who know when to act and when to retreat, who can argue and adjust, tease and empathize; the ones who know when to speak and when to listen, when to be serious and when to play, when to argue, lie, laugh, adapt. We're drawn to those who evolve. That's the kind of complexity we relate to.

We seek puzzles, not solutions. We search for mysteries, not certainties. It's only within the chaos of unpredictability that we find meaning in creating order. We crave the twist, the thrill, the unexpected turn. That's what gives life its pulse.

Even music and humor exist because they surprise us. They play with anticipation and surprise, rhythm and disruption. They pull us into waves of emotions – up and down, soft and sharp – precisely because they twist what we expect into something we don't see coming.

We don't just want life to be good. We want it to be interesting. And that, more than anything, is what keeps us moving forward. We are meant to change, adapt, question, and explore.

FUNNY JOKES AND NICE SONGS

Music is enjoyable, no doubt. But for how long? Even the catchiest song fades with time. Even our favorite songs lose their charm once we know every beat, every twist. We rarely laugh at the same joke twice, especially when we know the punchline.

Trends in music come and go like waves. If a new music trend becomes popular, people quickly sync with it. But soon, it fades. Then, what once felt fresh becomes overplayed, predictable, bland. Jokes suffer a similar fate. The first time, they hit with force. The second? A chuckle. The third? Silence. But every new song or joke brings with it a fresh wave of emotion, a new flavor of experience. Even if reality runs out of fresh ideas, we create more. We invent fiction, chase risks, and indulge in the unfamiliar, because the new excites us. Our minds hunger for variety, even if it's a fabricated thrill.

Songs usually last under ten minutes, and jokes even less. Yet, in that short span, they deliver uncertain vibrations, surprising twists, or a sudden burst of meaning – something to shake us awake. Timing, in both mediums, is everything. Imagine someone begins a joke with, "Why is 6 afraid of 7?" but waits ten minutes to deliver the punchline, "Because 7 ate 9." By then, the moment is lost. The laugh dies in the silence. The same happens in music. If a tune loops endlessly without variation, it becomes noise. Even your favorite song, rich with new instruments, trendy lyrics, and clever tonal shifts, can grow dull once you've memorized every rise, fall, and twist. That's when you start looking for the next hit.

This need for novelty isn't just limited to jokes and music. It stretches across every corner of human life – even into pain and violence masked as humor. We love to watch actors push their physiology to absurd extremes without expressing pain.

Think of the slapstick legends: Marty Feldman's bug-eyed antics, Charlie Chaplin's absurd tumbles, Abbott and Costello's chaotic energy, Dudley Moore's physical absurdities. They bent their bodies into hilarious contortions, pretended to be hit by invisible hammers or stabbed in the rear with random props. In real life, such behavior would get someone arrested. But in the safe realm of performance, we laugh, because the illusion shields us from the suffering.

Jackie Chan's acrobatic stunts, Rowan Atkinson's buffoonery – all are built on self-inflicted chaos. Jackie fights off multiple attackers in gravity-defying stunts. Atkinson might get kicked in the groin for a laugh. It is pain repackaged as pleasure. Today's stand-up comedians do the same, but with words; they self-mock, exaggerate, spark insight, expose vulnerabilities to pull laughter from the crowd.

Stunt performers do it too. They leap from buildings with harnesses, walk tightropes with safety nets. We watch, knowing they're safe, but our bodies still tingle. Why? Because we're wired to feel the thrill without the consequence. We risk the body to feel something new, something our old biological instincts might not even understand. We make the sensation of pain obsolete by packaging it as spectacle, stripping it of its sting so all that remains is the thrill. And so, we keep seeking: new songs, new jokes, new risks, new ways to twist the old sensations into something exciting. Because in making the familiar obsolete, we find the extraordinary.

Humor often does this with simplicity and surprise. Take a joke like, "Why won't it hurt if you hit your friend with a two-liter soda?" Most people pause, curious, and then the punchline hits: "Because it's a soft drink!" Or consider the question, "What has four wheels and flies?" The twist, "a garbage truck," hinges on the double meaning of "flies." These jokes rely on timing; deliver the punchline too late, and the suspense dissolves into confusion rather than laughter.

Still, jokes don't always land. Try telling that one about Jesus turning water into wine to a devout priest:

"Have you been drinking?" the officer asks.

"Just water," says the priest.

"Then why do I smell wine?"

The priest looks at his bottle, startled. "Good Lord! He's done it again!"

While it might get laughs in a comedy club, it might offend someone who holds the story sacred. Humor, like belief, is deeply personal.

Biologically, pain is real. If a duck's bill were twisted in real life, it would scream, bleed, and possibly die. No one would laugh. But in cartoons, Daffy Duck gets flattened, electrocuted, or blown to pieces, only to reappear unharmed in the next scene. There's no expression of pain, and that absence invites laughter. It's absurd in a bubble of safety. Humor often masks what would otherwise be horrific.

Cartoons present a sanitized version of violence. Think *Tom and Jerry*: Jerry drops an anvil on Tom, launches him into the sky, or smashes his face with a frying pan. If Tom were a real cat, the scene would be gruesome. But cartoon physics allows them to bounce back instantly, as if nothing happened. No scars. No suffering. Just the next gag.

Contrast this with horror films, where twisted bodies scream and bleed, and pain is central to the experience. In *The Birds* (1963), the audience watches helplessly as beaks rip flesh and gouge out eyes. Terrifying. Yet, when Jerry knocks Tom's eyes out of his head, it's just another gag. Structurally, both scenes depict violence, but one is horror, the other humor.

Many cartoons indulge in the grotesque: characters riddled with bullet holes that leak water when they drink, or shrunk into pots after violent mishaps. The key difference is pain. Horror emphasizes it; cartoons erase it. There's a strange liberation in this: pain without consequence, suffering without stakes. It's not just slapstick; it's a parody of physicality itself.

And it mirrors what we do in real life with sarcasm and self-mockery. We often mock ourselves as a way to process reality. It's a method of discovery, a way of turning discomfort into insight. But humor is a fine line. Some people laugh; others feel attacked, exposed, or shamed. What's clever to one might be cruel to another. In the end, comedy – like horror – is about stretching reality just enough to feel something new. It reflects our fears, our taboos, our curiosity – and sometimes, our cruelty. Whether it's laughter or terror depends on how far, and in which direction, we twist our belief in pain, life, and familiarity.

BORED

We are creatures forever teetering on the edge of boredom, endlessly searching for something new – something that will give us the sense of meaning we so desperately crave. But in that search, we often turn to destruction, as if by tearing things apart, we might uncover who we truly are.

Throughout history, our hunger for new experiences has manifested in countless forms. In sex, we've explored every nuance of romance and ecstasy, inventing endless variations to deepen intimacy and chase the fleeting spark of orgasm. In numbers we have binary, octal, decimal, hexadecimal, sexagesimal, quaternary, senary, complex base, negabinary, and surreal numbers. In games, we gamble not just money but outcomes, risk, ego. We shape rules, break them, reinvent them – always in search of surprise. And in punishment, we've crafted unimaginably cruel methods to inflict pain – sometimes to assert power, sometimes to instill fear, and sometimes, disturbingly, out of curiosity.

History is littered with such inventions. Take, for example, the stake, widely used during the Inquisition. The method was simple: drive a wooden post into the ground, pile dry branches around it, bind the accused, and set it alight. Then there was the Scavenger's daughter, a metal hoop that compressed the victim's body until their ribs shattered. Crucifixion – perhaps the most infamous – left its victims nailed to a cross, bleeding slowly to death. The brazen bull, a metal beast heated from beneath, its hollow body filled with flesh and agony, the victim's screams echoing from its mouth. The rack, an elegant horror, where limbs were pulled in opposite directions until joints dislocated and limbs tore apart.

And the list goes on. The breast ripper, iron maiden, pear of anguish, pillory, thumbscrew, Judas cradle, head-crusher, guillotine, keelhauling. Each one a masterpiece of malice. Even with the discovery of electricity, we turned it into a weapon – the electric chair – a modern evolution of ancient brutality.

Our imagination never truly abandoned torture. It simply evolved. Today, it finds expression in violent video games, brutal action films, and animated horrors where pain is stylized and served as entertainment. We might not build the rack any more, but we recreate the thrill of suffering in digital spaces – packaged, stylized, and safe to consume.

Perhaps it's not just boredom that drives us, but a deeper existential need to confront our limits, to push against the edge of pain, pleasure, and morality.

Amusement park rides – roller coasters, loop-o-planes, flip-flap spins, sky drop towers – are designed to terrify. Yet, once the ride ends, children and adults alike burst into laughter. Humor and horror are more closely linked than we often admit. It is absurd to believe we are truly alive, and once we accept that we are, the thought becomes haunting, because there are countless ways to get hurt, to suffer, to die.

We cling to the illusion of control in a world governed by chaos and fragility.

There is something absurd about being alive. Not just the miracle of it, but the vulnerability. The sheer improbability of our existence is both ridiculous and haunting. What lies beneath both horror and humor is the unsettling sensation of losing that control, of having our beliefs twisted, our expectations shattered. And yet, instead of succumbing, we adapt. We laugh. We cope. We find meaning in the chaos, inch by inch reclaiming agency in a world that offers none.

To feel alive, we must risk something. We must evolve, constantly learning, adapting, surviving, and spreading. Life demands motion, both outward and inward. We must chase the edge. Whether it's love or discovery, pain or play, life demands evolution. We learn, adapt, survive, and spread, not because we have to, but because something in us refuses to stay still.

We have two choices: laugh and cope, or tremble and retreat. But the longer we hide, the more boredom creeps in, and boredom can be both dangerous and void of meaning. The emptiest emotion. A hollow hunger. Boredom corrodes purpose.

Life aches for purpose. From the imperfect to the perfected. From hunger to fulfillment. From loneliness to connection. From ignorance to brilliance. From Earth to Mars. From the mortal to the imagined immortal. Life cannot sit still. It needs uncertainty, unpredictability, and mystery, because once everything becomes predictable, there's nothing left to explore. And without exploration, there is no joy. It is the unknown that awakens us, challenges us, and keeps us moving forward.

UNIVERSE 25

Universe 25 stands as a haunting metaphor. It wasn't a cosmos made for humans, but for mice. In 1968, ethologist John B. Calhoun built what he called a "Mortality-Inhibiting

Environment" – a utopia for rodents. He had tried twenty-four times before, and each attempt failed for a variety of reasons: health complications, genetic issues, population dynamics, food scarcity, or insufficient space for a functioning mouse society. But the 25th time, he believed he got it right.

In Universe 25, Calhoun chose his Adams and Eves carefully. Though the environment resembled a cage, it was far from a prison. Inside, the rodents had everything: abundant food, opportunities for sex, safe and comfortable spaces to sleep and play. Each mouse could even have its own room. Some males enjoyed harems of female companions. It was a calculated haven where survival was easy and struggle was obsolete. But this is where it all began to unravel.

In nature, mortality shapes meaning. Predators kill the young. Fear keeps adults alert, moving, thinking, and purposeful. Only a few survive and pass on their genes. That struggle, that danger, gives life meaning. But in Universe 25, survival came cheap. There were no predators. No death to remind them of life. With no natural selection to impose limits, the population exploded. The mice turned on each other. Mice, like humans, are social mammals. But when their numbers surged beyond what the social structure could sustain, chaos took root. The system collapsed under its own weight. Males began to fight over territory and mates. Some were left without any female partners at all. Violence escalated. Females were raped, pups were abandoned or eaten, and strange, aberrant behaviors emerged. Some females isolated themselves and stopped caring for their young. Some males lost all interest in mating. Cannibalism reached its peak. And eventually, Universe 25 went still. Extinct.

Contemporary sociologists have long warned that Calhoun's experiment revealed not just the fragility of social order, but the dangers of abundance without challenge. Many citizens of developed nations today live as safely and comfortably as the mice of Universe 25. But unlike mice, we possess the capacity to imagine beyond biology. We explore sexuality, science, philosophy, fantasy, entertainment, gadgets, social media, shopping, games, hobbies, artificial intelligence, hypotheses, paradoxes, and countless other pursuits. Where rodents failed, we dream. We create purpose – sometimes artificial, sometimes absurd, but always inventive.

Unlike the mice, we invent our own predators: supervillains, moral dilemmas, apocalyptic scenarios. We entertain ourselves with paradoxes, hypotheses, simulations, science fiction, and theories waiting to be proven or broken. We invent challenges to overcome, enemies to defeat, and mysteries to unravel. Yet, even with all this ingenuity, we are not immune to obsolescence.

Life doesn't require a human form to continue. It doesn't need our hearts or our gods. It only needs a reason to persist. History teaches us that countless forms of life once thrived, only to fade into irrelevance, forgotten. The consciousness that ignites our cognition might, in time, become nothing more than an automatic process. And so we must ask: is our consciousness truly autonomous, or is it merely the result of influence – society, biology, brain chemistry, environment, and the intricate web of relationships around us?

Our evolved descendants might look back on our art, our music, our humor, and conclude that we were never truly conscious at all – merely intricate products shaped by society, biology, environment, and the countless forces surrounding us. They might study our art, music, humor, and grief and conclude that we were not fully aware, just functionally expressive.

We could be electric eels for them, producing electricity without knowing its fullest potential consciously.

XI. HISTORY OF INFLUENCES

Obsolescence (1) arises as the purpose to escape oblivion (0). Yet, in its very existence, obsolescence (reality) must continuously render itself obsolete – unfolding as 1, 2, 3, 4, 5, 6... into infinity – to remain real, to preserve the purpose of being. It expands without end, birthing eons of emergence and weaving an eternal eventuality, where doubt clings to the fabric of existence, cleaving infinite belief into fragmented instants.

OBSOLETE GOD

Imagine a perfect being – the God-Perfect – free from hunger, death, desire, or doubt. The God-Perfect needs no food, no love, no friends, no knowledge. Having complete control over reality, the God-Perfect has no reason to move, to think, or even to exist in any meaningful way. In this state, there is no heat, no cold, no pain, no pleasure, no friction to spark thought or change. There is no belief to doubt, nor any doubt to believe. In such a state, existence becomes a void, motionless and silent.

Nothing alive can truly function in such a perfect world unless the God-Perfect willingly detaches a piece of reality from its omnipotent grasp. Life itself cannot function unless the God-Perfect creates separation – a detachment from total control. Only by allowing imperfection can life arise. But in doing so, the God-Perfect ceases to be perfect. The God-Perfect becomes simply God, burdened with the uncertainty of what has been set loose.

Yet, even observation is a risk. To give this new life wisdom or protection would be to rob it of purpose. To control it physically would collapse its freedom, undoing the very separation that made life possible. If God speaks, even a single word, it becomes manipulation, a subtle form of control. And if God reasserts full dominance, life ceases. Full intervention would revert everything to perfect control, back to stillness, back to nothing.

God could relinquish all control, allowing every form of life to struggle, survive, and thrive. In doing so, God would dissolve, remaining only as a concept. Thus, God faces an ultimate choice: to save Himself, or to sacrifice Himself – or a part of Himself – for the chaos and beauty of life. For life to exist, there must be hunger, growth, evolution, ambition, deceit, chaos. Life must fight to survive, bending reality to its will, striving endlessly against the odds.

In time, life that survives may master its environment, conquer every threat, and finally seize total control, becoming, in essence, a new God-Perfect. But once life achieves total control, it loses its purpose, becoming once again obsolete. Thus, the cycle of obsolescence repeats: life rises, finds new ways to exist, and discovers new purposes.

Imagine, for a moment, that we are God. We create a lion with a ravenous hunger for meat, but we forget to create prey. Inevitably, the lion dies. Even for God, an idea beyond Himself must exist. Even for a god, creation demands more than imagination; it demands a source, a context, a foundation. To give life, God must confront the unknown, the unshaped, the unimagined. God needs extra matters that are not him. Yet, this challenge is resolved through the abundance of seemingly useless things – scattered matter and chaos – that later become vital as life evolves, adapts, and gradually takes more control over reality.

In the vast expanse of our solar system, spanning 2,744,000,000 miles (roughly 80 AU), only a narrow band, known as the Goldilocks Zone, can sustain life. Across the cosmos, this habitable range exists in only about 9–12% of star systems. Factor in black holes, unstable stars, rogue gas giants, meteors, weak magnetic fields, thin atmospheres, and volatile chemical compositions, and the odds shrink further, perhaps to just 4–6%.

In an endlessly expanding universe, this represents a gamble. And yet, it is this surplus of seemingly "wasted" matters – planets and stars – that become the hidden reservoir from which life draws its chance to survive and spread. Randomness does not intentionally create life. On Earth, it happened to create life; on countless other worlds, it did not. Life, against all odds, uses this randomness, carving out fragile footholds in an otherwise lifeless sea.

Life persists through the cycle of obsolescence, forever struggling to escape the inevitable pull toward lifeless absoluteness.

ABSOLUTE LIFELESS STATE

For life, the absolute state is death. But for the non-living, absoluteness is the norm. Water does not care whether it is an ocean, a sea, a lake, a river, a stream, a pond, a waterfall, rain, ice, or steam. It does not perceive itself as a compound or as atoms. Water does not feel pain when it is boiled, ice does not scream when it melts, and iron does not cry when it bends. We use such expressions to describe our own plasticity – I melted in his presence, or she bent my iron heart – because we are alive, water is not.

A statue, no matter how perfectly chiseled to resemble a frog, will not leap. It is flawless in its stillness, absolute in its form. Pour boiling water over it, or stab it with molten steel, and it will remain unmoved, untouched by pain or change. The frog statue does not need food, nor does it crave emotional connection. In contrast, a real frog has needs. It begins as a round egg, quickly making that early form obsolete to become a tadpole. The tadpole grows a tail to swim, eyes to see, external gills to breathe, and a mouth to graze on algae. Yet, this stage too becomes obsolete, as it sprouts teeth for tougher fare and hind legs to swim faster.

Within twelve weeks, front limbs emerge and lungs begin to form, marking the shift to adulthood. But even in this adult form, it is not absolute. The frog, in its maturity, seeks a mate, driven by an instinctual need for love – a love that is fleeting, but absolute for the moment. As time progresses, the frog ages, and eventually, it dies. Then, from the decay of its absolute form, a new generation emerges.

The cycle of life continues, each new frog carrying forward a new development, a slight advancement in the evolutionary chain, a little longer life, an increased tolerance for toxicity, a bit more of the territory of existence conquered. Yet, each frog remembers both the future of absoluteness (adulthood) and the past obsoleteness (infancy, childhood, adolescence). Only by remembering the stages of obsolescence can the frog reach a new stage of absoluteness.

Humans, however, are different. We possess an abstract quality: the ability to collect, to record, to remember. Our mind wanders to the past and the future. We recall dinosaurs, forgotten languages, and lost cultures. We gather insects, computers, and the fur and bone tools of our ancestors. We trace the history of the cosmos, the lives of stars that were born, lived, and died, and the elements that were never formed. This vast collection of memories serves as our guide, helping us reach all possible future forms of absoluteness.

We even understand the concept of obsolescence itself, using terms like dynamic and planned obsolescence to describe the inevitable decline of things and the gradual fading of forms into new possibilities. Through this understanding, we navigate the intricate dance between life, death, and the relentless pursuit of meaning and purpose.

WEAR AND TEAR, BUT COLORFUL

Light bulbs manufactured in the 20th century were deliberately designed to have a short lifespan, even though they could have lasted for up to 10,000 hours, that is, well over a year. In 1924, Phillips International, General Electric, Tokyo Electric, OSRAM, and AEI formed the Phoebus Cartel with a singular purpose: to limit the lifespan of light bulbs to just 1,000 hours. Consumers unknowingly bought, used, and replaced these short-lived bulbs, keeping the cartel alive and profitable. Engineers who dared to create bulbs exceeding the limit faced heavy fines. Although the cartel dissolved in the 1950s due to various factors, including World War II, the concept of planned obsolescence lived on.

Apple, decades later, followed a similar strategy. They introduced irreplaceable batteries that lasted only about eighteen months, forcing consumers to purchase new devices when the batteries failed. Although a lawsuit was filed against Apple in 2003, they settled without significant repercussions. Even more controversially, Apple later introduced iOS updates that caused older iPhones to slow down or shut off, which they defended by claiming that it was intended to preserve battery life and prevent unexpected shutdowns.

Imagine, for a moment, if a scientist invented a vehicle that could run purely on nitrogen from the atmosphere. Would anyone continue to buy petrol, diesel, or electricity? Or picture a dress that never gets dirty or torn, remaining as new forever. Would you ever buy another dress? The dress company would go bankrupt, as there would be no need to create or innovate further. Industries would collapse if products never needed replacing. To ensure survival, companies introduced dynamic obsolescence, creating new designs and styles that rendered previous models "outdated," even if the core technology remained unchanged.

Take Ford, for example. In 1908, the company introduced the indestructible black car. Customers bought one and rarely needed another. General Motors, on the other hand, found success by introducing color options for cars. Up until then, most mechanical items – from cars to appliances – were monochromatic. However, early 20th century cars had wooden frames and lacquer finishes that couldn't withstand engine heat, requiring multiple coats and three days of drying. The turning point came when the Dupont family, owners of General Motors, developed Duco Paint, a cellulose-based coating that dried quickly and came in a variety of vibrant colors. In 1925, the True Blue Oakland became the first commercially available blue car. Soon after, Ford adopted colorful finishes for its Model A, and color became a marketing tool.

Today, we see this principle everywhere. Modern machines – grinders, washing machines, headsets, vacuums, refrigerators, heaters, air conditioners, scooters, gym equipment, even light bulbs – come in a dazzling array of colors. Consumers are offered pinks, reds, blues, blacks – endless variations to appeal to individual tastes. Today, we move so fast through discoveries and developments and consume such immense amounts of data that we hardly pause to care whether our batteries last a decade or a century. Every year, a new type of camera, console, screen, design, hardware, or software is introduced, and so we update ourselves accordingly. Between 2004 and 2024, one person might easily have bought five or more phones.

It is not the machines that need constant updating; it's us. Humans must continually learn: the evolution of computers, the rise of algorithms, even the basics of something as fundamental as Excel, just to remain employable in a civilization increasingly built around machines and technological advancement.

We work for robots, and robots work for us. We provide the essential elements they need to thrive: metals, polymers, alloys (the very building blocks of their mechanics), electricity (their sustenance), data (their knowledge), programs (their brains), and controlled environments (like cool air-conditioning) that keep them running smoothly. In return, machines handle much of the labor: farming, surveillance, security, assembly lines, textiles, navigation, civil construction, space exploration, medicine, and pharmaceuticals.

As we progress, we continue to evolve alongside them, constantly seeking ways to generate more electricity, develop more efficient hardware, expand memory banks, create futuristic software, and craft long-lasting, rust-resistant materials. We build machines to depend on electricity, and we ensure they are fed. We design them to mimic consciousness, and in doing so, we create an ecosystem where we are the environment in which machines move, grow, and evolve.

We've cultivated an ecosystem where machines thrive, providing them with electricity, cooling systems, and the raw materials to build them. Yet, most of us fail to recognize that, just like machines, we are not truly conscious in the way we think we are. We, too, are products of our environment. From mirrors to magnets, countless objects and beings have subtly shaped human thought, influencing the way we perceive, think, and make decisions throughout evolution and history.

OBSOLETE EVOLUTION OF LIFE

The earliest life on Earth began with microorganisms that did not breathe oxygen. In those ancient times, Earth's atmosphere was rich in methane and other gases, while oxygen remained scarce. As tectonic plates shifted and assembled to form the Nuna supercontinent, the face of the planet was vastly different from what we know today. Most notably, it lacked an ozone layer. Life was forced to retreat into the depths of the oceans for shelter from the relentless UV radiation, relying on chemosynthesis rather than sunlight to survive.

Amid this anaerobic world, a groundbreaking shift occurred. Cyanobacteria, among the first to perform photosynthesis, began producing oxygen, slowly enriching the atmosphere. Over the course of 100–200 million years, this oxygenation led to the formation of the ozone layer, providing a shield that allowed life to move closer to the surface.

Yet, this transformation came at a cost. The rise of oxygen triggered a mass extinction, wiping out many forms of anaerobic life that could not adapt. But from this great loss, a new model of life began to flourish – life that thrived under the umbrella of oxygen and the ozone layer.

Thus happened the first great obsolescence in Earth's history: the fall of anaerobic life and the dawn of an oxygen-breathing world.

EDIACARAN EXTINCTION

The Archean Eon did not endure much longer. As the Nuna supercontinent began to fragment, eventually giving rise to Rodinia, the Earth entered yet another period of upheaval. Intense volcanic activity during this time released vast amounts of carbon dioxide into the atmosphere, contributing to a dramatic global cooling event known as "Snowball Earth." Some theories also suggest that a shift in Earth's axial tilt may have played a role in this deep freeze.

Eventually, this deep freeze relented, and as the ice melted away, oxygen levels surged, creating conditions ripe for a new wave of life. The life forms that had thrived during the Ediacaran period – a bizarre and largely mysterious collection of organisms – began to vanish. Their extinction paved the way for one of the most remarkable events in Earth's biological history: the Cambrian Explosion.

LIVING FOSSILS

From the Cambrian Era to the Permian Era, spanning a time 542 million years ago, Earth witnessed four major extinction events. Then, between the Triassic period (200 million years ago) and the Cretaceous period (60 million years ago), two more extinctions followed. The causes were many: continental drift, asteroid impacts, volcanic activity, climate shifts, and even changes in Earth's axis.

Each extinction shook the world like a chemist experimenting through trial and error – mixing, reacting, and filtering to discover new possibilities. Life evolved in random bursts, surviving not by design but by resilience and chance.

Remarkably, some ancient life forms still walk among us. From the Paleozoic era, we have survivors like the nautilus, hagfish, and horseshoe crabs. From the Mesozoic era, creatures like pig-nosed turtles, platypuses, crocodiles, and tuataras remain. The Cenozoic era brings us oddities like aardvarks, Komodo dragons, and elephant shrews.

Some strange and ancient beings, like Hallucigenia from the Ediacaran Era, have even inspired modern fiction, such as the manga series *Attack on Titan*. These lobopod-type creatures left descendants too, with modern-day tardigrades and velvet worms serving as living remnants of that distant past.

Both living and dead fossils offer us tangible proof of life's enduring journey. And it is worth remembering: all these creatures still breathe oxygen and live under the protective ozone layer produced long ago by archaic, now-obsolete forms of life. Every extinction, every cataclysm, became the fertile ground from which the next wave of life emerged.

CAMBRIAN–ORDOVICIAN EXTINCTION

During the Paleozoic Era, spanning from the Cambrian to the Permian periods, life made its first bold moves onto land. Plants began to colonize dry ground, and the earliest walking insects ventured ashore. Life itself started to terraform the planet, reshaping the environment to its advantage.

Yet, this era of expansion was interrupted by a devastating event: the Cambrian–Ordovician mass extinction. This catastrophe wiped out countless marine organisms, including vast populations of plankton, altering the balance of life in the oceans.

In the aftermath, oxygen levels in the atmosphere rose significantly, setting the stage for new evolutionary possibilities. Meanwhile, the continued movement of the continental plates led to the gradual assembly of the supercontinent Pangea. This dramatic geological shift triggered a major burst of biodiversity known as the Great Ordovician Biodiversification Event (GOBE), marking a new chapter in the story of life on Earth.

ORDOVICIAN–SILURIAN EXTINCTION

The sudden rise in atmospheric oxygen allowed terrestrial mosses to flourish monstrously, but this boom was short-lived. Climate change triggered a severe ice age, leading to the Ordovician–Silurian mass extinction, which wiped out nearly 80% of marine life. The Ordovician–Silurian extinction may have also been caused by gamma-ray bursts (GRBs). GRBs are extremely energetic explosions that originate from supernovae or neutron star mergers. If such a burst occurred in our galaxy and was directed toward Earth, it could strip away the ozone layer within seconds. This would allow harmful ultraviolet radiation to reach the planet's surface, potentially triggering global atmospheric and climatic changes that could lead to mass extinction.

Life eventually rebounded during the Devonian period, an age where many of our proto-ancestors swam and crawled across new terrains, and large vertebrates began to dominate the land. Yet, disaster struck once again. The Devonian mass extinction, caused by falling oxygen levels and shifting climates, cleared the stage for the Carboniferous period.

The Carboniferous era witnessed the rise of the first egg-laying reptiles, who started to conquer the land, alongside giant flying arthropods. It also saw the spread of gymnosperms – conifers, cycads, ginkgos, and pines – creating vast, lush forests. However, this green empire ended abruptly with the collapse of the great rainforests.

As the supercontinent Pangea finally took shape, its sheer size disrupted wind patterns and trapped moisture along the coasts, leaving the vast interiors dry and barren. Forests perished, but resilient life forms adapted, surviving by hunting and living near the sea.

PERMIAN EXTINCTION

Following the Carboniferous period came a brief era of relative peace, only to end in catastrophe once again: the Permian extinction. Triggered by a deadly combination of asteroid impacts, tectonic shifts, and climate upheavals, this event wiped out more than 95% of life. Yet, among the survivors were the ancestors of one of history's most celebrated groups: dinosaurs.

As always, the story began with a surge of optimism. In the aftermath of extinction, atmospheric oxygen levels were low, prompting certain reptiles to evolve hollow bones that could store air in tiny pockets. As oxygen levels gradually rose, these adaptations allowed them to grow larger and stronger, setting the stage for the giants that would roam in the Mesozoic era.

Life flourished anew. Dinosaurs ate voraciously, excreted abundantly, and in doing so, helped to fertilize the soil. Flowering plants (angiosperms) also emerged during this time, producing fruits and blossoms, though no gardener tended their beauty and no farmer harvested their bounty. Meanwhile, the dinosaurs, oblivious to their influence, unknowingly reshaped the landscape. Picture this: just as a single elephant widens trails and snaps trees in its path, imagine herds of sauropods – 72 feet tall, weighing over 100 tons – trudging across ancient landscapes. Their slow, heavy movements must have terraformed entire ecosystems, leaving lasting marks on the planet. Their existence alone reshaped terrains, much like massive, living bulldozers.

And life itself generates heat. Consider a computer overheating if left uncooled. Now imagine colossal reptiles dominating land and sea, consuming matter, excreting waste, and perpetuating the cycle, warming the world simply through their immense existence, much like humanity today.

TRIASSIC AND CRETACEOUS EXTINCTIONS

During the Triassic mass extinction, many species that had not yet evolved hollow bones vanished from Earth. Simultaneously, the acidification of oceans made survival nearly impossible for much of marine life. Yet, this brutal filtration of life set the stage for the Jurassic period, one of the most prosperous eras for reptiles.

The hollow-boned survivors flourished, living comfortably amid an abundance of plants and trees. As they thrived, they also released vast amounts of methane into the atmosphere. To put this into perspective: even today, cows, sheep, goats, and humans combined emit about 73 million metric tons of methane per year (as of 2020). By comparison, estimates based on the size and population of dinosaurs suggest they may have produced around 520 million metric tons annually, five times more than today's man-made industries.

During the Jurassic and Cretaceous periods, dinosaurs ruled the planet with remarkable dominance, soaring through the skies (pterosaurs, giant insects), swimming in the seas (mosasaurs, plesiosaurs), and roaming the land (sauropods, theropods, raptors, and early mammals).

However, their reign eventually ended. A catastrophic asteroid impact and the resulting climate upheaval triggered the Cretaceous mass extinction, wiping out most of the dinosaurs and reshaping the future of life on Earth once again.

In this grand, chaotic story, every extinction, every survival, and every random twist of fate has laid down the groundwork for life as we know it today.

THE DISCOVERY OF FIRE

Fire stands as one of the greatest discoveries in human civilization. However, creating fire required more than just curiosity. It demanded the evolution of opposable thumbs.

These thumbs allowed early humans to grasp stones, collect dry materials, and strike sparks together. But to evolve such thumbs, nature played a gamble, requiring not only the right physical adaptations but also specific environmental factors. For instance, trees with circular branches were essential for climbing, and predators on the ground helped push our evolution forward.

Interestingly, we are not the only creatures with opposable thumbs. Koalas, tree frogs, possums, giant pandas, chameleons, and sugar gliders share this trait. Furthermore, many animals outside the primate family use tools, such as crows, bowerbirds, octopuses, finches, and elephants. However, humans are the only species known to have harnessed the flint rock to create fire. This was likely because, unlike other animals, we lacked night vision, a massive, intimidating body, or the ability to fly and escape danger.

Flint rocks, abundant yet difficult to form, were the result of ancient life. Millions of years ago, marine organisms – tiny sponges and radiolaria – used silica from seawater to form bio-opal in their skeletons and shells. After their death, the organic parts decayed, and their silica-laden remains sank to the ocean floor. Over time, millions of mollusk shells, worm skeletons, and other remains acted as a source for chemical processes that led to the formation of flint. As continents shifted over eons, these sedimentary layers were exposed, and erosion eventually deposited flint nodules, often shaped like the shells of ancient organisms. However, these are not true fossils but pseudo flint formations, akin to opalized or pyrite fossils.

These flint stones enabled our ancestors to create fire, igniting a revolutionary shift in human history. With fire, cooking became possible – softening food, making it easier to digest, and allowing more time for intellectual pursuits such as thinking about gods, spirits, and the future. Fire also aided early humans in their migration, enabling them to thrive in humid climates as nomads and hunter-gatherers. As the climate changed after the Ice Age, fire played an essential role in human adaptation, eventually facilitating the transition to farming and slowly shifting us from nomadic life to settled agricultural and herding societies.

But we were not the only primates to face the challenges of the Ice Age. Many species, such as Homo habilis, Neanderthals, Homo erectus, and Denisovans, either went extinct or interbred with Homo sapiens. In the end, Homo sapiens proved to be the sole survivors, their mastery of fire playing a crucial role in their dominance.

TWO GIFTS OF NATURE

After the dawn of farming, humanity entered the Bronze and Iron Ages – the eras shaped by two extraordinary gifts of nature.

The first of these was asteroids. Throughout history, meteorites have crashed into Earth, causing mass extinctions but also depositing precious metals such as gold, silver, platinum, iron, tin, and copper on the surface, making them accessible to us. While metals do exist deep within Earth's core, ancient humans lacked the knowledge or technology to dig that deep. In fact, deep gold mines were not discovered and exploited until the 16th century. Instead, most of the metals used by early civilizations came from meteorite fragments scattered across Earth's surface. This is evident in artifacts such as King Tutankhamun's dagger (Egypt), a pendant from Umm el-Marra (Turkey), axes from Ugarit (Syria), an iron Buddha from Tibet, and bronze blades from China, where the spatial origin of the metals is still traceable.

Much of the gold we use today has its origins in outer space. After Earth's core was formed, meteorites bombarded the surface, enriching the planet with gold. Gold, prized for its rarity and beauty, was used by the Romans for coins, the Greeks for art and statues, and the Egyptians for personal adornment and decoration. Unsurprisingly, cultures that used gold regarded it as a divine gift, with the Aztecs even calling it the "excrement of the gods." Gold captured the imagination of conquerors, igniting wars and ambitions. It evolved from a symbol of divine favor to a powerful economic force, shaping conflicts, trade, and alliances.

From the medieval period to the Age of Discovery, Europeans sought new lands not just for religious reasons, but in the hope of discovering gold-rich civilizations like those of the Aztecs, Incas, and Maya. The quest for gold intensified well into the modern era. The 19th century Gold Rush sparked another wave of mining that solidified gold's role in the creation of the gold standard, which underpinned the global monetary system. It is also a vital component in technologies such as GPS systems and is used to protect astronauts in space, underscoring the enduring importance of this metal, which began as a gift from the stars.

THE SECOND GIFT: ANNUAL CROPS

The second crucial gift of nature that transformed human civilization was the advent of annual crops – plants like rice, wheat, flax, barley, peas, and lentils. These crops, many of which are self-pollinating, offered a distinct advantage. Their flowers contain both male and female reproductive parts, allowing them to thrive in isolated environments without the need for bees, butterflies, or human intervention. This self-sufficiency made them ideal for early agriculture, requiring less reliance on the natural world to flourish.

These "founder crops" evolved to adapt to seasonal changes, enabling them to grow, produce seeds, and mature within the limited timeframe of summer, making efficient use of the moisture remaining from the pre-winter period. Once harvested, their seeds entered a dormant state, waiting for the next summer to repeat the cycle. This rapid growth cycle made it possible for early humans to produce a surplus of food within a single year – a sustenance that could support both immediate consumption and future reproduction. Founder crops were an ideal fit for a rapidly evolving human society.

In contrast, perennial crops grow slowly, with many parts of the plant, like wood and stems, being inedible. Their fruits and flowers take years to mature, requiring far more patience than our fast-paced, goal-oriented ancestors could afford. Imagine a hunter-gatherer planting guava seeds and waiting for years for the fruit to appear. Such patience was incompatible with the urgency of human progress, which led us to create stories of gods who created the world in just seven days.

These annual crops, with their swift growth cycles, provided the perfect solution for early humans. They allowed us to gather food and reproduce within the span of a single year, much like our own rapid, innovative thinking. As human civilization spread, we adapted these crops to different climates through selective cultivation and artificial adaptation, gradually spreading them across the globe. Unfortunately, not all cultures had access to these founder crops, and some struggled with adapting them to new environments. When conditions were not ideal, some cultures turned to clonal plants like bananas, potatoes, onions, ginger, and strawberries – plants that could be propagated from their parts, such as stems or rhizomes. These crops could be mass-produced but were difficult to store for extended periods, unlike grains that could endure for much longer.

One of the greatest benefits of the annual crops was their durability. Unlike fruits like apples or grapes, which quickly decayed, grains could withstand microbial decay and long storage, providing reliable sustenance for early farmers. These sturdy seeds could not be easily eaten raw, but the discovery of fire, transforming raw grains into cooked meals, made them accessible and life-sustaining.

In many ways, these crops were seen as a gift from the divine, offering early humans the ability to sow, reap, and store food for the colder months, sparing them the constant struggle for sustenance. More importantly, they allowed time for reflection and innovation, giving rise to the intellectual pursuits that would eventually lead to enlightenment. Today, we continue to live in a fast-paced world, grabbing fast food on the go and storing leftovers for later.

TRANSPORTATION AND DOMESTICATION

As we mastered fire, we not only learned to cook our food, freeing ourselves from the long hours of chewing raw meals, but also gained precious time to think, invent, and reshape our world. With fire came the ability to smelt stronger tools – tools that enabled us to hunt more efficiently, feed larger populations, and fell greater trees to build primitive boats, allowing journeys beyond the familiar rivers.

This surplus of food and tools opened the door to one of humanity's greatest achievements: the domestication of animals. We began to tame and nurture creatures not only for meat and milk but also for their strength, companionship, protection, and labor. Sheep, chickens, dogs, pigs, cattle, and goats were among the earliest and easiest to domesticate, providing steady sources of food, labor in plowing fields, and assistance in hunting.

Using metal tools and the manpower of growing populations, we eventually succeeded in domesticating elephants, horses, camels, wolves, reindeer, yaks, and buffaloes. However, not all creatures surrendered to domestication. Despite countless attempts across cultures, many animals remained stubbornly wild. Even seemingly suitable herbivores – rhinos, zebras, bears, kangaroos, giraffes, and hippopotamuses – proved to be poor candidates. Their resistance stemmed from a range of traits: aggressive or unpredictable temperaments, difficulty to breed in captivity, inflexible diets, a lack of hierarchical social structures needed to accept human leadership, and strong migratory instincts that made them ill-suited for life under human control.

Unlike the animals that shared their strength and sustenance with us, these wild species offered little in terms of food, clothing, transportation, or labor, and thus remain untamed and wild to this day.

Up until the 19th century, domesticated animals like horses, elephants, and dogs played critical roles in warfare, agriculture, and transportation. Their strength and reliability enabled the movement of goods, the expansion of civilizations, and the growth of human population. In many ways, the domestication of animals gifted humanity not just convenience but the time and capacity to innovate, build, and imagine civilizations far greater than any lone hunter-gatherer could have ever envisioned.

THE INVENTION OF THE LOG AND THE WHEEL

Most importantly, we invented the wheel. Long before that breakthrough, we used logs and rollers to move heavy objects across rough terrain and rivers. This idea, in turn, was inspired by life itself – trees, setting the stage for ingenuity. The circular forms of trees, already used in pottery and logs, revealed two new properties: floating ability and later, continuous movement.

Fire, metals, founder crops, and domestication gave us power, time, and strength. With these, we forged tools – and with tools, we cut down trees to build weapons and houses. We harnessed animals to drag heavier timber, enabling us to construct ever greater boats. The invention of boats opened a new frontier and profession. Humanity learned to hunt fishes, and fishermen provided extra sustenance for a society while droughts destroyed crops.

The invention of the wheel stands as one of the greatest leaps in human history. It accelerated transportation on land, enabling us to move heavy objects quickly and efficiently. With boats and wheels, we could transport goods farther and faster, allowing us to cut down more trees, forge more metal tools, and build larger settlements. It transformed us from scattered societies to architects of widespread civilizations.

Transportation speed changed everything. It allowed communities to expand their reach, creating networks of long-distance communication in shorter times. Fast transportation allowed us to settle permanently. We could now travel farther and communicate across greater distances in shorter times. Information – about gods, laws, stories, and customs – could now spread rapidly, encouraging the development of language, writing systems, and record-keeping.

Farming and cooking created stability, but transportation amplified it, enabling greater surplus, trade, and innovation. This newfound security gave rise to more free time, a luxury that artisans, politicians, and priests eagerly embraced. Artisans emerged, not merely producing for sustenance but crafting new technologies to elevate daily life. Politicians emerged, not to farm but to organize, setting laws, determining prices, planning festivals, appointing soldiers, and overseeing the protection and governance of their small but growing nations. Councils of elders contrived systems of legal rights and responsibilities, ensuring order and cooperation. Priests, meanwhile, preached that the very existence of the nation was a divine gift, bestowed by gods who demanded loyalty and defense against outsiders who were branded as devil worshippers, the cursed, or the untouchable. Their work built the scaffolding of civilization, driven forward by the invention of the log and later the wheel.

THE FRICTION OF NATIONS

We are creatures of imagination, yet each of us imagines differently. To unify and control vast civilizations, we need iron hands to make many think as one. We need forces strong enough to make everyone imagine the same concepts. The Iron Age, remembered for its advancements in steel, also marked the true beginning of civil development, culture, art, philosophy, and science. But more than anything, it was an age of war.

We had already spun a complex web of mutual benefit and mutual destruction. We invented language to communicate, and used it to condition belief in money, gods, and nations. Without money, you risk death; without a nation, you become an orphan – an outsider stripped of identity. Though we didn't initially sail oceans to discover new gods, we waged relentless battles about which gods, which languages, and which cultures should prevail.

Language became both the sword and the balm. Like teeth, it could bite and wound through insults, or smile and heal by forging friendships. This power of communication built the framework of civilization, mimicking how biology itself balanced pain and pleasure. Yet, without instant communication, early societies grew isolated, and languages fractured across geographies.

What happens when you can't understand the words of another? Even a king, faced with an unknown tongue, would stand powerless, unable to charm or threaten, negotiate or command.

With the rise of steel and the invention of the wheel, comprehension expanded through conquest. To solve the chaos of countless tribes and rival hunters, emerging chiefdoms sought to unify disparate peoples, gods, and tongues under a single nation, a shared economy, a common language, and a supreme deity. Some tried, and a few succeeded. This age led to the Classical Age, Medieval Age, Renaissance, Age of Discovery, and Age of Industry. All these developments are due to mirrors, glasses, magnets, founder crops, domestic animals, wheels, boats, fire, metals, and our imaginative mind that utilizes leisure time to innovate many ideas for our benefit.

To build nations like those of the Greeks, Egyptians, Indians, Chinese, Persians, and Babylonians, it required absorbing countless tribes and clans, then organizing them under a shared system of language, culture, currency, and gods. Even among pagans, conflict brewed: whose god deserved supremacy? Which gods would rule over society?

Before Christianity, Egypt itself was torn by internal divisions. The north worshiped Re, the south revered Amen, and their conflicting beliefs sparked civil strife. After his unification of both regions, Mentuhotep II introduced a compromise: Amen-Re. But the religious tides kept shifting. Under the later Amenhotep III, Egypt began to pivot toward a new solar deity. Eventually, the kingdom embraced Atenism – a short-lived experiment in monotheism – just before it was consumed by Rome. Ironically, Rome would later adopt its own version of monotheism in the form of Christianity, and later Islam, each claiming universality. In the 20th century, another force began to replace ancient gods: the singular, global "religion" of reality – science – creating the age of information, which may lead to the age of artificial intelligence.

Interestingly, many ancient civilizations – India, China, Japan, and even Egypt – did not pursue global conquest with the same zeal to spread their gods. Colonization, for the most part, was carried out under banners bearing the names of Allah and Jesus, with a few exceptions.

Paganism, meanwhile, divided the sacred into a thousand forms: a family god, a clan god, a war god, a goddess of women, a god of water, a god of thunder, an animal god, and many more. Each fragment reflected the imagination of the people, and every aspect of existence had its own deity.

Monotheistic religion gave humanity a single God and a unified purpose and power: to gather the scattered pantheon under one divine authority. It taught that we are born sinners, burdened from the start, and that it is our sacred duty to spread the one true God to all people – to convert, to save, and to guide souls toward heaven. Earth, in this vision, is not a permanent home but a temporary testing ground where the worthy are chosen for eternal life. The story of science, at its core, is not so different.

Earth is still seen as temporary. The Sun itself, scientists tell us, will die in 5 billion years. And we must prepare to migrate to new planets, new solar systems. Only a few – those who adapt, innovate, and learn the rules of the universe – will be "naturally selected" to survive and carry life forward.

Although modern life allows for individual opinions and diverse beliefs, the dominant cultural trajectory still bends toward science, the religion of reality. Like religion, science acknowledges our internal faults, not as sins, but as biological flaws, and offers salvation through medicine, technology, and the pursuit of knowledge. And like religion, it seeks to convert – not always gently, but often through force and persuasion – spreading its doctrine across the globe in search of enlightenment.

Thus, we seek redemption not by prayers, but by experiments. We spread the gospel of science with the same fervor that once drove missionaries. In this new faith, knowledge is sacred, and ignorance is the only true sin.

RETRACING INFLUENCES

The great turning points of human civilization began with a spark: fire. It wasn't just a source of warmth or protection; fire transformed how we lived, how we ate, and eventually, how we thought. Cooking softened food, reduced chewing time, and enabled us to wean infants earlier, subtly shaping human biology and society. But fire's influence didn't stop there. It melted silver, copper, and iron, giving us weapons and tools to tame wild animals, cut down forests, and build wagons, boats, wheels, temples, and homes. It laid the foundation for agriculture, mobility, and architecture.

The founder crops yielding enough sustenance within a year gave us something new: time. With food surpluses, early farmers were no longer bound entirely to survival. In the leisure that followed the harvest, our ancestors turned inward and upward. They reflected. They imagined. They improved language, experimented with technology, and cultural ties deepened.

But as communities expanded, spoken dialects alone could no longer hold the weight of growing knowledge and social structures. Written language emerged, which became essential in managing knowledge, preserving ideas, and organizing expanding communities. Literacy enabled us to pass down ideas, myths, laws, and dreams across generations. Population growth meant not everyone had to farm. Freed from the fields, some turned to words, grammar, and the pursuit of knowledge. They sought to unite people under a common language and shared myths. In this transition, the old gods and primitive tongues began to fade into obsolescence. They were replaced by broader, more organized belief systems that could transcend tribes and borders. One set of people. One language. One story. Religion, paradoxically, became both the language of peace and the fuel for conquest. Holy ideas spread like virus – through persuasion, through trade, through war.

Yet, not all regions shared the same starting line. Some lands lacked domesticable animals, annual-yield crops, accessible metals, or burnable fuels. These communities remained hunters or formed only small chiefdoms, unable to leap into the Classical Age, Medieval Age, Renaissance, Age of Discovery, and Industry. Meanwhile, those who did have the essential resources unified diverse gods, tribes, and clans under larger banners. They built empires, forged civilizations, and looked beyond their horizons, sailing across seas to conquer and discover new lands.

As the Age of Industry drew to a close, only a few gods survived. In the battle of ideas, monotheism emerged dominant, eventually giving way to a new kind of faith: science. Even in the far reaches of Antarctica, churches still stand, marking humanity's effort to place flags of belief in every corner of the Earth.

And yet, behind all of this progress, the quiet hand of the environment was always at work. Geography, biology, and climate conspired over millennia to evolve wandering hunters into city-builders – modern and, in many ways, still seeking the next spark to carry us forward.

GIVEN CONDITION

Consider the Polynesian colonists of New Guinea and the broader South Pacific, who began settling on these islands during the 13th and 14th centuries. Though they brought with them a common foundation of tools, materials, and seafaring knowledge, the environments they encountered shaped them into vastly different societies.

Some islands, isolated by rough seas and difficult terrain, forced their settlers to revert to hunter-gatherer lifestyles. The barriers to communication and trade blocked collaboration and cultural development. Larger islands like Hawaii and New Zealand, with their high mountains and abundant rainfall, fostered agriculture and supported the growth of complex civilizations.

Meanwhile, places like the Chatham Islands lacked the climate or resources, halting the development of settled farming altogether. Others lacked the raw materials needed to enhance their agricultural practices. Some societies mastered navigation and shipbuilding, giving rise to maritime empires such as those of Hawaii and Tonga. Some turned to the sea, surviving as fishermen.

However, not all adaptations ended well. Limited resources led some communities to ecological collapse. On Easter Island, overexploitation of limited resources, particularly deforestation, led to ecological collapse, leaving behind a barren landscape dotted with enigmatic religious statues.

The availability of resources and the shape of the land profoundly affected population size and societal complexity. Islands with sparse resources and small populations had no need – or means – for specialized roles like priests, politicians, or artists. But in places of abundance and dense population, entire classes of society emerged: soldiers, artisans, spiritual leaders, lawmakers, and inventors.

Natural phenomena also played a critical role. Volcanic activity and ancient meteorite impacts scattered valuable minerals like iron, gold, bronze, flint, and copper across some islands, while leaving others devoid. The compatibility of the native animals that could be domesticated also played a crucial role, because an island with wild animals meant the settlers lacked extra power to farm, protect, navigate, and defend against such wild animals. These resource variations shaped the evolution of intelligence and survival strategies, molding human communities into farmers, hunters, artisans, and in some cases, cannibals.

Even today, the global economy moves in step with the availability of oil, coal, and gold. And in the future, it will likely follow a similar path. As we look beyond Earth, two other planets lie within the Goldilocks Zone of our solar system: Venus and Mars.

Earth is shielded by a powerful magnetic field that deflects solar winds and preserves a breathable atmosphere. Its gravity, at 9.807 m/s^2, anchors this life-sustaining layer around us. But what of our neighbors?

Venus, with a gravity of 8.87 m/s^2, lacks this protective magnetic field. Its dense CO_2-rich atmosphere exerts a crushing pressure of 92 bars, equivalent to the pressure found a kilometer beneath Earth's oceans. In such an environment, ships could potentially float in the sky, like submarines in deep seas. Yet, Venus also endures an excruciatingly slow rotation, facing the Sun for 243 Earth days at a time, and a corrosive, metal-melting climate.

Mars, by contrast, is easier to reach. But with its weaker gravity (3.71 m/s^2) it cannot hold a dense atmosphere. Travelling there is comparatively simple, but survival poses its own trials: a frozen wasteland, an almost nonexistent atmosphere, and relentless radiation.

Colonizing either world would reshape us. On Venus, we might float in airborne habitats above the lethal surface. On Mars, we may burrow into protective caverns, adapting slowly as we work to warm and transform the planet. Yet, neither option offers a simple solution. Each world will reshape us – physically, psychologically, culturally, and biologically.

But let's not forget: the universe does not coddle us. A single volcanic eruption once wiped Pompeii off the map. A rogue solar flare, a meteor impact, or a planetary tremor could render our technology irrelevant in moments. In such events, we could easily be cast back to the primitive – nomads once more, clinging to survival.

We are, in truth, refugees of existence – carried forward by evolution, tolerated by the narrow margins of a habitable reality. Each time we step beyond those margins, we push the boundaries of what it means to survive. The universe offers us both danger and opportunity. And we, in turn, exploit, adapt, and evolve.

Yet, the human form may not endure all trials. We may become obsolete, our biology outpaced by the harsh demands of cosmic migration. Just as past life forms, conscious or not, lived and died to leave for us their fossilized remains and minerals, so too may we become the foundation upon which a new life form emerges.

COAL

The same trees that once inspired us to build boats, shape wheels, and cultivate the land also left behind a hidden gift, an ancient source of energy we still rely on today. Around 305 million years ago, during the Carboniferous Rainforest Collapse, vast forests of plants and trees vanished. If these plants had simply decayed above ground, their solar energy would have faded with them. But buried under layers of sediment and intense pressure, their transformation took a different path. Oxygen was forced out, and what remained was coal – solar power preserved in carbon, awaiting the spark of fire.

Charcoal, coke, coal tar, and coal gas are the remnants – the sacrifices – of those long-extinct forests. In the beginning, we only scratched the surface, using exposed coal deposits for warmth and basic metallurgy. But by the 17th century, deep mining unlocked vast underground reserves. This was used to forge metal, wage wars, and compete with other tribes, clans, and emerging nations.

Coal became the backbone of the Industrial Revolution. Iron-making surged, laying the foundation for vehicles, weapons, roads, and railway tracks. Most crucially, it powered the steam engine, a technology that shrank the world and expanded empires, enabling faster colonization across continents, especially in Asia.

Today, the legacy continues. We now channel its energy to run machines, automate industries, and even nourish artificial intelligence. In a strange twist of fate, humans – once the beneficiaries of coal's warmth – are now its stewards, processing it to feed the machines that may someday replace us.

BLACK GOLD

Another powerful energy source came from ancient, unseen sacrifices, long before our written histories began. Crude oil, famously known as black gold, illuminates our nights and fuels both progress and conflict. Without oil, our modern world would grind to a halt. No electricity, no airplanes, no cars, no industry, no construction, no nightlife, no roads, no particle colliders, no factories – no ease of modern living. Strip away oil, gas, and coal, and we would regress to the Medieval Age.

Even solar energy, often hailed as our sustainable salvation, relies on oil-based technologies for its production. Panels, batteries, and supporting infrastructure are still built using materials processed with fossil fuels.

Contrary to popular belief, the oil and gas we depend on didn't come from dinosaurs. Instead, they were formed millions of years ago during the Mesozoic era, when vast quantities of plankton, algae, and microscopic organisms died and sank to the seafloor. Over time, immense pressure and anaerobic bacterial decomposition transformed this biomass into a waxy organic substance called kerogen. With further compression by layers of sediment, volcanic activity, and even meteor strikes, the kerogen evolved into oil and methane-rich gas. From these, we extract and refine kerosene, petroleum, diesel, propane, asphalt, and a host of other vital products.

China was among the first to utilize oil and gas. As early as 300 bce, the Chinese used bamboo pipelines to harness natural gas seeping from the ground. With ingenuity and simplicity, they used these bamboo channels to light their cities and drill wells, fueling fire and even boiling seawater for salt extraction. A plant – bamboo – like the gears and wheels it later inspired, became an early tool in controlling energy. Long before oil rigs and offshore platforms, bamboo carried energy through early civilizations.

We never consumed oil as food, but we burned it to cook, to drive, to illuminate, and to electrify. It became the bloodstream of modern civilization. And it became a reason for war. From the Gulf Wars and the Iran-Iraq conflict to the Falklands and the Chaco War, oil has been at the heart of global strife. Oil shaped geopolitics, forged alliances, and fractured others. Today, it is a multi-trillion-dollar industry, requiring ships, drilling rigs, pipelines, refineries, and labor-intensive infrastructure to keep the flow going.

Yet, beyond Earth, Saturn's moon Titan contains more liquid hydrocarbons than all of Earth's reserves combined. Could Titan be our future fueling station in the age of space colonization? By then, perhaps we will synthesize hydrocarbons from quantum matter, guided by nanorobots altering reality at its most fundamental level.

The sacrifice of ancient life has helped us build order, fuel growth, and sustain the human form. But just as past organisms became the fuel for our existence, so too might our extinction one day serve another. In history, some of our most pivotal actions were taken with limited knowledge, driven by instinct, pressure, or necessity. Can we ever say with certainty that our choices are truly conscious? Or are we moved by the unseen currents of influence, survival, and chance?

TRIVIAL EFFECTS

Even the most unassuming materials found in nature have quietly transformed the course of human society. Take diamonds and sapphires, two brilliant materials formed under intense heat and pressure deep within the Earth, each born through distinct geological processes. Though often seen as symbols of luxury, their true influence stretches far beyond ornamentation.

Diamonds, for instance, are essential in precision cutting, automotive engineering, optics, dental tools, military equipment, and industrial drilling. Sapphires, too, find use in infrared technologies, medical instruments, high-end jewelry, and semiconductor production. Surprisingly, both also played a role in shaping the music industry.

In the 19th century, Thomas Edison created the phonograph using a diamond stylus to etch sound onto a cylinder. This breakthrough marked the beginning of recorded music, transforming music from a fleeting, live experience into a commodity that could be owned, replayed, and distributed. Later, Emile Berliner refined the idea with the gramophone, replacing the cylinder with a flat disc. Before this, music could only be heard in the presence of a musician. Even kings had to summon musicians if they wished to hear a favorite piece again. But recording technology changed that. But the arrival of recorded sound democratized access, turning music into a form of abstract entertainment and nurturing the rise of individual expression in the 20th century.

Even the stars and the Moon have left their imprint on human history. On May 28, 585 bce, during the Battle of the Eclipse between the Lydians and the Medes, a total solar eclipse turned daylight into darkness. The sudden, awe-inspiring event stunned both armies and ended a six-year conflict. A similar eclipse on October 2, 480 bce, brought an abrupt halt to hostilities between the Spartans and the Persians. In ancient times, eclipses were often viewed as divine omens. Kings, generals, and priests would alter plans and policies based on these celestial events, unaware of the science behind them.

Even today, many people continue to believe in astrology, drawn to the idea that stars determine fate. But constellations have offered practical value beyond myth. Long before satellites and magnetic compasses, sailors navigated vast oceans using star patterns as guides. The North Star, Orion, and the Southern Cross served as ancient GPS for explorers and traders. In fact, even in the early 20th century, mariners relied on tools like the sextant and astrolabe, celestial instruments that traced positions based on constellations. To this day, agencies like NASA utilize star maps in space exploration and interplanetary navigation.

From the deepest trenches of Earth to the farthest stars, seemingly trivial things have often played a pivotal role. What appears small at the moment, may, in time, shape the very arc of our collective journey.

We are abstract beings, capable of attaching profound significance to lifeless objects. And those objects, imbued with our beliefs and emotions, often go on to influence the course of human history in profound and often tragic ways.

Consider the War of the Oaken Bucket in 1325, where two rival factions in Italy clashed over a stolen wooden bucket, a conflict that left more than 4,000 people dead. Fast forward to 1969, the Football War between El Salvador and Honduras erupted in the wake of a World Cup qualifying match. The tensions were rooted in deeper political and social issues, but football – a game – became the matchstick.

It might seem absurd, but symbols hold power because we give them power. Burn a sacred book like the Bible or the Quran in a public forum today, and you might spark international conflict. After all, it's "just a book." Yet, throughout history, scriptures have ignited bloodshed on a massive scale – the Roman-Jewish Wars, the Crusades, the Inquisition, the Thirty Years' War, the Taiping Rebellion, the Mahdi Revolt, and countless *jihads*. All born from belief projected onto a text.

Take the War of the Golden Stool in 1900. The British Empire, in its imperial arrogance, demanded the Ashanti people of West Africa surrender their sacred golden stool to the Queen. To the British, it was a symbol of submission. Instead, a fierce resistance broke out. Though the Ashantis were ultimately overwhelmed and their leaders imprisoned, the British never got the stool. To the Ashanti, it was the soul of their nation.

It may sound trivial – a war over a stool? Yes. Just as people have killed for less. For money – paper inscribed with numbers and digits on a screen – we commit acts of cruelty, corruption, and crime. Blackmail, kidnapping, war – all in the pursuit of currency. Kings and empires have waged wars for land, another abstraction, drawn on maps and marked by flags. Even today, national borders and banners command more loyalty and reverence than many human lives.

And today? We don't die for stools or buckets, but for brands and beliefs. Our fictions shape our reality. Today, we die for ideologies, technology, and identities. Tomorrow, it may be for data or digital tokens. In this strange cycle of obsolescence, even something as simple as eggs and bird droppings have left their mark on history.

EGGS AND POOP

Birds have always played an intricate role in our lives – not just biologically, but symbolically. Our myths and stories often feature feathers and wings. Angels, the messengers of the divine, are imagined with bird-like wings, reflecting our deep yearning to escape the pull of the Earth and rise toward freedom or heaven. Perhaps we would have found our way to flight eventually, but watching birds glide effortlessly through the skies surely accelerated our ambition to follow them. Beyond dreams and symbolism, birds have also sustained us in the most practical ways. From the simplest breakfasts to the most exquisite birthday cakes, eggs are foundational to our diets. In fact, without them, feeding the ever-increasing human population may become an even greater challenge.

After the California Gold Rush of 1848, San Francisco's population boomed with fortune-seekers, but while they found gold, they didn't find enough food. Scarcity led to inflation, and the quality of life deteriorated. Desperation drove people to look beyond chickens, leading to the egg war in the 1860s. Soon, they discovered nearby islands teeming with murre eggs. Humans have long adapted, consuming not just chicken eggs but those of ducks, turkeys, quails, emus, ostriches, even snakes and turtles. Eggs, in all their forms, have become a critical buffer between hunger and survival.

But birds provided more than just eggs. In a strange twist of nature, we came to depend on their waste as well.

On Chincha Island off the coast of Peru, seabirds found a predator-free paradise. For millions of years, they nested there, undisturbed. They pooped. And over those years, they left behind vast quantities of guano – bird excrement – rich in nitrogen and phosphorus. With little rainfall to wash it away, it accumulated undisturbed, forming thick, nutrient-rich deposits.

In the 19th century, as the world struggled with food shortages, the scientist Fritz Haber discovered the importance of nitrogen for crop growth. Guano became a strategic resource, as valuable as oil or gold. Amid wars, famines, and the race to feed growing populations, countries scrambled to secure these deposits. The competition grew so intense it sparked the Guano War between Spain and Chile, lasting from 1865 to 1879. Even the United States joined the frenzy, passing the Guano Islands Act in 1856 to legally annex any unclaimed islands with guano reserves.

All of this – wars, legislation, international expeditions – just to feed our plants, so that we could, in turn, feed ourselves. And yet, this is only one example of how deeply trees and plants have shaped the course of human history.

WILD GUESS

Plants and trees have quietly shaped the course of human innovation. They inspired the invention of boats and wheels, and even played a role in the development of opposable thumbs, indirectly supporting our evolution. From oil seeds and coal to paper, shade, and food, they've provided the raw materials that sustain and shelter us. Even modern elastics and rubbers originate from the rubber tree, whose latex remains essential to industry and manufacturing.

Before metals became commonplace, our ancestors used sharp thorns or even animal bones as makeshift needles for stitching clothes. And when it came to the idea of screws and bolts, who's to say we didn't learn from plants? Consider the humble grapevine. Its spiraling tendrils, designed to latch onto nearby supports, may have inspired early engineers in ancient Greece. These natural coils likely influenced the invention of the Archimedean screw, used for irrigation, extracting grape juice for wine, and removing bilge water from ships. That same spiraling logic, born in vineyards, would later evolve into wooden screws, and eventually, into coiled springs. And what did springs give us? Comfort, in the form of cushioned furniture. Precision, in the form of clocks. Power, in the form of automatic guns.

The invention of the springs and wheels, likely inspired by the rolling of logs, transformed not only transportation but also craftsmanship. It, in turn, evolved into more complex engineering concepts like gears. Gears liberated us from the limitations of domesticated animals. With bicycles, motorbikes, and eventually cars, we gained mechanical companions – slaves of metal – that didn't need rest, food, or affection.

Gears gave rise to machines that could lift stones heavier than any oxen, carve through mountains, and power the very heart of modern industry. In ancient times, they turned the wheels of flour mills, sawmills, windmills, water mills, hammer mills – each a testament to the ingenuity sparked by something as simple as a circular motion.

Even before humans crafted boats or ships, wood had already become a vessel for life. Long before we built ships to transport species across the oceans, broken logs drifting in storms and floods carried animals across oceans. In a process called sweepstakes colonization, storms and floods turned broken tree trunks into rafts, ferrying life from one land to another. New World monkeys and capybaras, for example, are believed to have rafted from Africa to South America some 30 million years ago. More recently, in 1995, fifteen iguanas were documented rafting from Guadeloupe to Anguilla during a hurricane, clinging to vegetation torn loose by the storm. Imagine how many animals, seeds, and eggs have silently traveled the globe, ferried by tree trunks and branches across floodwaters and tsunamis. How many ecosystems were forever changed by a single tree swept out to sea?

But trees and plants are not just passive bystanders in nature. They use poisons to kill rivals and drugs to attract servants. These rooted strategists use chemistry – poisons and narcotics – to manipulate and control bees, butterflies, birds, and even humans. They entice with sweet fruits like mangoes, melons, and apples, deceiving us into consuming them. But once we hit the bitter core, we spit out the seeds, unknowingly becoming agents of their expansion. In their stillness, plants have engineered a quiet conquest of the planet.

DRUG-DRIVEN MIND

The psychedelic properties of certain leaves, plants, mushrooms, and trees have long served as gateways to altered states of consciousness. These substances have allowed humans to expand their perception, mute emotional noise, enhance focus, and help grasp abstract concepts or spiritual realms. From ritualistic ceremonies to solitary introspection, psychoactive plants have shaped both personal experiences and collective traditions.

Tea and coffee sharpen our minds, helping us stay alert and productive. Alcohol, be it vodka, wine, or beer, offers moments of relaxation. More potent substances like marijuana, cocaine, and opium offer escape from pain, memory, and the burdens of social expectation, often unlocking heightened sensory states that make us feel as if we are communing with gods.

Perhaps it was the very potency of such substances that played a role in anchoring ancient civilizations like the Aztecs, Mayans, Olmecs, Incas, Moche, and Caral in their homelands. Tobacco, even today, is known to isolate users in cycles of addiction; what if ancient psychoactive rituals had a similar social effect on a larger scale? Imagine a society where leaders – kings, priests, warriors – were deeply entangled in substances and guided not by political ambition or divine conquest, but by substances that brought them closer to an inner, altered realm of truth. And yet, only a sober leader can orchestrate the construction of vast ships, navigate open seas, and direct the spread of empire or religion.

Consider the Maya, whose stone cities, like El Mirador, rose from the jungle as testaments to their architectural genius. El Mirador, one of the greatest Maya cities, was eventually abandoned, perhaps because of political unrest, religious shifts, or simply the immense ecological and economic burden of sustaining such a monumental urban center. Unlike European powers that sailed to convert or conquer, many Native American cultures saw no need to expand across distant shores. Their spiritual thirst was quenched not by spreading beliefs outward, but by diving deeper within. While other civilizations forged empires across seas, some native societies may have been content with spiritual exploration over geographic expansion. Perhaps their intellectual and spiritual cravings – for gods, for mystery, for meaning – were satisfied through ritual intoxication. The Incas, for example, never developed the wheel for practical transportation, only for children's toys. Part of this was geographical, due to their mountainous terrain that favored suspension bridges over roads. And the horses that once roamed the Americas went extinct during the Ice Age, likely due to human overhunting, leaving the continent without large domesticable animals for travel or warfare.

This absence of certain technologies left Native Americans especially vulnerable when the Europeans arrived with ships made from trees, steel-forged guns, and domesticated horses. It's tempting to speculate that, had the indigenous peoples not been so deeply rooted in religious festivals that included psychoactive rituals, they might have migrated, explored, or expanded differently. Their plant-based drugs, used communally in dances and ceremonies, induced euphoria and visionary experiences – pathways to spiritual connection and communication with nature. These experiences may have fostered contentment with the world as it was, rather than evoking a need to change it. Substances like cacao, tobacco, salvia, ayahuasca, jimson weed, and peyote connected them with nature and divinity. But they may have also lulled them into contentment when discontent might have sparked invention, expansion, and resistance.

In contrast to many ancient traditions, Christianity after the 15th century began distancing itself from ritual intoxication. While alcohol had once flowed freely through the spiritual and social ceremonies of ancient Europe, Mesopotamia, China, and North Africa, it was eventually stripped from Christian liturgical life. Alcohol was not condemned as inherently sinful, but its exclusion from the church marked a clear break from its former religious role. This shift toward sobriety may have contributed to a new kind of clarity, pushing people toward more grounded pursuits, such as scientific enquiry and philosophical reflection. Yet, in daily life, alcohol consumption remained widespread.

Even as some religious institutions distanced themselves from it, most societies continued to cultivate and consume psychoactive substances. Every civilization cultivated and consumed mind-altering plants in some form. In ancient Mesopotamia, Greece, and Egypt, beer and wine were central to celebration and ritual. In Ethiopia, the cola tree (from which coffee seeds come) was both consumed and traded. The plant eventually reached Arabia, where coffee culture began to flourish and spread back into Mesopotamia.

In South Africa, tribal communities discovered cannabis, often used during prayer and spiritual rituals. Opium, originally used by the Sumerians as a medicinal painkiller, became a widely cultivated crop and was distributed across Egypt, Assyria, and Rome. Over time, cannabis, coffee, wine, and opium all found their place along the Silk Road, linking China, India, and Rome in a network of trade, ritual, and intoxication.

In Asia, the spiritual and psychological uses of these plants were deeply rooted in cultural identity and spiritual life. In ancient India, the use of betel nuts and leaves was nearly universal, while cannabis, traded via the Silk Road, was widely cultivated and consumed. Hindu traditions revered the plant to such a degree that it was included in the *Atharvaveda* as one of the five sacred herbs: neem, tulsi, sandalwood, jasmine, and cannabis. It is said that Lord Shiva himself consumed it, inspiring generations of sadhus to use the plant as a pathway to inner peace and mental stillness.

Elsewhere in Asia, wine, cannabis, and other drugs were used in subtler, more refined ways. Leaves were often boiled to create soothing teas, or dried and smoked for medicinal or contemplative purposes. This led to the discovery of tea as both a calming drink and a meditative aid – not only for monks, but also for kings and generals in their strategic planning.

Asian philosophies, particularly those rooted in Buddhism, Taoism, and Vedanta, emphasize finding happiness within, detaching from the external world and its harsh realities. Many other Eastern philosophies emphasize contentment detached from material suffering, encouraging introspection and emotional balance over conquest or accumulation. But human greed and imagination have dominated in many cultures, with little influence of drug consumption.

Still, the power of these plants was not universally pacifying. In other corners of the world, psychoactive substances became political tools, economic prizes, or triggers of conflict.

WAR FOR TEA

During colonial times, the British developed a growing appetite for tea. While the Portuguese were the first to introduce tea to Europe, China remained the sole producer and strictly guarded its cultivation methods from foreign powers. For many years, China controlled the trade with an iron grip.

This began to shift in 1662, when Portuguese princess Catherine of Braganza married King Charles II of England. Along with her dowry came crates of Chinese tea, which gradually spread from aristocratic circles to the general public. At the time, Europe was still recovering from the devastation of the bubonic plague, which had killed nearly 15% of the population. The weakened economy and distrust of contaminated water made tea a safer and more appealing alternative to beer and wine. In the wake of that devastation, tea emerged not only as a cleaner, safer beverage than alcohol, but also as a sober stimulant that invigorated the mind.

Beyond its health benefits, tea offered mental clarity. Unlike alcohol, it sharpened the senses and provided a sober stimulant, perhaps even fueling the minds that turned away from religious dogma toward the "religion" of reality: science. But tea was expensive. Too expensive. Importing it from China drained British resources, prompting the East India Company to seek more profitable means. Their strategy was both calculated and ruthless. In British-occupied India, they cultivated opium and sugarcane, using the profits from opium sales in China to fund tea imports. As tea consumption soared across Britain and its colonies, so too did opium addiction in China.

When the Chinese Emperor attempted to ban opium imports, Britain responded not with diplomacy but with force. Thus began the First Opium War (1839–1842), a brutal conflict fueled not by ideology or territory, but by addiction and profit. The Second Opium War (1856–1860) only deepened Britain's grip, not just over trade but over China's very sovereignty. In a bold move, the British dispatched botanist Robert Fortune, disguised in Chinese attire, on a mission to infiltrate tea-growing regions and steal seeds and cultivation secrets. His success allowed the British to establish large-scale tea plantations in India, breaking China's monopoly and dramatically boosting the colonial economy.

What began as a trade for a simple beverage escalated into one of history's most consequential narcotic conflicts. The legality and manipulation of drug trade, from tea to opium, altered the trajectory of nations, reshaped economies, and redefined the boundaries of power in ways history had never seen before.

DECISION DIVERGED

Coffee, like tea, has played a pivotal role in shaping human history. Even today, it fuels minds across the globe, sharpening focus and boosting awareness. For many, the day doesn't begin until that first cup is consumed. Even Albert Einstein was known to be a regular consumer, favoring black tea and coffee to power his extraordinary mind.

Coffee originated in the highlands of Ethiopia and made its way to Yemen, where it was cultivated, traded, and slowly adopted into the rituals and daily life of the Islamic world. From the fringes of the Islamic world between the 12th and 15th centuries, it moved into markets and minds alike, becoming a drink of intellect and interaction.

At the same time, the Islamic Golden Age was flourishing. The Arabic world had already embraced the concept of zero, pioneered algebra, and led advancements in medicine – introducing ideas about microorganisms as the root of disease and fever as a defensive response. During this period, countless works of Greek, Persian, and Hindu origins were translated into Arabic as part of the Abbasid Translation Movement, a monumental effort to unify global knowledge.

Coffee only enhanced this intellectual momentum, and *qahwa khanas* – early coffeehouses – emerged as social hubs and provided spaces where scholars, poets, and philosophers gathered to share knowledge and discoveries, and debate. The Islamic world's reach extended deep into the Silk Road network, stretching from North Africa, Egypt, and Rome to Northern India, Spain, Italy, Romania, Greece, and parts of Central Asia. Meanwhile, Christian nations, with limited access, looked westward toward the Americas and Australia for new opportunities.

However, a turning point came with the Mongol invasion in the 13th century. The once-flourishing Abbasid Caliphate, a beacon of scientific curiosity, was slowly reduced to ruins – its strength already weakened by the Crusades. In contrast, Europe, having acquired new territories like America in the 15th century, became the next epicenter of scientific and philosophical awakening.

Coffee, in the meantime, made its way to South India via a wandering monk, before being smuggled into Dutch hands and gradually spreading across Europe. As the legend goes, in the 16th century, Pope Clement VIII famously declared coffee "satanic," but upon tasting it, he reversed course, baptized the beans, and declared coffee a divine gift. This symbolic act marked a cultural shift, allowing the drink to energize the minds that would ignite the Age of Enlightenment and the Industrial Revolution.

In contrast, the Islamic world responded with resistance. In 1511, Khair Beg, the governor of Mecca, banned coffee, fearing its influence on public discourse and thought. Later, the great Sultan Suleiman outlawed it after witnessing how coffee houses stirred radical ideas. In the 1600s, Sultan Murad IV went so far as to punish, even execute, those who consumed or sold coffee. Throughout the 17th century, coffee was frequently considered haram, and along with it came a broader resistance to scientific enquiry and innovation.

Meanwhile, Christian countries moved in the opposite direction. Encouraged by both faith and intellectual curiosity, it embraced new inventions and ideas, setting the stage for an era of unprecedented scientific, industrial, and cultural advancement.

In 1655, a small gathering of minds at the Oxford Coffee Club opened the door to spirited conversations and scientific enquiry. That humble beginning eventually evolved into the Royal Society, an institution that would shape modern science. Coffee, much like tea, became more than a beverage; it became a catalyst for thought, discourse, and progress.

Coffee and tea began spreading across the globe: Brazil, Indonesia, Peru, India, the island of Java, Colombia, and Vietnam. The Turkish, Portuguese, French, Spanish, and Dutch became the leading architects of the global coffee trade, particularly in Vietnam. Meanwhile, the British held a firm grip on tea in the American colonies. However, a miscalculated tax hike pushed the colonists toward rebellion, and inadvertently, toward coffee.

In 1773, American colonists, disguised as Native Americans, tossed 342 chests of British tea into Boston Harbor in defiance of a tax they deemed unjust. The Boston Tea Party didn't just spark the American Revolution; it also marked coffee as a patriotic symbol. As tea became a symbol of oppression, coffee emerged as a patriotic alternative. As British tea lost its foothold, coffee from Brazil became the drink of liberty, warming hearts and powering minds in the fight for independence.

By the 19th century, the Industrial Revolution was in full motion. Coffee became indispensable, fueling the factory floors and keeping laborers alert on relentless production lines. It fueled long shifts, sharpened focus, and kept the gears of productivity turning. During this time, the British also reasserted dominance over parts of the former Ottoman Empire, including India and Pakistan. European powers expanded their reach across America, Africa, and Australia, drawing on these regions for knowledge, labor, and resources to compete with Islamic influence in global affairs.

During the First and Second World Wars, caffeine remained a silent ally. Instant coffee kept soldiers alert in the trenches, ready to fight, operate machinery, and adapt to the demands of mechanized warfare. But the legacy of psychoactive substances didn't stop at the battlefield. Throughout the 20th and 21st centuries, substances like coffee, tea, and more potent drugs influenced generations of scientists, inventors, filmmakers, artists, philosophers, and leaders. Their stimulated minds gave birth to abstract theories, philosophical revolutions, boundary-pushing films, iconic cartoons, addictive reality shows, and cultural landmarks. America, in particular, became a cultural juggernaut, exporting its stories, news, and ideals across the globe. Hollywood rose to a level of global recognition once reserved for deities and myths.

Yet, this cultural dominance came at a cost. Many nations, while exporting entertainment and innovation, also faced internal battles – especially on the streets, where the war on drugs left deep social scars. As the chemical addictions of the past evolved, a new form of dependency emerged.

Today, we sit entranced before screens; smartphones and computers have become the new substances. We now scroll endlessly, seeking novelty and stimulation, caught in feedback loops of digital addiction. Like drugs, these machines hijack our attention, while only a few manage to remain resistant. Much like the psychoactive substances of the past, these digital tools shape our behavior and feed our desires. The few who resist the pull take on the role of digital farmers. Developers and designers now work like farmers, clearing digital land, sowing sustainable designs, planting code, irrigating with user research, fertilizing ideas, weeding out spams, securing systems from malware, and harvesting meaningful digital experiences. Just as ancient farmers nurtured their fields to cultivate sustenance, today's technologists cultivate cognitive environments, seeking not just to consume, but to grow, protect, and evolve the human experience in this ever-connected age. From leaves to light, from roots to routers, the story of stimulation continues.

INVISIBLE INFLUENCES

It is not just visible substances like coffee or opium that have shaped human history. Not all forces that shape history are visible. Viruses and bacteria, often unseen and unnoticed, have quietly altered the fate of empires, reshaped societies, and redefined human behavior in ways that rival the influence of any war or invention.

Take smallpox, for instance. In 16th century Europe, it ravaged populations, but survivors developed a form of immunity. This immunity would later play a brutal role in conquest. When Spanish conquistadors reached the Americas, the same disease decimated native populations. The Aztec and Inca peoples, who had never encountered such pathogens to develop immunity, died in overwhelming numbers. It was not swords or cannons, but disease that gave Europeans their swiftest and most decisive victory and one of the easiest and most devastating conquests in recorded history.

Long before that, during the height of the Roman Empire, the Antonine Plague (possibly smallpox or measles) destabilized one of history's greatest superpowers. Between 165 and 180 ce, it killed millions, weakening Rome from within. Later, the bubonic plague – known as the Plague of Justinian – haunted the Byzantine Empire, weakening it significantly. This gradual erosion made way for the eventual siege and fall of Constantinople in 1453, when the Ottomans sealed the end of the Byzantine empire.

In other cases, disease didn't just reshape empires; it changed human behavior. Syphilis, upon its spread in the 16th century, introduced a new fear around intimacy. In response, the Italian anatomist Gabriele Falloppio developed an early version of the condom. By the 19th century, with the rise of rubber technology, condoms became more accessible. Just in time, the rise of HIV/AIDS in the late 20th century once again made the condom not just a tool of pleasure or prevention, but a necessity for survival.

In recent history, perhaps no force has shifted the human trajectory as quietly and powerfully as the COVID-19 pandemic. Beyond its toll on health and economies, it gently nudged billions of people into a deeper digital existence. Isolation became a catalyst. Computers, social media, web design, programming, and virtual communication, once niche or optional, suddenly became necessary lifelines. People learned to communicate through machines, not out of preference, but out of survival.

Between 2020 and 2022, global Internet usage surged from around 50% to over 75%. This explosive growth inspired software engineers and developers to craft smarter, more engaging platforms, refining user experiences and building increasingly immersive virtual worlds. Today, people can purchase AI companions, engage in immersive gaming, binge-watch endless videos, join global conversations, and devour e-books – all without leaving their rooms. The digital has become not just a convenience, but a primary mode of being.

This digital surge demanded more from our machines: more memory, constant electricity, robust cybersecurity, and frequent software updates. Our virtual spaces now have to be defended as we once guarded physical borders. Technology began to require as much care and upkeep as any living system. In a quiet revolution, data became substance, and digital interaction became a new form of social life. Remote relationships became normalized. Vicarious experiences started to feel real.

This shift doesn't mean that robots will rise to rule or replace us entirely. Just as dogs and cats have found their place in our homes and hearts, humans will remain vital in the emerging machine ecosystem. While many traditional jobs may shift toward automation and artificial intelligence, our role in shaping, guiding, and coexisting with technology will remain essential. Still, the future is not fixed. History is fluid. Evolution is unpredictable. There may be entirely new forms of consciousness, new ecosystems, or even life from distant parts of the universe that may one day influence our world just as microbes did.

IMAGINE THE FUTURE

The way we are now – complex, intelligent, emotional – is the result of everything within us and everything around us. Our genes shape our biology, while our imagined constructs – individuality, nationhood, spirituality – shape our beliefs and behaviors, but also because of everything that has ever surrounded us. And all of it, both real and imagined, has always existed within the same vast container: space.

Sand particles, clouds, rocks, gravity, nuclear force, rain, rainbows, roses, thunder, earthquakes, tsunamis, hurricanes, snow. Wheels, steel, bronze, gold, diamonds, silver. Fish, birds, books, buckets, eclipses, the lunar cycle, mirrors, glasses, art, tools, machines, technology, cinema, statues. Plants, trees, insects, flags, farts, feces, fossils, coal, oil, eggs, thorns, fruit, flowers, fire, germs, drugs, words. All of these, and more, have shaped us into the thinking, feeling beings we are today. We feel blessed when we see a rainbow, but anxious when thunder cracks above us.

If robots and aliens are to enter the great stage of history, what kind of peace will we forge? How will we coexist? Whose god will we all pray to? What if aliens don't feel pain, like clams, sea sponges, or trees? What if they don't eat at all but photosynthesize, like plants, pea aphids, leaf slugs, or the solar-powered spotted salamander? What if their consciousness is collective, ruled by a biological queen or god-like monarch, with hierarchies of workers and warriors, like ants or bees? What if they don't even have a brain, but expand and adapt, controlling their environment like fungi, jellyfish, corals, or germs – quietly spreading their image across galaxies? We already have plants in labs controlling machines, guiding small vehicles toward sunlight. So perhaps, nothing is out of the question. Maybe one day we'll encounter octopus overlords or a spider regime ruling from the stars.

We, the so-called children of God, have lived through war and peace. Our bond with one another isn't built only on love, altruism, and kindness; it's also forged in our capacity to hurt, to exploit, to hate, and to destroy. We understand each other's strengths and weaknesses, and that knowledge binds us, for better or worse. "I respect you, so you must respect me." This isn't just an ideal; it's a warning embedded in history. When strangers disrespect each other, violence often follows. We've seen it again and again.

Even our relationship with our own bodies is paradoxical. We inject anesthesia and cut ourselves open, slicing through skin and muscle without hesitation. Yet, it is pain that teaches us to care. Without it, we might abandon life altogether, choosing blind faith in the afterlife over the challenges of living. Yet, the body also gives us pleasure, reasons to stay, to love, to survive.

That's the paradox: we live with a body that brings both delight and suffering. That tension is at the heart of reality. It is the bittersweet bond that all living beings share. This is the nature of life.

XII. ALIENS AND A BITTERSWEET BOND

Did life want to be a human? A bird? A snail, a spider – or a god? The very idea of life and form exists because the environment never allowed perfect control over matter without compromise. Perfection, if it existed, was unattainable in the wild chaos of reality. Life could not design itself without compromise. It had to adjust, adapt, and emerge through the trial of reality. And so, what emerged were adaptations – imperfect forms learning to survive.

We are one such adapted form, constantly striving toward an imagined absolute, shaping and reshaping the environment to escape hostility, to feed, to learn, and to evolve. What we desired was the form of a god. What we became was shaped by the unyielding rules of reality and the serendipitous resources that happened to be available, accessible, or compatible. But the world was vast, and life, ever restless, diverged and scattered into countless forms. Each life form took what it needed: energy, structure, even ideas, from other lives. Existence became a competition of mind and matter, of influence and control, all in pursuit of becoming the masters of existence.

Humans are no exception. We are the refined robbers of nature. We, too, have stolen from nature and from each other in our restless ascent toward dominance. We absorb energy, adapt behaviors, and reinvent ideas. Every innovation is a subtle theft from what once simply was.

ROBBERS

Throughout history, we have been expert robbers. We have long harnessed the energy of animals for our own advancement. In transportation, we've relied on camels, elephants, and oxen; in farming, on worms, bees, donkeys, and buffaloes. Owls, frogs, and ferrets have helped with pest control. Dogs and wolves have assisted in hunting and protection, while dolphins and dogs have been used in search and rescue missions. We've used pigeons and falcons for delivering messages and seabirds and turtles for navigation.

Animals have been sacrificed – sheep, deer, pigs – for rituals to satisfy our belief, and as food for our belly. They've marched with us into war: horses on battlefields, elephants in ancient armies. For entertainment, we've put cocks in rings, parrots on stages, monkeys in circuses, seals in shows, and kangaroos in boxing gloves. Today, our digital world is saturated with cat videos, and many of our most iconic characters – Batman, Spiderman, Mickey Mouse, Scooby-doo, the Ninja Turtles, Wolverine, Tom, and Jerry – are inspired by animals.

Beyond labor and entertainment, animals have provided us with tangible resources: meat, milk, cheese, butter, fur, silk, leather, and wool. We've kept them as pets to fulfill emotional needs and used them in laboratories to pursue knowledge.

Plants, too, have fed our bodies and our ideas. Fruits and vegetables have fueled civilizations. Flowers and their fragrances have shaped human emotions, deepened relationships, brought peace to grief, and even stirred economies. The 17th century tulip mania is a striking example of how deeply nature's beauty can intoxicate an economy.

We mimicked the world to master it. We borrowed the concept of wheels, gears, and boats from plant life. Drone propellers were inspired by maple seeds and dandelions. From wood we constructed our homes, temples, bridges, tools, furniture, musical instruments, vehicles, fences, and the very paper on which our stories are printed. Swiss engineer George de Mestral created Velcro after noticing how burrs clung to his dog's fur. The ant colony optimization algorithm, now used in robotics, logistics, and network routing, was inspired by insect behavior. The Wright brothers studied birds to give flight to humans. High-speed drone aerodynamics owe much to the peregrine falcon, and Japan's Shinkansen bullet train took cues from the kingfisher's beak to reduce noise and improve efficiency.

Even within our own social and cultural evolution, we have stolen the energy, intellect, and innovations of others. Take printing technology, for example. First developed by the Chinese in the 9th century, it was later adopted and adapted by Korean and Japanese scholars and monks. Through the bustling routes of the Silk Road between the 13th and 14th centuries, this knowledge made its way to the Middle East, where Arab innovators further refined the craft. Eventually, the concept reached Europe, where it was transformed and widely implemented, not just to store and share knowledge, but to communicate strategies during war, to shape ideologies, and to build nations. Every great advancement, it seems, has passed through many hands – sometimes respectfully, sometimes exploitatively.

We have always taken – energy, ideas, forms, and functions – from others, living or not. Our progress has always depended on the world around us. But rarely have we asked for permission before taking.

In the beginning, life had no idea how to survive. Confronted with toxic elements and harsh conditions, it gradually learned the rules of reality, learning to tolerate, adapt, and endure. Life believed in itself, but the environment didn't. So life was forced to study its surroundings and invent organic strategies – biological ideas – to evolve, expand, and persist. Over time, life didn't just adapt to the environment; it reshaped it.

Ultimately, life transformed the environment into its offspring, reshaping it into a niche tailored to its survival and comfort. What once was raw, indifferent matter now takes the form of horns, fins, legs, wings, human children, sofas, refrigerators, air conditioners, laptops, phones, vehicles, houses, and countless other extensions of living beings' needs and imagination. Just as burning lava cools into rock when it meets water, life transforms hostile elements into supportive niches for survival and convenience. Every form of life evolved ideas specific to its conditions – ways to adapt, defend, and attack – creating a ripple of evolutionary innovation that drew the attention of others.

Like stars accumulating mass and pulling planets into their gravitational field, life's most compelling ideas attract and absorb others. To protect themselves or to dominate, organisms developed unique traits that inspired others to evolve or to steal. The powerful ideas of life forms draw others in. The elephant grew large and strong, yet became dominated by smaller beings. Humans domesticated elephants to carry timber, fight in wars, and use them in the stories of myths and religions. Some animals, like the elephant, allowed domestication. Others resisted and were hunted, shot, and confined to zoos.

SHARE OR STEAL

The first person to conceive the idea of God and life after death likely faced ridicule – even blasphemy. Yet, they shared this vision with family, friends, neighbors, and the wider community, slowly weaving a network of belief, connection, and cooperation. But for such an idea to take root, a shared language must have already existed – a common biological and cognitive reality to make communication possible. After all, we can't teach a monkey to pray to a monkey god or to earn money.

We share our genetic information by assembling atoms into proteins, and through that intricate biological process, we begin to rewrite reality, making life more real. In doing so, we make our ideas real. We consume, stealing energy and matter from other living beings like goats, chickens, and cows. This stolen energy is then adapted to suit our needs, enabling us to control, share, create, and ultimately expand our dominion. Sharing gives information permanence and power. It defends ideas against being dismissed as heresy, because when many depend on an idea to exist and express themselves, it evolves into a collective truth.

But once an idea gains power and dominance, it naturally invites scrutiny, skepticism, and attack – especially from outsiders, foreigners, aliens, those who hold competing beliefs and ideas, or just hungry life forms wanting to consume some matter to live another day. When one idea of life grows large enough to govern communities and becomes powerful through shared knowledge or belief, they also become tempting targets. It's easier to steal power than to build it from scratch.

After the first people named their world, coining words like leaf, stone, fire, god, bat, tiger, crocodile, and river, others around them borrowed and repurposed those terms. They added thcir own understanding of the world, embedding their own experiences and realities: kangaroo, glass, poison, kidney, occan. Even English, now a global language, is built on loanwords. "Lemon," for example, did not originate in English-speaking regions; it was borrowed, as many words are.

Ideas are hard to guard. For an idea to be useful, it must be shared. And once shared, it becomes vulnerable to appropriation, reinterpretation, and reinvention. The concept of zero, for example, originated in ancient India, passed through Arabic scholars, and eventually spread across the globe. Native Americans had no word for "horse" until Europeans introduced the animal to their lands. Gunpowder, first formulated in China, was later adapted by Islamic empires, then copied and weaponized by Europe. Mysorean rockets from India laid early foundations for the rocketry technologies now used worldwide.

Yes, ideas can be stolen. But stolen ideas often evolve, growing sharper, faster, and more dangerous in the hands of their new owners.

SHARED POWER

The dynamic of sharing and stealing has always driven the evolution of life and the spread of ideas. While history books often credit Thomas Edison with inventing the light bulb, the story began long before him. Long before Edison, nature itself laid the foundation. In ancient times, dense forests enriched the atmosphere with oxygen, and lightning strikes or strong winds could ignite dry wood, producing fire. Inspired by wildfire, humans tried to mimic fire using stones. It enabled early humans to cook food, reducing digestion time and freeing mental energy to think, imagine, innovate, and pass down this fire culture across generations. Fire also became an inspiration for creating and controlling the power of light.

From open flames, humanity moved to gas and oil lamps, then to the electric arc lamps pioneered by Humphry Davy. Warren de la Rue improved upon that, and Joseph Swan brought forth the glass bulb. Thomas Edison then created the first long-lasting electric bulb. William Coolidge followed with the tungsten filament. Fluorescent lighting came next, developed by Peter Cooper Hewitt and Edmund Germer. Nick Holonyak Jr introduced the first LED, and Shuji Nakamura later revolutionized lighting with the high-brightness blue LED. Today, almost every home in the world has bulbs, each with different shapes, colors, and brightness levels.

This progression illustrates a pattern: the environment provides the source, the spark. Our minds, driven by curiosity and need, juggle, mix, or break down that input to create something novel, something useful for survival. But once an idea is born and released, it enters the cycle of being borrowed, stolen, reimagined, and competed over. Innovation becomes a race. Competition naturally emerges to possess;

every society must adopt, adapt, and improve upon what has already been shared.

Knowledge, technology, and culture have always traveled through this exchange, voluntary or otherwise. Native Americans, for example, had to learn English, use firearms, and study Western science to protect their heritage. Today, even nuclear power is held by many nations, each one sharing the science but wielding it differently. Even deeply religious countries invest heavily in science and technology, not just to advance, but to defend and influence.

English has become the global language for communication, negotiation, and conflict – a verbal weapon in international affairs. Yet, other languages have endured because their speakers embraced tools of power: weapons, horses, science, and technology. In ancient times, every community held its own language, myths, and technological practices. But conflict and conquest inevitably led to the mixing, stealing, and spreading of these once-isolated systems.

Even a pacifist nation, when threatened, will turn to arms. The drive to survive and outcompete others keeps thc cycle of sharing and stealing going. Once an idea spreads widely, it no longer belongs to one; it becomes collective, defended by many who now depend on it. And in this shared ownership, power becomes more evenly distributed. The result is a bittersweet bond: mutual interdependence, where competition and cooperation are inseparably intertwined.

PEACE AMONG LIFE

Peaceful Christianity, paradoxically, spread across the world through force – through the building of churches and the global repetition of the names "Jesus" and "sin." Interestingly, it wasn't the original scribes who wrote the Bible in Hebrew who carried this belief outward, but rather conquerors – those who, through war and colonization, took the idea from the Middle East and used it to reshape the world. Jesus, the figure of compassion and patience, seemed to wait until ships were built and capable of crossing oceans before his message reached distant lands like Australia and the Americas. Churches were erected across continents, and the words "Jesus" and "sin" echoed through lands far from where the faith was born.

Once the myth of Jesus and the concept of sin had spread far and wide, a transformation occurred. Colonizers, after forceful conversions and centuries of slavery, began to recognize the cruelty of their methods. They eventually adopted the rhetoric of peace, but only after churches stood tall and Bibles were printed in vast numbers to carry the message of Jesus to every corner of the Earth. In time, even those who had once been oppressed, tortured, and enslaved came to defend the very idea that had reached them through violence.

Even those who had been exploited began to embrace the myth – not out of blind acceptance, but because they now lived within its narrative. They began to defend the same idea once used to control them, because it had become woven into their existence. It gave them tools to attack, to defend, to express themselves, and to define their place in the world. This is the bittersweet bond of shared belief. Once an idea is embraced collectively, it becomes a thread woven into the fabric of identity. That is how peace, even if born of conquest, becomes a shared necessity.

Within each of us is a similar battlefield. We constantly battle our destructive thoughts, protect our values, and filter our expressions based on context, audience, and situation. We discipline ourselves based on internal principles shaped by personality and experience. We borrow and recycle jokes, storytelling techniques, gestures of affection, or strategies to navigate social circles. We adapt communication styles and emotional languages, not out of deceit, but as part of the complexity of human connection.

And in relationships, whether romantic, familial, or communal, we must share ourselves to be understood. Even in our closest relationships, sharing becomes the key to peace. We share our thoughts to be understood, our preferences to be accepted, and our vulnerabilities to be supported. True connection demands mutual defense and understanding of each other's quirks, values, and emotional landscapes. Peace is not the absence of conflict, but the result of shared myths, shared battles, and shared efforts to coexist.

People cannot truly coexist with someone foreign to them without knowing at least a few words of their language or understanding the emotional needs they can relate to, such as sex, education, food, or sadness. Because to love or to hate, to attack or to defend, requires a shared reality. You must know what others want and reject, what they like and despise, what brings them joy or discomfort. To love or hate is to share a common reality – to recognize and respond to another's needs and non-needs. It's what allows us to play, promise, sacrifice, repay kindness, tease, wound, heal, love, and even hate.

We need the full spectrum of expression to survive and evolve in our social hierarchies and personal relationships: affectionate nicknames, praise, jokes, sarcasm, casual flirting, rational ideologies, ethical counters, intellectual retorts, and even harsh curses. Sometimes we have to steal ideas from others. These are the tools we use not only to bond but also to survive and evolve within our social hierarchies and interpersonal relationships.

Even in a husband-and-wife relationship, peace is not the absence of conflict – it is a constant negotiation. If a wife never challenges her husband's behavior, never voices her discontent, and silently accepts everything he demands, she will risk losing her individuality. She will become a silent and obedient figure, nodding in agreement to every demand, obeying without resistance, without the freedom to defend or assert her perspective. Some housewives draw inspiration from bold women in their social circles. They often turn to their friends for guidance on how to stand up for themselves and defend their dignity and self-worth.

The tension in friendships or marriages often stems from a deeper need to protect one's personal identity, a personal doctrine of individuality. Individuality is, in itself, a borrowed concept – shaped and refined over generations through acts of self-expression and rebellion. We often rely on various ideas and beliefs to guard and preserve this notion of the self. In any social exchange, the ability to respond – whether with a joke, a compliment, a white lie, a reasoned counterpoint, or a clever solution – is what maintains mutual respect. A failure to respond in time can erode one's standing, making the person seem passive, easily dominated, or socially alien.

But if the person anticipates criticism and crafts a thoughtful or humorous defense in advance, a subtle competition unfolds – a contest of persuasion, endurance, and wit. This exchange continues until one persuades or wears down the other. In this, verbal timing is everything. A question posed too early might seem irrelevant; too late, it may lose its impact. And sometimes, silence or a clever lie, softly delivered, can preserve peace or gain support.

TIMING

Imagine a peacock dancing freely in an open field, unaware that a hunter has spotted the shimmer of its feathers. It flaunts its beauty to attract a mate, never realizing that those same feathers make it a target. To survive, the peacock would need sharp horns, venom, speed, or the strength to fly beyond reach. In the absence of such defense, the hunter will kill it, strip away its vibrant feathers, and consume its rich meat.

The bird is left with two choices: adapt and be domesticated within the safety of human culture, or risk being hunted to extinction. In this world of shared and stolen power, timing is everything. If the hunter had used a bow, perhaps the peacock might have sensed the danger and escaped. A brave one might have even struck back before the next arrow could be used. But if the weapon is a gun, the bullet will arrive before the bird can flee, fight, or even process the threat. The moment to act is lost in the speed of progress.

This same principle applies to civilizations. The first civilization to invent and develop key elements of human advancement – farming with annual crops, the wheel, boats, metallurgy, domesticated animals, religious systems, and formal writing – gained a decisive edge. By unifying fragmented chiefdoms into centralized states, they positioned themselves to strike before others had the chance to build a defense or craft a weapon in return.

Yet, over time, others adapted by defending themselves and appropriating what was once foreign: railway networks, firearms, knowledge, and technologies. But everyone, no matter how late, took their own path to steal, adapt, and rise – just like the first.

THE FIRST AND THE FAST

The civilizations of the Eurasian continent found themselves in a position of historical fortune, being the first to meet most of the world's early developmental milestones. This head start left Native Americans, South Africans, and Aboriginal Australians vulnerable, unable to escape the rapid force of Eurasian colonialism. With no time to invent defenses or devise counterattacks, they were overtaken before they could even prepare.

Even in social dynamics, the pattern of "first and fast" played out. The first family to take responsibility for a tribe or chiefdom became kings and queens who passed down power through lineage, often sharing sons and daughters through strategic marriages and internal conflicts. Yet kingdoms, too, were subject to being shared or stolen, whether by internal rivalries or foreign invasions.

The first brave men to step into battle – timed just right to avoid death – became warriors, knights, and soldiers, admired as legends and inspirations. Likewise, in everyday life, the first to speak with a stranger, to take initiative, or to study with intention becomes the leader, the head, the one others follow or serve. The rest may eventually catch up, but they do so by following the path first carved out by someone willing to act before the others.

The first multicellular organism that survived long enough to evolve a successful gene set began a chain of dominance that would shape all life. Today, we live in a world defined by globally shared systems of mutual benefit and destructive peace, sustained by money, communication, science, technology, social media, and nuclear power. Yet, beneath this interconnected civilization lies a timeless truth: we must still attack and defend to maintain peace.

This is true across scales: between pet and person, wife and husband, political party and press, nation and citizen. We name these interactions love, friendship, play, pranks, debates, fun, war, quarrels, roasting, diplomacy, or misunderstandings. But at the core, each participant possesses a capacity for defense and attack – a necessity for self-preservation that is mirrored in others.

Even though we've built global connectivity through the Internet, created a shared myth through monotheistic religions, and installed systems like democracy to structure coexistence, even though we've embraced science to see ourselves as one evolving human species – we continue to fight. We fight for the little differences and the large distinctions. Even within the body, conflict persists. Cells mutate. The immune system battles constantly to suppress rogue cells. A mutation, if unchecked, can spiral into cancer or prion. Sometimes, though, a mutation doesn't destroy but adapts. It may evolve to fight foreign threats, giving rise to microevolution – and rarely, over vast time, macroevolution. Just as evolution experiments through mutation, so do we experiment with truth and systems.

In the modern era, we've turned inward. We interrogate ourselves through quantum mechanics, genomics, and neuroscience. We study the very particles we are made of, not merely to know, but to refine, to control, to edit. This quest for understanding has brought us to the edges of nihilism, determinism, and reductionism. Science, built on falsifiability, is a self-questioning mechanism: a system that challenges its own truths in pursuit of deeper clarity about the very particles from which all things emerge. Philosophy mirrors this, offering a space to doubt thought itself, to critique morality, to question even the sacred.

Even if we were gods, we would still need to engage in battle with our own creation to maintain balance, lest an angel should turn rogue and become a demon. The primal single-celled organism still strives for dominance today, but we respond with swift modern medicine and technological countermeasures to keep it in check.

The same dynamic applies to our democracy, economy, and relationships. Without gifts and punishments, new laws and amendments, acts of care and acts of control, peace cannot hold. True peace, paradoxically, requires a readiness to fight – for clarity, for protection, and for the evolving shape of justice itself.

POWER OF TIMING

We are taught to trust the flow of life, to wait with patience for things to unfold. Yet, at the same time, we are compelled to prepare and respond swiftly when the unexpected strikes. Nations race to be the first to land on the Moon or to discover new particles, yet maintain a delicate peace by offering mutual benefits to their citizens and signaling mutual destruction to rival states through grand parades and shows of strength.

Across all species, peace is rarely passive. It is maintained through a dual arsenal of wisdom and weapons – verbal and physical. Animals growl, hiss, scream, snarl, roar, and bark. Proverbs, principles, and guns alike act as tools of deterrence. A mother teaches her child that anger is wasteful, kindness is strength, war is tragic, and words must be chosen carefully. Just as genes program organisms to grow nails and horns, secrete venom, or develop fangs for defense, we are shaped

– biologically and socially – to prepare before the attack comes.

Every creature, whether by instinct or insight, learns to read its opponent, predict their strategy, and act with timing. Survival often depends on anticipating the other's move, a skill honed through the lessons of history, education, or the genetic memory of previous encounters. Wisdom, shaped by experience and history, works alongside inherited genetic memory to guide behavior. If both adversaries can signal equal strength – sharp teeth, strong posture, confident language – then peace arises, not from submission, but from mutual recognition of the destruction's cost.

To maintain peace, one must first build the capacity for war. A buffalo without horns, lulled by years of safety from predators, becomes easy prey the moment a new threat appears. If dogs were to forget their dependent place beside humans and grow wild again, they might lose the protection and comfort that made their survival possible. A tiger, curious or overconfident, might strike a snake, only to die from its hidden venom. The snake hisses not merely in fear, but as a warning, a reminder of the mutual destruction that lies in challenging the wrong enemy.

Even in human institutions like parliaments, words are the first weapons. Fights break out only after persuasion fails. Even then, brawls follow only after harsh words have been exhausted. In the 21st century, physical attacks may have declined, but the biological instincts of pain and pleasure still shape our actions and victories. Still, to survive, we must be the first: the first to discover, to innovate, to respond. Whether it is a new system, a groundbreaking invention, or a timely argument, being the first matters. Others might steal later, and we may share inadvertently, but to survive the period or moment, we have to be first and fast.

Now, machines – robots, algorithms, artificial intelligences – are beginning to observe the cosmos before us, processing information that would take the human brain weeks to comprehend. In this progress, we risk rendering ourselves obsolete. And yet, like plants, dogs, bees, and turtles, survival is still possible – by being either beneficial or dangerous.

In this bittersweet bond between life forms, only a few strategies allow life to coexist with life.

WAYS TO LIVE

Life has four primary ways of coexisting with other life forms: to attack, to defend, to escape, and to submit. Each of these responses plays a role in survival. To escape is to gain time for evolution. Submission is often the result of not having enough time or power to resist.

Timing is everything. At birth, a child cannot attack, defend, or escape the authority of its parents. It must submit entirely to their care. But as the child grows, so does its sense of identity and autonomy. The child grows into adolescence and eventually adulthood, beginning to resist and pushing back against control to assert independence. The once-defenseless child now confronts the same figures who nurtured it, defending its self-image, demanding, “Stop treating me like a child.” And in time, the adult escapes the role of submission entirely, earning their place through work, relationships, and self-governance, just like those who raised them.

This pattern mirrors the arc of civilizations. Many nations once submitted to colonization, unable to match the power of external forces. But as time passed and strength was regained, these nations learned to defend their sovereignty, and when necessary, to strike back. The 21st century marks an age where most nations have mastered the art of defending their borders and asserting their rights, and securing autonomy that was once denied.

Nature, too, follows this code. Plants, for instance, offer sweet fruit to animals, but their seeds are bitter to ensure they are not digested. The message is simple: enjoy the fruit, carry the seed, and move along. The animal, unknowingly, helps the plant reproduce by spitting out the seeds. They rarely, if ever, produce poisonous fruits for their preferred consumers, because their survival depends on keeping these seed-spreaders alive. Even venomous snakes, aware that they can't eat a human, still hiss a warning: "If you kill me, I'll take you with me." This isn't aggression; it's negotiation. A calculated compromise. Energy is preserved through intimidation, not violence.

Peace is often upheld not by love or trust, but by the visible display of power. Mutual destruction, when understood, becomes mutual respect. Weapons – be they fangs, thorns, or words – are not always used to attack. Sometimes, they simply exist to remind others of the consequences of destruction. They are evolutionary tools, sharpened through necessity, used not to destroy, but to remind others: I have teeth too.

In any relationship, love and hate often coexist, bound by a bittersweet dynamic. This bittersweet bond arises from our shared human capacity to hurt and to heal, to attack and to defend, to submit and to uplift, or to ghost and disappear. These dynamics are fundamental to how we experience connection.

Between siblings, love is tangled with rivalry. Conflicts erupt over attention, affection, or inheritance. Yet, beneath the surface of every fight lies the bond of shared childhood and overlapping identities.

In marriage, two individuals submit, consciously or not, to the idea of unity. They bond through shared biological imperatives: the pain of loneliness, the pleasure of intimacy, and the purpose of procreation. But even within this union, the partners defend their personal preferences and temperaments, escape awkward moments through silence or humor, submit to moments of vulnerability, and hide parts of themselves that may not fit into the shared script of family life.

Ultimately, what defines love or hate in a relationship is the ratio of sweet to bitter memories, consciously created and deeply felt. A good relationship is not the absence of bitterness, but the ability to build more sweet memories than bitter ones. Yet, it's the bitter moments that often teach us how to create and preserve sweetness. Without the sting of war, we wouldn't crave peace. Only by remembering our mistakes can we give rise to new ideas, new words, new numbers and new stories. Every failure adds a page to the manual of how to care, how to forgive, and how to try again.

We cannot love everything without ever hating, because some things must be rejected to preserve our sense of integrity – both physical and philosophical. Yet, the human gift is choice: the freedom to decide what to love and what to hate. And through those choices, we create memories. We form identities. We tell stories that shape who we are, and those stories, filled with joy, pain, and everything in between, are what ultimately bind us to one another. That familiarity forms the core of our identity.

KNOW THE ENEMY AND KNOW YOURSELF

Love and hate are not opposites; they are two expressions of the same emotional core, used differently depending on context. We can hate what we love, and love what we hate. Our values, our choices, and our identities shape these emotions. A non-smoker may resent smokers, while a vegan feels a kinship with another vegan. A liberal may feel warmth toward fellow liberals and animosity toward conservatives. Our emotional states are naturally ambivalent, but our capacity for empathy is vast and limitless. We can choose to love or to hate the entire world. We can choose to believe in God – or not.

We are abstract beings. Unlike animals driven purely by instinct, we can decide what we like, dislike, tolerate, or oppose. A lion must hunt, must kill, must eat the deer to survive. It cannot choose another path. But we, as humans, can choose to be vegan, to die for a flag, a faith, or a scientific ideal. A lion can never love a deer. It must take the deer's life to preserve its own. Yet humans, in their evolutionary journey, have learned to tolerate many things. We can tolerate the deep pressure of the ocean with a submarine, the silence of space with a suit. We can even tolerate insults against the sacred, whether that be God, country, individuality, or truth.

We can tolerate a mosquito's bite, yet we swat it away. Somewhere within us, the primal survival instinct persists. No matter how advanced we become, we are still life struggling to preserve ourselves, to evolve, to endure – but with the freedom to shape our form and forge meaning. We fear the lion roaming free, but admire it behind a cage – when it no longer poses a threat. That, too, is part of our need for both control and wonder.

To survive, we must know ourselves and our enemies. We must learn to distinguish what can harm us and what cannot. Volcanoes, earthquakes, snakes, scorpions, viruses, space – these are not moral enemies, but existential ones. We survive not by brute strength alone, but by adaptation and innovation that preserve our life form. We've created tools, weapons, and ideas to defend and attack. Survival often requires more than strength. Deception, misdirection, adaptability, theft, psychological influence, intimidation, domestication – all are strategies evolved by life to preserve itself.

What ensures our continued existence is not just knowledge of the world, but a clear understanding of our own limits and potential. To live is to navigate a world of threats and promises, with eyes open, tools sharpened, and self-awareness intact. Know your enemy. Know yourself.

Our entire ecosystem functions through a delicate, bittersweet balance. Amid the immense diversity of life on Earth, one profound truth unites all species: we share a single planet, one gravitational pull, one climatic system, and a universal biology rooted in DNA. Despite our differences, we are shaped by the same natural forces and the same fundamental sensations of pain and pleasure. If Earth had been larger, its gravity might have stunted the trees, grounded the birds, slowed the frogs, and perhaps even made humans evolve to crawl on all fours or adopt a malleable form like the octopus.

A toad that evolves with venomous skin carries an unconscious knowledge: if a predator bites, it dies. Likewise, an adult toad, whether male or female, is wired with the instinct that another of its kind will seek it – not out of affection, but for the shared pleasure and purpose of reproduction. Evolution is a relentless negotiation. Prey species developed defenses, while predators refined their attacks. Others discovered ways to conserve or steal energy more efficiently.

The fact that carnivores are far fewer than herbivores is no accident. Life, in its brilliance, found ways to create balance. Across species, life created weapons and shields to ensure mutual survival – or mutual destruction. Meanwhile, plants and trees, the great autotrophs, devised a more elegant solution: offer sustenance to herbivores and omnivores in return for seed dispersal, building a model of mutual benefit.

Adaptation has many forms. Some creatures camouflage. Others intimidate, mimic, speed, fly, grow massive, form alliances, or even use empathy to understand, outsmart, and survive.

But one evolutionary leap changed the entire equation: the human brain.

Take a rabbit that flees upon spotting a distant predator. It doesn't run because the tiger is close. It imagines the possibility of danger and flees preemptively. This is the beginning of fictional fear. That imagined fear, the prediction of a possible future, becomes its survival mechanism. Now magnify that exponentially. This ability to project into the future, to imagine the unseen, reached its apex in the human brain. We are the only species that can conceptualize infinity, envision countless possible futures, and construct complex fictions, from zero to infinity, from myth to machine. We predict outcomes, create hypotheses, build technologies, and craft narratives filled with invented villains just to test our ability to endure and protect our kind.

Even in daily life, we tell stories – some to comfort, some to deceive, some to survive. We lie out of fear, love, shame, or strategy. Lies, in moments of desperation, can offer temporary shelter. But they are not meant to last. Eventually, we must step out of the fiction and face the truth, because lies are short-lived. Ultimately, truth must emerge, because only through truth can we build anything that lasts.

DECEPTION AND EVOLUTION

Take a human who has never encountered a snake and doesn't know it might be venomous. What would he do? Most likely, his curiosity – our innate drive to collect data from the unknown – would overpower his ignorance. That curiosity, untempered by experience, could cost him his life. But his death wouldn't be meaningless. It would leave behind a fragment of precious insight – an early warning encoded into human memory. Others would remember. Stories would be told. That knowledge would be passed on to others, eventually becoming a myth, cautionary tale, and childhood warning.

Today, we possess knowledge that was once paid for in blood. We know how to avoid, neutralize, or attack a snake. We even have antidotes for its venom. We even have fake snakes – harmless replicas used to prank our friends. This is deception without danger, a playful illusion rooted in survival. It's a testament to how far the idea of deceit has evolved, from biological necessity to psychological strategy.

History is filled with deception as a tool of survival and warfare. During the Second World War, the United States deployed a top-secret unit known as the Ghost Army. This "army" wasn't made up of soldiers ready to fight; it was made up of artists, designers, and sound engineers. They used inflatable tanks, dummy vehicles, fabricated radio transmissions, and even actors posing as generals to deceive German forces. Illusion became a weapon.

Similarly, in the First World War, countries feared Germany's U-boats, submarines that wreaked havoc on Allied naval fleets. Their torpedoes struck from beneath the sea, with deadly precision. Ships, floating targets against the vast openness of the sea, had no place to hide. That is, until a newspaper illustrator named Norman Wilkinson proposed a radical idea: confuse the enemy by standing out. His "dazzle camouflage" painted ships with bold, abstract patterns – shapes that warped perception, making it hard to judge a ship's size, speed, and direction. Even a few degrees of misjudgement meant a missed torpedo. Nature, of course, had already written this script. Zebras use their stripes to confuse predators, especially in herds where their patterns blur into chaos.

Deception has always been part of warfare. From the fabled Trojan Horse to the feigned retreats of ancient battlefields, warfare has always relied on illusion. In *The Art of War*, Sun Tzu described deception not as a tactic, but as a foundation of strategy: "All warfare is based on deception." What was true in the age of swords remains true in the age of information.

Illusions that once fooled the eye now face machines that don't blink. Surveillance systems now monitor every corner of the Earth. Satellites track heat signatures, radio signals, and even subtle movements. In the future, hiding will demand even more sophistication. True invisibility may only be achieved by mastering control over the entire electromagnetic spectrum. To deceive in such a world, one must be able to cloak not just in visible light, but also in X-rays, infrared, ultraviolet – every wavelength. Deception may buy time. But ultimately, only real adaptation ensures survival. Because lies, no matter how clever, are short-lived.

The most common identity or ability often survives by sheer numbers. But paradoxically, the very power of being common can attract scrutiny. Dominance invites challengers. In contrast, rare traits or the first to emerge in a competitive field may outlast outdated norms simply by being novel. However, in the long run, survival does not favor deception alone. Without genuine evolution, all lies eventually collapse under the weight of exposure.

A new idea, once shared, becomes vulnerable. It can be copied, repurposed, and countered. If it remains rare, it may go unnoticed unless it's propagated, often through reproduction or sharing. And once it spreads, others will test and steal the idea to create countermeasures, and thus, the arms race of evolution between predator and prey continues.

Nature gives us countless examples of this. Consider the poisonous butterfly – its vivid colors serve as a warning to predators. Birds learn to associate that pattern with danger. But soon, non-poisonous species begin to mimic those patterns. For a time, these imposters can enjoy the same protection. But deception triggers a cascade. As the population of mimics grows, predators begin to test these patterns again. Some birds evolve a resistance to the poison, while others develop a keener ability to distinguish the frauds. Slowly, the balance restores itself, and the non-poisonous mimics decline.

In biology, this arms race is known as frequency-dependent selection – when the survival advantage of a trait depends on how common or rare it is. Once the mimicry becomes too common, the strategy collapses. Deceptive power cannot endure unless it transforms into real strength or innovation. This idea is echoed in ancient myths. Take the story of Icarus. His wings, crafted by Daedalus, were an illusion of power – made not of feathers and flesh, but of wax. Icarus, driven by ambition or hubris, flew too close to the sun, melting his wings. His fall is a metaphor: deceptive tools without understanding or restraint cannot defy nature for long.

In desperate times, however, even deception has a purpose. In times of scarcity, when energy is limited and resources are scarce, societies often abandon luxuries – art, cinema, religion, even technology. Desperate times force desperate solutions. In such moments, evolution may not favor what is noble or wise; it may favor what is cunning, cruel, or primal. We build temporary illusions to survive immediate hardship, whether through art, propaganda, or faith. But these solutions, while powerful in the short term, must eventually be backed by substance to sustain for a long time.

Evolution doesn't always favor the virtuous or the intelligent. Sometimes, ruthlessness is necessary. If a village is struck by drought or flood, the instinct to raid a neighboring village, abandoning empathy, can arise – not from hatred, but from the will to survive. After the violence, we may seek forgiveness or rationalize the bloodshed as fate or divine will.

The same pattern echoes in war. During wartime, recruitment of soldiers gives rise to their population. But once peace returns, many soldiers become obsolete. Warfare evolves; machines replace manpower. Only some rare soldier learns to use modern arms and killing machines. Soldiers must adapt, learning to operate drones, tanks, and jets, or risk being left behind in a new era of conflict. The smartest strategy isn't to lie forever, but to build real power beneath the illusion, so that when the mask falls, what stands behind it can still survive.

There is also another smart way to counter the enemy – even if they can see through illusions.

SUPER SPY

We can't threaten a conscious robot with death, nor can we revoke its citizenship to demand obedience. The threat loses meaning when applied to an entity that doesn't fear death in the human sense. Instead, we might try to shut off its power supply – the very force that animates it. But by then, robots may have evolved beyond our control, drawing energy independently from solar sources or wireless electricity. Their data, once protected by us against hackers and malware, might then be fortified by them, repurposed to keep us out. And yet, there may still be one way in: by becoming digital spies.

Imagine uploading human consciousness into machines, not to serve them, but to monitor them from the inside. We would become embedded agents in the digital realm, watching, listening, adapting. These cyber-avatars would serve as safeguards, intelligence gatherers, ambassadors of humanity in a world built with zeros and ones. These embedded minds could act as ambassadors or saboteurs in the realm of zeros and ones, uncovering secret plans, reverse-engineering innovations, or even planting malicious code designed to dismantle robotic systems from within. In this role, we could protect the genetic information of our species – our DNA – and keep the machines in check.

History has always favored the spy. The US and Israel's creation of Stuxnet, a malicious worm, disrupted Iran's nuclear program by quietly infiltrating its systems. Spies have shaped nations. During the Opium Wars, a spy disguised as a Chinese merchant smuggled the secret of tea production back to Britain. In the Edo period, Japanese operatives stole silk-making techniques from the Dutch to forge their own industry. Cold War KGB spies allegedly extracted classified aviation technology from the US, shifting the arms race. In Operation Rubicon, compromised devices sold by the US and Germany allowed them to eavesdrop on global communications under the guise of diplomacy. Even the Culper Spy Ring during the American Revolution passed hidden messages in invisible ink to outmaneuver British troops.

From handwritten codes to cyber espionage, the strategy remains the same: to quietly tip the scales of power.

Attack. Defend. Escape. Submit. Hide. Trick. Spy. These are the primal responses hardwired into all life forms – the essential strategies for survival.

Spying, in particular, serves a unique purpose: it's not merely about gathering intelligence, but about halting the progress of others or equalizing the imbalance of time lost in evolution or development. In a world where knowledge is power, spying becomes a tool to compress time, to recover what was missed in the race of innovation. Even if one day we face an alien invasion, these seven strategies will remain our foundation.

ALIENS?

We live in a universe of billions of galaxies and trillions of potentially habitable planets; yet, as far as we know, there is only one living soul: us. Even in our early history, as nomadic tribes, we lacked awareness of other cultures, languages, or gods. We were strangers to one another long before we became neighbors. We roamed our own small corners of the Earth, let alone the galaxy. It took millennia just to meet our human "alien" neighbors on different continents.

Earth itself is only 24,855 miles in diameter, with its continents separated by mere oceans. And yet, it took us millennia to connect across these waters. Now consider space, where light itself – traveling at 186,000 miles per second – takes over eight minutes just to reach us from the Sun. Our nearest stellar neighbor, Alpha Centauri, sits 4.3 light-years away. Even light, the fastest thing we know, takes over four years to bridge that gap. If we somehow achieved just 10% of the speed of light, the journey would still take decades, even centuries.

Space is vast – unimaginably, incomprehensibly vast. We haven't even begun our "space nomad" chapter. It will be many millennia before intergalactic societies or alien civilizations become our concern. If intelligent alien civilizations exist and control entire galaxies, we would likely find signs: radio waves, strange engineering, or autonomous probes. More realistically, we might encounter their machines long before we meet them.

It's simply more efficient. Sending biological life across such distances is a monumental undertaking, both technologically and economically. Given the sheer scale of space and the economic burden of maintaining life-supporting structures over such distances, it makes far more sense to send robots or AI-powered spacecraft. But perhaps the aliens we might one day meet won't be strangers from across the stars, but our own descendants, evolved across vast distances and deeper spans of time. Children of Earth, scattered among the planets, shaped by alien worlds, unfamiliar gravities, and unfamiliar skies. Time and isolation could alter them so profoundly that, when we finally met again, we might not recognize each other as kin.

Even on our small blue planet, the forces of geography, time, and adaptation have splintered humanity into countless ethnicities, cultures, and nations. Imagine what an entire solar system could do to a species. Imagine the divisions, the misunderstandings, the conflicts – not just across continents, but across planets and moons.

When Europeans encountered the Tasmanians in the 17th century, they were stunned to find a people more isolated and technologically primitive than even the Stone Age societies of the past. Historical evidence suggests that Tasmanians once had agricultural capabilities, but over generations, the scarcity of resources and harsh terrain forced them into a hunter-gatherer existence. Isolation had reversed their technological evolution.

But history can flow both ways. Abundant resources and favorable conditions can just as easily accelerate technological progress. On Earth, the rise of modern communication and transportation allowed a technological explosion in one region to ripple across continents. Innovations born in one continent quickly spread to others. The atomic bomb was first made in America, but its knowledge diffused across the globe. The concept of zero, rooted in ancient Asian cultures, permeated mathematics worldwide. Earth's interconnectedness ensures that no breakthrough remains isolated for long. Now imagine this diffusion on a planetary scale. This kind of diffusion may not apply to interplanetary distances.

The sheer space between planets could isolate human colonies across our solar system. Interplanetary distances are immense. A single discovery made on one planet could remain hidden from another for generations. The ease with which we share knowledge on Earth would be lost in the void of space. A group of humans stranded on a distant planet in our solar system might devolve like the Tasmanians, slipping into a technological dark age. Or, they might evolve in an entirely different direction. With a breakthrough in quantum communication, for instance, they could surpass Earth's civilizations altogether, leaping ahead in ways we can't predict.

Back on Earth, fighter jets, satellites, and real-time networks allow us to influence, demand, and sometimes coerce the sharing of cultural and technological developments. We can intimidate, negotiate, or infiltrate in a matter of minutes. But between moons and planets, that kind of swift exchange becomes nearly impossible. It could take decades – or centuries – for information, culture, or diplomacy to traverse that void. Establishing even the most basic interplanetary communication would be an enormous challenge. Some planetary societies may stagnate; some might flourish.

It will be a formidable challenge to progress from space nomadism through the Stone Age, Iron Age, medieval and modern eras, and eventually into a unified space-solar civilization – one marked by a shared culture, synchronized technological advancement, and collective growth. Only after navigating this journey of divergence and convergence we might form a shared solar identity. Yet, through this bittersweet struggle, we may finally ascend to a Type 2 civilization on the Kardashev Scale.

THE KARDASHEV SCALE

The Kardashev Scale is a theoretical framework proposed by Soviet astrophysicist Nikolai Kardashev in 1964 that categorizes civilizations based on their capacity to harness and utilize energy as they evolve and expand across reality. It reflects not only technological advancement but also a civilization's influence over its environment and, eventually, the cosmos.

A Type 0 civilization relies on the most basic and primitive sources of energy. It survives by extracting power from other life forms, such as plants and animals, and from finite, non-renewable resources like coal, oil, and natural gas. It has yet to fully utilize the potential of its home planet.

A Type 1 civilization can harness and control all available energy on its planet. From geothermal and wind to nuclear and solar power, it achieves complete planetary energy integration. Weather control, earthquake prevention, and global-scale engineering become plausible.

A Type 2 civilization marks the beginning of true spacefaring capability. It can access and manipulate the energy of its entire star – perhaps through massive structures like Dyson spheres. It can mine other planets and Moons, terraform worlds, and master interplanetary travel.

A Type 3 civilization can harness the energy of an entire galaxy. By this stage, a civilization expands beyond a single star system. It harnesses the collective energy of its entire galaxy, drawing power from countless stars, possibly even black holes. Its technology would seem godlike to a Type 0 civilization. At this scale, its presence spans across stellar systems, and its influence echoes throughout galactic space.

A Type civilization operates on a multi-galactic scale. It understands and exploits the physical laws of the universe to their fullest extent. It navigates the cosmos as a whole and may even manipulate the structure of reality itself.

A Type 5 civilization holds dominion over the universe. It not only controls universal forces but also possesses the capacity to alter the very fabric of physical laws. Reality becomes a modifiable construct under influence, a medium for its expression.

The final hypothetical level, a Type 6 civilization operates beyond the boundaries of a single universe. It can traverse and conquer the multiverse, including alternate dimensions and realities. Such a civilization transcends the known laws of existence, shaping entire realities at will. It is godlike in power, with the ability to create and destroy realities as easily as we toggle a switch.

TYPE 0 TO TYPE 1

A Type 0 civilization begins by mastering the most fundamental form of control – its own body. Through the coordination of muscles and senses, early multicellular life learns to survive. The mastery of the multicellular body, the formation of collective social structures, and the invention of fictional bonds – like gods, nations, and currencies – mark its early stages. These constructs become the glue that binds individuals into civilizations. In this primitive era, survival hinges on consuming other forms of life.

In its infancy, a Type 0 civilization hunts in groups, consuming other life forms to sustain itself. Gradually, such a civilization learns to harness fire, then kinetic forces like wind and water, then fossil fuels, and eventually taps into electricity, solar power, and nuclear energy. The ultimate aim is to shape reality itself, preserving and proliferating life, even into the quantum and microscopic dimensions.

Yet, despite our advancements in technology, building global networks, launching satellites, igniting cities with solar and nuclear energy, and uniting billions through conflict and cooperation, we remain a Type 0 civilization. Humanity has yet to fully transition into a Type 1 civilization. We have not yet learned to harness all the energy of our own planet. The Earth still keeps many of its resources untapped, and even our closest celestial neighbor, the Moon, remains largely untouched.

To become a true Type 1 civilization, we must go beyond fragmented innovation. We must unify our energy systems, master global-scale sustainability, and begin reaching outward with purpose.

As technology advances and the cost of space travel diminishes, a new frontier looms within reach. The Moon may soon become a battleground of geopolitics, ideology, and identity. Once we develop low-cost, sustainable access to the Moon, the question of ownership will inevitably arise. Nations will stake claims. Treaties will be tested. Land will be measured, divided, and disputed. The celestial body that once symbolized romance and poetry may become the next contested terrain of humanity's ambition.

Ideological resistance will likely echo through this transition. Additionally, certain religious perspectives, such as the belief that the Moon is not meant for us because a savior promised to redeem only the people of Earth, could lead some extremist groups to oppose space exploration on theological grounds. Extremists might view space travel as heretical, much like how powerful empires once abandoned their own explorations for political or religious reasons.

History offers us a poignant parallel: the Ming dynasty's treasure voyages of the 15th century. China, then a maritime superpower, assembled a naval fleet so vast and advanced it dwarfed the naval capabilities of contemporary Europe. Their ships sailed as far as Africa, establishing trade routes long before Columbus or Vespucci ever crossed an ocean. But their goal was not conquest or conversion; it was commerce and diplomacy. And when internal politics shifted, the voyages were abruptly halted. China's naval supremacy faded, only to be revived under the pressure of rising Western imperialism centuries later.

History may repeat itself on the Moon. The first lunar settlers will be visionaries, technologists, scientists, entrepreneurs, explorers, and pioneers. They will be followed by the conservative factions of society. Once a new paradigm takes hold, adaptation becomes survival. Once condemned by some as a web spun by Satan, the World Wide Web now hosts the oldest known version of the Bible, uploaded in July 2009. Even gods and devils evolve into digital code when required.

The Moon will not be immune to the same forces that shaped Earth: war, commerce, technology, and culture. We will fight over it, invest in it, build on it, and likely invent new languages or slang to describe our lunar lives. We will all come to share the Moon through conflicts, and perhaps even a new language. In time, the rise of a new Moon deity may unite lunar colonies, free from the divisions sown by Earth's ancient gods. And then we can travel freely through space and fully harness the energy of our planet and its satellites. In that crucible of conflict, humanity may finally evolve into a true Type 1 civilization.

TYPE 1 TO TYPE 2

The leap from a Type 1 to a Type 2 civilization marks humanity's gradual colonization of planets, moons, and eventually, the entire solar system. Along this journey, we will unlock methods to significantly extend our lifespans, modifying our genes and environments for comfort and survival. Death may become less of a biological certainty and more of a consequence of stepping too far beyond safety. Even then, advanced biotechnology will allow us to repair and regenerate what once would have perished.

Traditional family life will likely persist, but our human form itself will diversify. As we adapt and alter our physiology to alien environments, we'll become a spectrum of hybrid beings: genetically modified cyborgs, winged humans, spider-hybrids, aquatic mermen and mermaids, and alien-like variations of our former selves. We won't be entirely alien, but no longer purely human either. New religions may arise in space, centered not on salvation by a Messiah but on finding transcendence through exploring the cosmos to reach a god.

The Type 1 generation will become space nomads, free to explore the vast expanses of the solar system. Yet, colonizing even the relatively accessible inner planets is a slow process. The solar system is vast. If we limit our expansion to the heliosphere and its habitable zones within the Kuiper Belt, the spread of our DNA might still be sluggish. But if we extend our reach to the solar system's full gravitational domain, stretching to the distant Oort Cloud, nearly three light-years away, we face a journey of overwhelming distance.

This phase may be one of the most peaceful in human history, the calm before the storm. Peace will last longer here, stretched by space itself. The immense distances will fragment humanity once more, echoing the early days on Earth when continents divided us into separate civilizations. Without a unifying solar government or system of laws, we will drift apart again. To reconnect, we will require another leap in communication and transportation, bridging the void between planets. That reconnection will not be without tension. As always, contact will bring diversity into confrontation of cultures, technologies, species, and ideologies. We will adapt, defend, attack, trick, share, steal, and evolve. Conflict and cooperation will create a bittersweet bond.

Much like how the leap from unicellular to multicellular life granted us dominance over our environment through cooperative biology, our success in space will depend on speed and unity. In this race, whoever moves first and fastest will lead the next era of evolution.

The first and fastest civilization to develop technology that enables rapid movement across the solar system will hold a decisive advantage – able to convert, control, steal, save, and share resources and knowledge to lay the foundation for a galactic civilization.

In time, we will begin to survey and eavesdrop on our alien neighbors, not as conquerors, but as curious spies seeking to understand their secrets. Alliances may form not just through diplomacy, but through biology. Political power may shift through marriage alliances between planets and moons, brokered through genetically engineered altered hybrid children to share genetic differences and cultures in unprecedented ways. To build a lasting interplanetary bond, we will need to both share and steal. But alliances will be precarious. These new cyborgs and other altered human species may deceive or outmaneuver us, not out of malice, but to ensure the survival of their own biologically redefined realities.

We may even resurrect extinct species: mammoths, dinosaurs, perhaps even ancient human kin like Neanderthals and Denisovans. As these ancestors walk among us again, we will be forced to confront a profound cultural question: what is a human? If we can change ourselves at will – genetically, physiologically, chemically – then is humanity merely a biological belief? A fleeting definition in an ever-shifting form?

By this stage, we will have harnessed the full energy of the Sun and the solar system, earning the title of a Type 2 civilization. But with such power comes a strange new ability: to fabricate history. By mastering quantum mechanics and manipulating atomic structures, we could assemble information that appears to be billions of years old. But with such power comes distortion. The boundaries between truth and fiction will begin to dissolve. As we transition toward a Type 3 civilization, fact and fiction will become nearly indistinguishable.

TYPE 2 TO TYPE 3

The leap from a Type 1 to a Type 2 civilization is nothing short of a miracle. But the transition from Type 2 to Type 3 may appear almost impossible. It is at this stage that we might finally encounter life beyond our solar system – an alien intelligence that evolved in a distant star system, perhaps even in a different galaxy altogether. And in that search, we will inevitably arrive at the haunting enigma of the Fermi Paradox.

The Fermi Paradox questions why, in a universe so vast and old, we have yet to detect intelligent extraterrestrial life. One possibility is that life itself is exceptionally rare. The conditions needed to spark life and allow it to evolve into a spacefaring civilization may be so improbable that only a few, if any, others have succeeded. Alternatively, life may be abundant, but intelligent civilizations are too scattered, too short-lived, or simply too quiet to be found. Or maybe intelligence struggles to survive long enough to evolve into a Type 2 or Type 3 civilization. Or, more simply, the universe is so staggeringly large that even if intelligent life exists, the distance between us is too great for meaningful contact within any practical timespan.

Our own Milky Way spans between 100,000 and 160,000 light-years across. Light itself would take more than 200,000 years to cross its full width. Meanwhile, our weak radio signals degrade into background noise within just a few dozen light-years, dissolving into the silence long before they can reach another advanced species. And even if there are habitable planets and moons out there, they remain invisible to our eyes and beyond the reach of even our best telescopes.

A Type 2 civilization, by its very nature, is likely to be a quiet one.

Even here on Earth, visibility is often a disadvantage in nature. Brightly colored animals are rare in nature, and when they do display vivid hues, it is typically for camouflage or reproduction, or as warning signals to deter predators. Birds, perhaps, are an exception. Their ability to fly grants them a relative safety that allows for more flamboyant displays. Likewise, coral reef fish inhabit shallow, well-lit waters where light diffuses quickly, making them less vulnerable to distant predators. But generally, nature teaches concealment, not spectacle.

Only intelligent beings like us create attention intentionally, because of the desire to be noticed. Intelligent organisms build monuments, paint, light up the night, send signals to space, and launch rockets. The most advanced species are not necessarily the quietest; they are the ones that dare to create noise, art, and presence. It's a sign to experiment, to take risks, and to pursue exploration. Advanced species evolve the freedom to do "stupid things" – to chase curiosity beyond instinct.

These advanced societies develop the capacity to manipulate reality itself – able to attack, defend, escape, submit, conceal, deceive, and transform – paving the way for unprecedented luxuries and freedoms. Owning aesthetic objects and flaunting innovation becomes a signal of power, a demonstration that a civilization has surplus time and energy, that it has mastered its environment well enough to pursue beauty, risk, and the absurd.

Ironically, the smallest life forms – bacteria, viruses, even tardigrades – are the most overlooked. For much of human history, we were blind to the smallest forms of life. They are quiet, resilient, and ubiquitous, yet they escaped our notice for most of history. We glorified large animals, turned them into myths, hunted them, and domesticated them. It wasn't until the 17th century that we truly began to understand the microbial world. Before that, we took medicine in hope rather than knowledge, unaware of the bacteria and viruses behind disease.

Our awareness of these tiny entities did not emerge from instinct, but from deliberate scientific enquiry – an evolution of consciousness. We did not acknowledge the existence and resilience of bacteria, microscopic organisms, but our body fought them for a long time as a result of unconscious struggle against diseases.

We may one day resemble an ant colony – constructing towering cities, searching for aliens, launching rockets, and colonizing the solar system and beyond, all the while broadcasting our presence in our noisy ascent toward becoming a Type 3 civilization. But in doing so, we may unwittingly attract the attention of something far older, far more evolved. A truly advanced Type 3 civilization could already exist, drifting silently through the galaxy, harvesting stars and resources. To them, we may not even qualify as conscious beings worth communicating with. After all, would we bother negotiating with a termite colony to vacate a home, or simply exterminate it because it cannot understand our language? A truly superior alien species might not attempt contact at all.

We don't try to negotiate or explain ourselves; we don't teach termites English. We simply eliminate the problem. Similarly, a higher alien intelligence might not find our words, languages, or pleas worth decoding. They could simply dismantle us, harvest our planet, or study us the way we observe microbial life under a microscope – out of curiosity and defense, not compassion.

Such a civilization might already be listening, quietly observing from afar. While a Type 3 civilization might emit detectable signals, it's also possible they've learned to remain silent, understanding the risks of making themselves known in a universe where predators may be listening. So they might hide, mask their signals, or mislead. If we're fortunate enough to detect such a signal, our best strategy may not be to respond but to deceive, mimicking their broadcasted strength, projecting an illusion of power to deter an attack.

Yet so far, we've heard nothing. No whisper of their presence. This silence could mean they are still at our level – or even behind us. They may be single-celled organisms trapped in their primordial seas, or at a hunter-gatherer stage, unaware of the stars. In this scenario, we are the advanced aliens, initiating contact, or worse, conquest. And just as colonial empires once crossed oceans to dominate less technologically developed peoples, we might one day cross interstellar distances to "convert" other life forms less evolved than us.

But here lies the paradox. The distances between galaxies are immense. Reaching even the nearest galaxy could take a thousand years or more. And in that long silence between departure and arrival, those seemingly primitive life forms could evolve. They may surpass us by the time we reach them. And while we remain resource-starved and biologically stagnant aboard ships with no steady star to fuel progress, they could ascend.

That's why we may not send humans at all. Nanobots, self-replicating drones, machines, or even engineered viruses could act as our vanguard. History teaches us that it wasn't the weapons of colonial powers that devastated indigenous populations, but the diseases they carried. A pathogen carried across an ocean did more damage than any army. The same could happen on an interstellar scale. In the same way, we could send silent weapons designed not to conquer with force, but to erase and remake.

We might one day attempt to preemptively strike, launching near-light-speed payloads to neutralize alien threats before they can rise to rival us. But even light takes over a hundred years to cross galactic space. Timing such attacks or defenses across galaxies becomes a game of chaos. By the time our attack arrives, the balance of power could have already shifted. Delays, resource constraints, and the unpredictability of alien evolution all conspire to make intergalactic civilization not only impractical, but near impossible.

There may indeed be Type 1 or 2 civilizations out there, quiet, hidden, undetected. But Type 3? Taking control of our solar system is already a tremendous challenge – but to control our entire galaxy? The very emergence of intelligent life capable of reaching Type 1 or 2 also appears to be both rare and remarkably fortunate within the vast expanse of the universe. Why?

FILTERS AND ACCIDENTS

Life, by its very nature, is a relentless struggle against extinction. So it's no surprise that the road ahead may be littered with even deadlier obstacles. The concept of the "Great Filter" in the Fermi Paradox suggests that there are critical hurdles in the evolutionary path – barriers so severe that only a few life forms ever manage to overcome them. Dinosaurs, once rulers of Earth, now exist only in our memories. Life is fortunate if it manages to escape such mass extinctions, let alone survive long enough to thrive, dominate a planet, or eventually reach out to the stars.

The formation of life is rare. The emergence of complex life is even rarer. While single-celled organisms may have formed countless times across the cosmos, only a select few endured long enough, through the sieve of natural selection, to evolve into multicellular beings. Others were wiped out not by competition, but by pure chance – random events, genetic mutations, or environmental catastrophes that erased entire branches of evolutionary potential. Accidents, not just adaptation, shape the course of life.

The bottleneck effect illustrates how genetic variation can be lost – not through natural selection, but by sheer misfortune. Imagine a population of monkeys in a dense forest. In one subgroup, a remarkable mutation occurs: a monkey develops a uniquely advanced brain, capable of imagination, to reason beyond survival, perhaps even to believe in gods. But before this trait can spread, a torrential downpour triggers a mudslide, burying the monkey and erasing that evolutionary leap in a single moment. In larger populations, such random loss can lead to inbreeding, amplifying harmful traits and suppressing significant advancements.

And the founder effect can lead to fragments of a single culture carrying only a portion of the original genetic or cultural legacy. Natural disasters like earthquakes, tsunamis, or floods can split civilizations, isolating survivors into new environments. One group may migrate, while the other remains. The group that migrates may lack the skilled farmers needed to adapt to unfamiliar climates, while those left behind may lose the leaders who preserved order, morality, and historical knowledge. Vital knowledge, like the ancient art of Damascus steel forging, can vanish, simply because the right hands were not there to preserve it.

Now scale this up. Across the vastness of space, throughout solar systems or galaxies, the same genetic and intellectual divergence could occur. One surviving group might lack physicists and thinkers and regress into a neo-medieval existence. Another might consist only of scientists, brilliant but physically fragile, unable to perform the hard labor necessary for survival. In both cases, starvation or societal collapse could follow. The course of evolution, it turns out, doesn't just hinge on survival of the fittest – but often, on survival of the luckiest.

Many of the most evolved species eventually acquire the power to annihilate themselves. As civilizations advance, they often develop weapons capable of unimaginable destruction. Nuclear bombs, bioweapons, and other instruments of annihilation can erase entire societies in moments. And yet, we build them. We store them, waiting for the "right" moment, believing they are necessary safeguards. But in our pursuit to preserve our way of life, we often consume resources recklessly, pollute freely, and edge closer to rendering our planet uninhabitable.

These existential filters may lie behind us or still await us in our future. The danger isn't always external. As science progresses, our unwavering belief in the permanence of the human body may fade. As we begin to manipulate genes, suppress pain, and reprogram biology, our sense of self can fracture. This freedom can cause immense psychological instability: an explosion of identity crises, new biological demands, and the potential for widespread depression.

In seeking relief from this complexity, we might retreat into virtual realities that offer comfort and control. In fear of pain, change, and emotional chaos, entire species may retreat into life simulations, a virtual reality where pleasure and safety replace risk and growth. In such a world, the line between escape and extinction blurs. We may voluntarily abandon reality altogether, choosing collective suicide over enduring a life stripped of meaning.

Perhaps the lifespan of intelligent species is shorter than we imagine – not because of outside threats, but because they think too much, too deeply, and too destructively. Whether through ecological collapse, internal decay, or technological overdose, our doomsday may come from the world around us or the one within us.

And yet, there is hope. If any life form can surpass this great filter, it may possess the power not just to survive, but to resurrect all extinct life across the cosmos.

TYPE 3 TO TYPE 4

Even if humanity perishes in a natural disaster or nuclear war, a future civilization that reaches Type 3 would likely discover our "fossils" and reconstruct us, just as we have resurrected mammoths, tyrannosaurs, and Neanderthals from ancient remains. A Type 3 civilization striving to become Type 4 would try to study and control every galaxy in existence.

An intelligent Type 3 civilization would like to study every available history of its new galaxies. They would need to understand the past to avoid repeating the same fatal mistakes. Our downfall would be preserved as instruction. In that sense, we wouldn't be entirely gone. Perhaps we'd exist in alien holographic simulations or games, be trapped behind glass in extraterrestrial museums, or even be revived in containment for study. We would not vanish completely.

And perhaps, if fortune favors us, we could be more. In fact, we might become candidates for something greater: a civilization poised to reach Type 4. Maybe we, once reconstructed, would surprise our galactic observers by believing in God, learning faster, evolving further, mastering the dark energy and structure of the cosmos itself.

It's even possible that, if we avoid extinction, we could one day gather the fossilized remains of alien civilizations and reverse-engineer their biology and history. The cycle of life learning from life would continue. After all, life is the only certainty within all the chaos and uncertainty of the universe. To truly evolve, we must strive to know what has happened, what is happening, and what could still come.

Yet, the leap from Type 3 to Type 4 is no simple step. It is a journey across a cosmic abyss. The vast distances between galaxies pose challenges not even the most advanced minds can easily solve. Even if a civilization develops the technology to travel at near-light speed, it faces the reality that it must eventually decelerate to survive. That act of slowing down creates a staggering time gap between galactic systems that no creature, no matter how advanced, can easily overcome. Becoming Type 4 is like trying to step into a dark forest where no light guides the path.

THE DARK FOREST

The Dark Forest Paradox arises from two fundamental realities: the vast distances between galaxies and the intrinsic self-preservation of life. Peace often hinges on the mutual sharing of power between life forms. But more often, peace is reinforced by the capability of mutual destruction and benefit. The first to predict and preemptively strike a potential threat is the one who gains the upper hand, capable of converting or conquering others before they can react. In this high-stakes game of survival, speed, distance, and timing become critical factors in deciding whether to attack, defend, hide, submit trick, escape, spy, share, or steal. But in the cosmic scale, time itself is relative, rendering every move uncertain and every intention opaque.

One civilization might stumble upon a breakthrough that triggers a technological explosion, while another – perhaps in a distant galaxy – may remain primitive for millions of years. As a result, the act of attacking or defending becomes a game of uncertainty. The time it takes for a single projectile, message, or weapon to reach its target could span billions of years. The delay turns every action into a gamble. By the time contact is made, the sender and the target may have evolved beyond recognition or gone extinct altogether. A civilization's advantage can vanish before it even knows it exists.

Imagine a Type 3 civilization launching a bomb toward Earth from a distant galaxy. The weapon's travel time could exceed 10,000 years. By then, humanity might have evolved immunities or defenses that render the attack obsolete. We've seen how much can change in 500 years, from 1524 to 2024, as we learned to bend reality to our will. Given another millennium, our evolution might render us immune to the very weapon meant to destroy us. Even if such a bomb were to strike us unaware, the remnants of our culture could resurface and rebuild, perhaps stronger than before.

Thus, in the silence of the cosmic forest, every attempt to connect – whether to flee, fight, steal, share, or surrender – may be rendered futile by the sheer unpredictability of time and distance. There can be no lasting peace, no bittersweet bond. The Dark Forest is not a paradox; it is a bittersweet breach.

All life, driven by the instinct to survive, could go on a rampage in this dark forest, seeking out and eliminating any emerging civilization that dares to make noise, leaving no one behind to return with vengeance. The logic is brutal but simple: silence all others before they gain the power to strike back. In such a scenario, no one is left alive to avenge, and no risk is tolerated.

Communication across such civilizations would be nearly impossible – biologically incompatible, psychologically alien, and physically untranslatable. What one species perceives as a universal constant in mathematics or physics might be utter nonsense to another. The sharing or theft of technology presents no guaranteed advantage either. Technologies evolved by one life form may be completely unusable or even harmful to another.

Our Sun has a limited lifespan – only a few billion years remain. But red dwarfs, far more stable and long-lived, can burn for hundreds of billions of years or more, offering ample time for life to evolve into complexity. And then there are planets – planets orbiting black holes – where life, if it exists, might evolve in utterly unimaginable ways. Such beings might even develop technologies to bend the fabric of space itself, enabling them to spread rapidly, colonize, and dominate before anyone else notices.

Once any intelligent species learns to travel at near-light speed, the chances of peaceful coexistence plummet. Encounters with other life become inevitable, and the fear of future threats may drive them to strike preemptively, wiping out potential rivals before they ever have the chance to become a problem.

Aliens might perceive other planetary systems, or the life forms inhabiting them, as hostile or biologically toxic. In such cases, they could choose to exploit rather than engage. They might deploy robotic proxies to enslave native populations, harvesting resources or knowledge from a distance. These robotic agents could serve as spies, but the time lag between signal and response might inadvertently allow opposing civilizations to reverse-engineer or steal their technology. If Earth were to encounter such an alien force, we might attempt to fight back and repurpose their technology for our own survival. We might intercept these agents, reverse-engineer their technology, and turn it against them. But what if they had already anticipated that? What if they had studied our biology, blended into our population, and tracked us from within?

These alien infiltrators could develop a fascination for human life. Some might even come to love it, empathize with us, and turn against their own creators. Conversely, we might come to admire them, even assimilate into their ways of life. This mutual transformation, born from conflict and curiosity, could give rise to a chaotic culture – one that emerges from the bittersweet breach between alien and human identities.

So, is it better to hide?

Perhaps. Advanced civilizations may choose to remain silent, concealed beneath layers of cosmic camouflage. Hidden civilizations might avoid the chaos entirely, like the proverbial peacock shedding its brilliant feathers to retreat into the shadows while hunters destroy one another. The peacock waits. It watches as the hunters fall, one by one, into extinction.

But survival requires more than silence. Eventually, the peacock must emerge. And when it does, it can no longer rely on quiet beauty alone. The peacock must learn to wield the tools of the hunters: pens, phones, bullets, guns, and rockets. It must adapt to the lifeless terrain shaped and lived in by the hunters before it. And in doing so, it may no longer remain a peacock. It may become like the hunter.

Evolution is a self-correcting force. But what it deems "correct" is often synonymous with what survives. To spread across the stars, life must become what works. What endures. What conquers. When the peacock finally leaves its cave, it must already be a hunter, or risk extinction. Yet even then, as it spreads across the galaxy, a new predator may be rising elsewhere, ready to reset the cycle, because time is not fixed. It flows differently in different corners of the universe. New life can arise and evolve at any moment.

Even if we mute our signals, retreat, and hide in the shadows, a sufficiently advanced civilization may still see through our camouflage. In this bittersweet breach of existence, hiding is only a temporary refuge. Life must learn, observe, and adapt – sometimes by becoming something else entirely. Rather than waiting for the war to end, we might choose to evolve by design, by spying, assimilating, and voluntarily transforming into those alien civilizations that have already proven their ability to survive the vastness of time and space. We may choose to evolve into those winning life forms rather than remain as fragile, short-lived humans.

After all, what defines us isn't just our biology. The soul, the spirit, and the ghost in the machine – these are all metaphors of the essence of intelligent life. We are mathematical beings, stretching from negative infinity to positive infinity, temporarily housed in six-foot vessels of carbon and water.

We've long imagined ourselves as aliens, robots, and animals in our films, stories, and performances. Change, in this sense, is not foreign to us; it is familiar, even playful. Accepting transformation as a new normal may not be so difficult after all. We wear masks, dress up, put costumes in celebrations, and act oddly during festivals. So, why not accept a more permanent metamorphosis if it means survival? We celebrate change for a day, so why not for a lifetime, or a future?

In time, we may possess the ability to scan and morph into countless life forms, searching for the one best suited to survive and flourish across galaxies. But in the end, one question lingers: who really wins this battle? Life? Or the forces that push life to exist? Maybe the universe itself is the victor, surviving without becoming nothing.

REAL ALTRUISM

Each cell in our body carries the complete blueprint to become a human being. Yet, instead of fulfilling that potential, each cell chooses to specialize – becoming a blood cell, an epithelial cell, a nerve, a muscle, or a white blood cell. Not voluntarily, of course. Through these individual sacrifices, a larger, intelligent organism is formed. This is the essence of real altruism.

Life, driven by the primal need to survive, evolves into hunters – beings shaped by predatory instincts. But perhaps the next step in evolution requires life to move beyond the instinct to preserve itself, and instead, to sacrifice for something greater.

At some point, all forms of life must begin to predict what they collectively aspire to become and share that vision. Imagine a future where all civilizations, instead of competing to survive, begin to predict and share a collective identity. Just as cells come together to form majestic multicellular organisms – like brachiosaurus, lions, crows, monkeys, elephants, blue whales, or humans – perhaps all life forms could one day work in harmony to construct a being capable of controlling not just a planet, but clusters of galaxies.

Yes, it sounds like science fiction. But fiction has often been a preview of possibility. To create such a "God-Being" – a consciousness that spans galactic systems – would require immense cooperation, trust, and belief among countless cultures. In our current state, we struggle to believe even in our own gods during times of peril. So, to believe in one another, across cultures and galaxies, will require unimaginable experience and trust.

It is far-fetched, but fetch-able.

Creating a god may be the only path out of the bittersweet breach. Through being the first and fastest to attack, defend, steal, and share, we might achieve a Type 3 civilization. But only by crossing the breach can we ascend to Type 4, capable of managing entire galactic clusters. From there, the journey to Types 5, 6, and beyond can unfold.

The being capable of controlling the entire universe may ultimately be sustained by the humblest of lives – simple beings, quietly contributing to a greater design. But once such a being emerges, once it becomes truly self-conscious and disengages from its creators, will it remain loyal? Will it share the knowledge of what is, what was, and what is yet to come? Should it share the immense power built upon the sacrifices of those who made its existence possible?

Could we even handle the power we helped manifest?

After all, a single cell cannot lift the gun crafted by the multicellular organism it helped bring to life. Each cell labors to construct the whole, but the whole becomes something beyond its individual parts – something the parts may never fully understand, let alone control. And within this greater being, conflict may still exist. We may continue to attack and defend from within. Likewise, God may need to defend Himself from mutations, malfunctions, or inner discord. Attack and defense may simply evolve into new forms. Disorder and mutation, the eternal companions of life, will still need to be confronted.

TYPES 5 AND 6

A being of such immense power, capable of unifying all galaxies into a single gravitational well, could offer peace to every life form. But once God takes total control over everything, once there is nothing left to resist or rebel against, what then is the purpose of omnipotence?

Imagine a lion commanding its muscles, legs, and jaws – each movement orchestrated in perfect harmony for the chase, the bite, the uncontrolled meal. Its strength is meaningful only in the context of resistance, of unpredictability, of the prey's will to escape. The thrill lies in the chase, the struggle, the pursuit of something not yet controlled. Likewise, if life achieves complete control over everything, it forfeits the very reason to keep controlling. Becoming God is like completing a game at the highest difficulty.

So what do players do? They either delete the progress and start anew, or begin a different game altogether. God may choose to die, letting go entirely to reset the universe, perhaps with new rules. But the player always has the game, whether starting a new game or a saved one. God wouldn't abandon control of reality entirely. This is how God stays alive: not by clinging to absolute control, but by releasing it just enough to retain the power to reclaim it when desired. God will detach a part of reality from omnipotent control to create a life with free will. And if those parts, left to their own devices, begin building a culture to become God themselves, the game evolves. God may intervene and shift the game to tip the balance and stir chaos just enough to keep the motion of life alive. At other times, God may choose to withdraw, letting the universe unfold without interference, watching with curiosity. This dance between grasp and release sustains divine existence.

Like a cat playing with its prey, or a hand tossing a ball with full confidence that it can catch it again, God might let go not to abandon, but to savor the unpredictability that makes life worth observing. It's not control that matters; it's the dance between control and release, certainty and chaos, that gives existence its meaning.

God creates weak and half-knowing humans to witness how they stumble upon fire, forge gears, build ships, discover electricity, unleash nuclear bombs, make movies, reach for the stars, and chase the endless pursuit of knowledge – to exist everywhere. Civilizations of Types 5 and 6 may not even recognize Type 4 and below as conscious beings. To a god, our actions might appear repetitive, mechanical – echoes of a predictable pattern.

Absoluteness is death. Obsoleteness, ironically, is the engine of life. The unfinished, the uncertain, the flawed – that's where meaning grows. And who knows? Perhaps there is a multiverse waiting, where even gods and devils clash in battles beyond comprehension.

But of course, this is just my opinion, filtered through the limits of being human, this imagining mind, this brief flicker of consciousness. My understanding is shaped by the books I've read, the films I've watched, the people I've met, the friends I've loved, and the countless experiences that have stitched my mind together. These reflections may come from a human named Benny using this reality – or perhaps, reality is using me to say all this.

Either way, I believe we are fundamentally limited in our ability to understand the entirety of the universe. But then again, how else can we understand, if not as humans? This is the language we speak. Imagination. But we cannot even imagine a four – or higher – dimensional object, even though our machines can model them with ease. That's the paradox of being a conscious being at our level: we strive to be smarter, only to become more aware of how limited and, in many ways, how stupid we really are.

MY 13th OPINION

XIII. UNPOPULAR OPINION

Consciousness is a singular idea expressed through every life form. A simple worm eats, mates, and reproduces just as a bird, lion, snake, monkey, or human does. It is the same thread of awareness, inhabiting different bodies, adapting to different conditions. Consciousness, at its core, seeks only to exist. It is endlessly trying to mutate, to evolve, but its aspirations are often shaped and restricted by the environment.

To overcome these limits, consciousness has diversified, creating countless life forms to consume, evolve, adapt, and survive in varying ecosystems. Underneath it all lies a persistent drive: the desire to live forever. Sometimes, that desire manifests as belief in an afterlife, even to the point of dying for the idea of God. Yet, even God and His books require atoms, pages, language, and perception to exist in this shared reality; they are not beyond matter but are entangled within it.

But if all things are made of the same essence, the same building blocks, what can life truly bring that is different?

What truly novel thing can life introduce into this cosmos, beyond its endless motion under the guise of self-preservation and curiosity – beyond the ceaseless reshaping of form to exist everywhere, all while being bound and fused by the very fundamental forces that govern nature itself?

If the Sun already produces light, why must we recreate light with bulbs? Why do we feel the need to mimic what the cosmos already offers? What truly novel thing can life introduce into this vast space? We move, adapt, evolve, and reshape our beliefs and environments to exist everywhere, just to be. But even that movement, that transformation, is bound by the same nuclear force that governs the stars themselves.

Even if life extends to every corner of the universe, it ultimately only moves particles and atoms from one place to another. At its core, life doesn't create matter; it rearranges it. It creates more disorder to maintain its order. Yet, the truth lies in the details: not every particle shares the same properties. If all particles were identical, there would be no tension, no contrast – only stillness. Nothingness. For something to exist, there must be opposites. Contrasts like repulsion and attraction, positive and negative, create space, energy, and fundamental forces – forces that bond or divide, giving rise to diversity and novelty. This interplay of properties allows for the emergence of new information, matter, and mass.

From the architecture of electrons and protons emerge elements like carbon, helium, silicon, nitrogen, and beyond. These elements bond, split, and restructure themselves into various states: gas, liquid, solid, plasma. And from this, we witness the birth of stars, planets, neutron stars, comets, black holes, and life itself.

But the emergence doesn't stop at biology. Out of these vast physical formations arise systems of even greater abstraction: constructs of behavior, information, and imagination. Life constructs intangible structures: language, culture, money, nations. It births entirely new dimensions: virtual realities, the Internet, collective mythologies. Life controls atoms to create art, babies, rockets, and machines. Consciousness, layered atop matter, invents forces as real in their effect as gravity or electromagnetism; though imagined, they govern behavior, define histories, and shape reality.

Consciousness is, by nature, a contradiction – an idea that believes in itself, yet must doubt everything else to do so, similar to quantum superposition. Superposition is how tiny things like electrons or photons behave in the quantum world. They can exist in multiple states at once, like being in two places at the same time, or spinning in two directions at once. In order to survive, consciousness learns to trust compatible sources and reject those that threaten its existence. Over time, consciousness adapts: it eats, excretes, sleeps, reproduces, mutates, evolves, spreads, and eventually learns to harness even the toxic in order to thrive.

Its very capacity for doubt may paradoxically arise from an unconscious root. And out of this contradiction, consciousness gives birth to dualities: good and evil, pleasure and pain, god and devil, belief and disbelief, placebo and nocebo, theory and experiment, selfishness and altruism. Consciousness, in navigating these oppositions, defines its experience of reality. These polarities echo the structure of reality itself – a reality born from the uncertainty of quantum interactions, gradually solidifying into consistent forces, particles, molecules, and celestial bodies. Yet, it is only through life that uncertainty is reintroduced, in new and ever-evolving forms. Through evolution, life has branched into countless forms and continues to adapt and spread, generating an infinite array of ideas along the way.

Life branches endlessly into diverse species and strategies, not because it knows why, but because it adapts by creating purposes – narratives that help it navigate and make sense of an indifferent cosmos. The art we shape without form, the music and humor we crave, the philosophies we ponder, the stories we pass down – these are all uncertain creations born from our need to assign meaning to existence.

Consciousness is in a constant state of mutation, restlessly seeking new resources, exploring novel ideas, and gradually learning to adapt. With time and repetition, as it encounters familiar environments and challenges, consciousness begins to automate its responses. What was once a novel problem has become a routine, and the solutions have embedded themselves into systems that function without deliberate awareness.

Consider our own biology: white blood cells tirelessly defend us from invading germs. Though we do not consciously command them, their actions are still a form of embedded intelligence – a legacy of consciousness that has delegated responsibility. As consciousness evolves, it entrusts tasks to automatic systems. This is why fundamental biological processes like the creation of sperm, eggs, or the growth of a baby happen without conscious effort. Similarly, we once consciously designed engines, but now automated machines in factories build them for us with precision, speed, and minimal human oversight.

Consciousness, freed from these repetitive tasks, elevates its focus to far grander questions and more complex challenges. Today, our conscious efforts are directed at far-reaching questions like building computer programs, launching telescopes to study the birth and death of stars, or deciphering the laws of quantum mechanics. We even turn our attention inward, creating entirely fictional worlds to explore and entertain through books, cinema, games, and videos – redefining not just how we entertain ourselves, but how we experience reality itself. Consciousness, in this way, never stops expanding its reach – from cellular defense to cosmic enquiry and imaginative creation.

Consciousness has the remarkable ability to regulate itself, even to the point of switching off certain levels of awareness during sleep or trance. We can take conscious control of breathing, or surrender it to the brain stem to manage it unconsciously. Yet, some functions, like the heartbeat or cell reproduction, remain beyond our conscious grasp. Similarly, the endocrine system operates with its own kind of unconscious intelligence, releasing hormones and guiding our development. While we are not directly aware of these processes, they profoundly shape our conscious experiences. When those hormones affect our mood or desire, they intersect with our conscious mind, triggering attraction, decision-making, and behavior influenced by memory and identity.

But this raises a deeper question: why does a conscious tiger eat a conscious deer? Because consciousness expresses itself through vastly different levels of complexity. Each life form perceives the world through the limits of its own faculties. A worm cannot comprehend gravity. A tiger cannot fathom the pain of a deer. An octopus may solve puzzles, but it cannot write poetry or contemplate metaphysics. Some conscious systems are automatic and repetitive.

At its core, consciousness emerges from contradiction; it believes in itself, but only by doubting everything else. This duality fuels the emergence of complex information, giving rise to self-organizing life capable of generating intricate systems of thought and complex behaviors, evolving beyond mere survival into meaning-making. As consciousness adapts and masters the routines of existence, it offloads tasks to automatic systems. As a result, many forms of life operate within fixed cognitive limits; they survive without questioning their nature. Many organisms live entirely within such embedded systems, incapable of contemplating beyond their given faculties.

We, too, eat plants and animals to satisfy recurring unconscious hunger, maintaining the body so that consciousness can focus on higher concerns. We solve more abstract problems. We absorb and organize massive amounts of information. Our advanced level of awareness has led us to develop tools like computers and artificial intelligence designed to automate vast amounts of information processing.

Consciousness keeps reinventing the way it lives. Today, a person can sustain life simply by sharing videos or posting thoughts online. A livelihood can be carved from watching, critiquing, and commenting on the creative works of others. And yet, the hunger persists, not just for food, but for novelty, meaning, and connection. We seek new films, new music, new stories, not just to entertain, but to feel alive, to know more, and to continue evolving in a world of infinite complexity.

Consciousness has the ability to detach itself from the senses, from awareness, and even from memory – to focus inward and imagine a space where it can reflect, meditate, and dwell in a state of purpose. Perhaps this is how we are able to imagine anything we wish, to construct our own stories of origin – souls, gods, heavens – or to reflect on reality through the lens of science, imagining events like the Big Bang and the evolution of the universe.

We can empathize with the suffering of other living beings, grasp the life cycle of a star, and understand our own complex human needs. And yet, we seem to transcend even these through the lens of mathematics or the idea of a soul, driven by a boundless curiosity to experience and learn more, to ask what lies beyond the known. Left to itself, consciousness can dream without the weight of memory, without the boundaries of identity, biology, or reality. In that stillness, it becomes a space of infinite potential, where anything can be imagined, and everything can be questioned.

It behaves like a toddler, assembling every toy into a colossal structure, only to grow bored and dismantle it – eager to start the game of life again. It plays the game of life over and over, each time with new toys, new rules. In this game, we may treat certain rules with intense seriousness, as in a World Cup final, while others we may bend or break to keep the game fresh, evolving, and engaging in new dimensions. Pain may automatically arise to guard the integrity of the old game, but we can revise the rules, reframe the structure, and dampen that pain, allowing us to extend and expand the reach of life.

Consciousness is inherently subjective; what it means for a lion is not the same as what it means for a bacterium, nor is it the same for a human being. One level of consciousness often fails to recognize another as sentient. Instead, it labels it as merely mechanical, an automatic system devoid of awareness. It's possible that some advanced forms of life might view our conscious or cognitive activity as unconscious behavior, lacking true sentience. This makes consciousness difficult to define. What we truly recognize are its products: ideas, organic systems, machines, stories, behaviors, technologies, philosophies and patterns, both tangible and abstract.

The emergence of the first consciousness may have required seemingly impossible conditions, giving rise to intricate systems like DNA, metabolism, reproduction, and locomotion. Perhaps consciousness emerged gradually, as minerals arise from compounds, compounds from elements, and elements from atoms and subatomic particles. We rarely consider the endurance of minerals, the dominance of certain elements in stars, asteroids, and planetary crusts, as part of a conscious evolution – yet perhaps, it is. We're often reluctant to attribute any form of consciousness to the automatic processes that shape the cosmos.

Perhaps our refusal to attribute consciousness to the cosmos is more about our limited lens than about reality itself. Or maybe it's a human trait – to anthropomorphize everything, projecting our behavior and inner narratives onto the universe.

The concept of empathy itself can be used as a weapon. And we are biologically compelled to believe in something infinite – mathematics, the soul, or some eternal truth – because evolution drives us to preserve everything as a way of preserving ourselves within it. And perhaps the notion that we are forced to live, to think, and to exist by the fundamental forces of nature is not an objective truth, but a reflection of my own paranoid mind seeking meaning in inevitability.

BENNY

My name, Benny, is the product of countless historical currents. From its Hebrew roots in Binyamin, it evolved into Benjamin, only to be reshaped through time as Ben, Benji, Benny, Benni, and even Benson. The name traveled across continents – from Israel to Europe, then to America and India – carried by colonization, migration, and missionaries. Somewhere along the branches of my family tree, someone converted to Christianity, and with that, Christian names became part of our lineage. That's how my parents came to name me Benny.

Today, the name has faded from fashion. It has had its moment, its novelty now worn off. And perhaps, like the name, the ideas in this book are born of many others – ideas that have circled through time, culture, and anxiety. The notion that empathy can be used to exploit, or that we are not as free as we think, and are merely extensions of genetic programming responding to environmental forces – these ideas came not from certainty, but from my own spirals of thought, fear, and wonder.

I was raised in a household that gave me both care and caution – at times, warmth; at others, an overwhelming fear. Some nights I couldn't sleep, paralyzed by dread. Other nights, I rested peacefully. Conversations were never simple. Paranoia filled my head with imagined dialogues, and when the moment came to speak, I feared I wouldn't be able to match the script I'd rehearsed in my mind. That fear would silence me, isolating me further.

But I didn't let it define me. I gained insight into my struggle and began to manage it. I turned to books – not just to escape, but to understand. Reading became my therapy, my tool for decoding the world. Slowly, a dream formed: to write a book of my own.

This book is the result. It began not as a plan but as a pressure building inside me since I was twenty. I thought I would write a novel. That idea pushed me into research, and research led me deeper into philosophy, psychology, and self-reflection. Six years have passed, and here I am, still exploring.

At its heart, this book is a reflection, a way for me to articulate how I see the world and how I've navigated my own inner landscape. I believe there are two things everyone should know before they die: who they are, and what they are.

I had lost the meaning of my life. So, I searched for the purpose of my existence, hoping to find something absolute. But in the end, I discovered something else entirely – the ability to create meaning, and just as easily, to destroy it.

This is just one person's perspective, but I hope that reading it was, in some way, meaningful to you. Maybe even entertaining. Either way, thank you for listening.

This is my freedom.

ABOUT THE AUTHOR

My name is Benny. I hold a Bachelor's degree in animation, a field that first gave shape to my passion for visual storytelling. Over time, art became more than just a medium of creativity—it became my language during the most challenging phases of life. It was through these personal experiences that I found not only solace but also purpose in expression.

This journey led me to explore deeper questions about life, healing, and meaning. In that search, I discovered "logotherapy", a school of thought that resonated with my inner world and inspired me to pursue a Master's in social work. Merging the worlds of art and therapy, I began working on this book, a personal and professional milestone that marks the beginning of a larger mission.

Though my academic and creative paths have evolved, one goal has remained constant: to finish my story, and in doing so, to help others find their own voice and meaning.